What Peop

Frozen Tears is accurate, compelling and complete. J.B. King brought together this serious murder investigation by multiple law enforcement entities as they built the court prosecutable case against SP4 Johnny Lee Thornton, a military police game warden at Fort Leonard Wood, Missouri. J.B. collated, analyzed, and wrote this book based on his personal knowledge, and careful reviews of the investigative reports from the US Army Criminal Investigation Command (CID), The Federal Bureau of Investigation (FBI), The Missouri State Highway Patrol, The Pulaski County Sheriff's office and news media accounts of the murder. He did so in an excellent manner.

CW5 Willie J Rowell, CID Special Agent (Retired)

* * *

It is only fitting that a distinguished career law enforcement professional such as J.B. King should recount the history of such a ruthless and heinous crime, conducted by one who was entrusted with the distinctive responsibility of protecting the community. That special trust was broken when Thornton, a young military police patrolman, brutally and sadistically committed the "Crime of the Century" against the most young and innocent. How could this abomination have happened? As the initial responder, J.B. gives invaluable insight and first-hand description of the multi-jurisdictional investigation, arrest and ultimate prosecution of a sinister, evil and psychotic individual. A masterful job written from a human standpoint, not just the cold facts of an investigation file.

~Rex Forney Jr, Colonel (Retired), US Army Military Police

FROZEN TEARS

THE FORT LEONARD WOOD
MP MURDERS

J. B. KING

With Sandra Miller Linhart

Red Engine Press
Pittsburgh, PA

Library of Congress Control Number: 2019945260

ISBN: 978-1-943267-70-5 Paperback

Cover Design: Sandra Miller Linhart

Edited and Designed by Joyce Faulkner

Printed in the United States.

Red Engine Press

For the victims of Johnny Lee Thornton

Living and Dead

INTRODUCTION

THE PURPOSE OF THIS BOOK is to tell the story of Pulaski County's 'Crime of the Century' in detail and with clarity. The murders of three innocent young people shocked the community. Within a few hours after law enforcement learned of the crimes, officers identified and arrested Johnny Lee Thornton of the 463rd MP Company. This is that story.

> There will be people who might look upon this book as a condemnation of the United States Army Military Police Corps. They will be wrong.

I've worked in a law enforcement capacity since December, 1969. Pulaski County was my first assignment after I graduated from the Missouri State Highway Patrol Academy. During my 32-year career as a state trooper, I've worked side-by-side with many former MP officers.

They were fellow Missouri State Highway Patrol troopers and highway patrol radio dispatchers. They were part of every law enforcement agency in Pulaski County and surrounding counties. Later in my law enforcement career, as the elected Sheriff of Pulaski County, I hired former MPs. They proved to be some of my best deputies. I assure you, Johnny Lee Thornton was an aberration. The United States Army Military Police Corps is professional and highly-skilled.

For people who say things like, "This should never have happened," every officer I spoke to during the writing of this book agrees with you. It should never have happened. Speaking for these officers, I will tell you that we hate criminal acts or stupid behavior by law enforcement officers more than non-officers do because such behavior casts a black shadow on all of us.

In today's world and in past history, we've read far too many stories about doctors and dentists who molested their anesthetized patients. We've seen too many teachers sexually abuse their students. We've heard too many stories of hospital ward nurses who kill their patients. The bottom line is, all occupations draw workers from the general population — and that pool is often polluted. Two-legged sharks walk among us.

From the first minutes after this attack was reported, the United States Army, the Federal Bureau of Investigation (FBI), the Army's Criminal Investigation Command (CID), and the United States Attorney's office worked together to bring the killer to justice. This book is a first-hand, comprehensive look into the investigation.

This was a major case. The media, particularly the newspapers of the time, offered all-inclusive stories, complete with quotes — about every phase and minute detail of this crime. The investigation, the grand jury, the proposed trial dates and locations, and the actual trial appeared in hundreds of outlets.

The United States Federal Court held thousands of pages of documents and exhibits relating to the trial. For the purpose of this book, we procured numerous pages from these records. All of the contested evidence suppression and competency hearings were transcribed. We have copies of that testimony. Unfortunately, the main trial transcript was never completed. This meant I had to rely on media articles and 40-year-old memories of those who were there.

And then, lighting struck. I spoke with Patti Bates, sister of murder victim Anthony "Tony" Bates. She told me her mom, Marjorie Bates, compiled three scrapbooks of notes. Patti allowed me to examine them. To my surprise, I saw that Marjorie Bates attended the federal trial and recorded notes on each witness via shorthand. Then, after the trial, she typed out the testimony and her other notes. Patti Bates graciously gave me a copy of these materials. The words 'Thank You' don't go deep enough to express my joy at receiving them.

The federal court record listed 102 possible witnesses for the trial. There's no plausible way to locate that many people after 40 years. Many of them testified to one small issue regarding the case. So, for much of the courtroom testimony, we were left with the newspaper accounts, the memories of those who were there, and Marjorie Bates' notes — which focused on the main witnesses and their testimonies.

I interviewed several people who provided supplemental information. Most of the folks I talked with participated in some phase of this case and were more than willing to tell me everything they could recall about what happened or about the people involved.[1] To give the reader a better understanding of the case, I placed many of these recent interviews into the story at around the time each event occurred.

Some information might cause pain to surviving family members. For example, in general, there is no need to share the autopsy report. The reader need only know Thornton shot and killed the victims. However, sometimes a pertinent fact from the autopsy is necessary to understand key parts of the story. Ultimately, I decided to limit sensitive details to what appeared in the 1977 newspapers.[2] This was a complex investigation — especially during the first few days. I presented the case in the best chronological order possible, but one must understand there were a multitude of officers working the case. Several parts of the investigation were underway at the exact same time. I did the best I could in those circumstances to keep the information congruent. I also found a few instances where written records didn't line up with memories of agents who were on the scene. Since it's been 40 years, and in the interest of total accuracy, I've tried to include the information from both sides of these instances and let the reader decide.

In a major investigation, officers seize potential evidence and send it to the lab for evaluation. It may take weeks or months before the lab sends back results. Those results can shoot down your crime theory, send the case in a new direction, or prove the evidence submitted was pretty much what you expected. In order to better understand this case, I decided to eliminate the long waiting period. I inserted lab results into the story at, or about the time, the evidence was first obtained. The same holds true for witness interviews. I tried to highlight

---

1 Where an actual participant is deceased, family stepped in to tell that person's story.

2 This information is publicly available for those willing to look it up.

parts of interviews that later proved to be of value during the investigation or the trial.

Thanks to Pulaski County Prosecuting Attorney, Kevin Hillman for his patient explanation of legal issues connected to this case. Kevin is also a military officer and lawyer with the United States Army Judge Advocate General Corps. Thus, his explanations were balanced between civilian and military law. I'd also like to thank three members of his staff: Laura Cantrell, Hayley Eisley, and Verna Kline for their help in organizing hundreds of pages of documents.

In the same vein, Jeanne Keller, Operations Generalist for the United States court system's Western District of Missouri, was invaluable when it came to supplying court documents. She also provided all the copies we requested.

A special word of thanks goes to Shaun and Pam Collins who are both retired CID agents. They had nothing to do with the original case but joined me in trips to the federal court files in Springfield, Missouri, to research the case. In addition, Shaun had prior training in the criminal mind-profiling field and his insights were helpful. Pam was a forensic specialist and she had her share of questions to answer.

A special 'Thank You' goes to retired FBI agents, Bill Castleberry and Tom Den Ouden, along with retired CID agent, George Matthews. Their contributions to this book were crucial. Former MP Game Warden James Reist (who served with Thornton) offered insights into Thornton's work habits and professional demeanor.

I would also like to thank other FBI and CID agents, MPs, family members of the victims, and civilians who went out of their way to assist. When I first started this project, I hoped to find enough information for a book. Instead, I found myself buried under tons of information. I pray I didn't leave out any significant details or names or that I got a key fact wrong.

As word of my efforts to write this book became known, the Editor of the local Daily Guide Newspaper, Natalie Sanders, twisted my arm, insisting I give her an interview for a story on the book effort. Foolishly, I resisted her requests at first. But eventually I consented. As a result of her print story, several people who had connections to the case contacted me. Natalie, I apologize for the resistance. Thank you for your help.

Also, thanks to Red Engine Press. It was as a result of my presentation to members of the Military Writers Society of America at a Civil War and True Crime lecture session, sponsored by the Pulaski County Tourism Bureau in October of 2016 that I first met Joyce Faulkner and Pat McGrath-Avery — the co-owners of Red Engine Press. After hearing my story on the Thornton case, they talked me into doing the first true crime book their company has ever produced.

I would specifically like to thank co-author, Sandra (Sandi) Miller Linhart for her help running down several hundred newspaper articles about the case from across the USA. That information was invaluable. Sandi also proofread selected chapters during the writing of this book and gave me her gut reaction to what I had written — which helped me stay on course.

So, sit down, open the book, and read. I hope you'll find this case to be as compelling and interesting as I did.

J.B. King
P. O. Box 226
Waynesville, MO 65583

TABLE OF CONTENTS

1

JUANITA

A TREE LIMB CRACKED UNDER the weight of the snow. *Is HE following me?* Juanita tried to run but she couldn't breathe. She no longer felt her ears or her fingers or her toes. Trembling with cold, she looked behind her. No one there.

She was unsure where she was headed — but hopefully it was toward Highway 17. Away from Fort Leonard Wood. Toward someplace safe.

Did any of it even happen?

Maybe she was dreaming. If so, the images were nightmarish and she wanted to wake up. She buried her icy hands inside her coat pockets.

I am awake and I need help. They need help.

She choked back a sob. She didn't want to think about them — not yet.

Something flickered in the distance.

A light?

She squinted. *A house, maybe?*

The snow was over her shoes — up inside the legs of her jeans. She tried to hurry — and then stopped again.

What if HE lived there?

She was growing weaker. No matter who was behind that window with the light, she had to get inside before she died.

The sun's glow peeked over the tree line to her left.

How far have I walked?

Every muscle ached, but she put one foot forward — and then the other. Steady. Straight.

Maybe the people who live there have a phone. Or a car.

She looked over her shoulder again. What if he went back to the hillside where her friends were lying and noticed she was missing?

Her chest ached — and all the other places he'd hurt her.

Juanita stumbled on, wondering if he was behind her — hunting her.

What if there are other monsters — wild ones — out there too?

Had she been able to, she would've run. She would have run as if her life depended on it. Because it did. But she couldn't. She could only walk. And so, she did.

As the sun crested the sky, Juanita saw the mobile home. Smoke wafted from the chimney. It beckoned and — having no other choice, she followed.

What if the MP does live here?

She'd never been afraid of people before. There had been no reason before.

There was a swing set in the yard. An orange Maverick in the driveway, halfway buried in a snow bank.

A family?

Juanita took the stairs leading up to the trailer's door one at a time. She stood on the porch. Music from a television show seeped through the thin walls. She recognized it from the soap opera her mom watched, *As the World Turns*. Terrified, but without any other choice, she lifted her fist.

Please, God. Help me.

She took a breath and knocked.

There was movement inside. Juanita forced herself not to run — which is all she wanted to do — run away and hide. The door opened.

A woman — not much older than her — stood in the doorway. She looked up and down the road behind Juanita. "Where's your mom and dad?"

"I'm really cold."

The woman opened her door wider. "Well, come on in."

Juanita stepped inside the warmth.

The woman was a stranger, but she seemed kind. "What's wrong? Are you hurt? Should I call the police? An ambulance?"

Juanita needed to take a chance, but words wouldn't come.
"Are you hurt?" The woman repeated.
Can't you see? Of course, I'm hurt.
"Would you like a warm drink? Dry clothes?"
"My friends are all dead. He killed them," Juanita blurted.

Anthony "Tony" Bates
Courtesy of Patti Bates

Linda Needham
Courtesy Gatehouse
Media Daily Guide

Wesley Hawkins
Courtesy Gatehouse
Media Daily Guide

2

THE CRIME REVEALED

MY NAME IS J.B. KING. On Thursday, January 13, 1977, I was a trooper with the Missouri State Highway Patrol. Stationed in the Pulaski County Zone of Troop I, headquartered in Rolla, Missouri, which included the Fort Leonard Wood Army base. I was a fairly new and young trooper. However, fate made me the first law enforcement officer to gather facts about our area's 'Crime of the Century.'

Trooper J. B. King, #733
Photo Courtesy of J. B. King

When the original call came in to the Troop I communications division at 1:18 p.m., dispatch told me they had information from a Mr. Needham. He was the father of a runaway girl, aged 16. He knew the location of his daughter and the other three missing youths. He also told Troop I that one of the girls had been shot. He gave his location as 12 miles south of U. S. 66 (I-44) on Missouri Route 17.

This scenario didn't make sense to me — runaways, missing kids, but one was shot? I reminded myself that first reports on breaking situations are almost always wrong or misleading on key points. Our initial confusion on this call stemmed from the fact we had no prior reports about missing kids. As I drove toward Mr. Needham's location, Troop I radio-contacted the Military Police (MP) on Fort Wood and learned that four teenagers were reported missing Wednesday night. That was all the information the MPs had to share with us.

When I got the call that Thursday afternoon, the temperature was in the low twenties with a 10-to-15 mile-an-hour north wind. We had eight inches of snow on the ground — some of it freshly fallen. The roads weren't in the best shape and I was operating a rear-wheel-drive patrol vehicle. As a result, I didn't locate the Needham car parked alongside Missouri Route 17 until 2:15 p.m.—almost an hour after I received the initial call-out.

Upon my arrival, Mr. Needham exited his car and approached mine. Nearly hysterical, he yelled at me for a minute or so. At first, I couldn't comprehend a word he said. Finally, in frustration, he paused and pointed at his car. "Well, do something. She's been shot in the chest."

When I got to the driver's side door and looked in, I saw a slender, young female sitting in the passenger-side front seat. Neatly dressed and very clean, she did not look like a gunshot victim. She was crying. Her eyes, reflecting a mixture of terror and horror, were the epitome of the 'thousand-yard stare' I'd seen on the faces of combat veterans. *This is going to be bad*, I thought.

My initial words to her were, "He said you were shot?"

In response, the young lady lifted up her left forearm and showed me what appeared to be an uncovered bullet-crease wound.

"He said you were shot in the chest."

She lowered the neckline of her blouse. She had a clean and uncovered, major-caliber bullet-entry wound near the top of her breast. The entry site was not bleeding. Slightly glazed or crusted over, it was many hours old. Despite the fact it was a large caliber bullet wound, it didn't appear to be serious.

Time stopped briefly as I ran over the facts at hand in my mind.

- Missing kids from the night before.
- A young woman with two, real-live bullet wounds.

This is going to be a big case, I concluded. *Law enforcement was not going to like this.*

It was obvious that the girl was not in the best condition for questioning. However, with three kids missing and two bullet wounds in this one, we needed immediate answers. I had no choice but to question her further. As we talked back-and-forth, her soft-spoken short responses were loaded with details.

She told me her name was Juanita Deckard. The night before, she was on a double-date with three friends. She named her companions as, Anthony Bates, age 18, Wesley Hawkins, age 18, and Linda Needham, age 16. Juanita said all four of them lived in the Plato, Missouri area.

As they drove across Fort Wood on the south side of the base, not far from the airfield, an MP vehicle, using red lights, stopped them. A uniformed MP ordered them out of their car. Handcuffing her two male companions, he arrested all four of them for armed robbery and ordered them into his vehicle.

The MP started to drive off, but then stopped. Without warning, he drew his gun, turned in his seat and shot the two boys sitting in the back. Then he drove to a secluded cabin on the Roubidoux River in a remote part of the base. There, he sexually assaulted the girls before shooting them. Finally, he buried all four of his victims in a snowbank and drove away.

Miss Deckard played dead when he kicked snow over her body. After he drove away, she tried to rouse her friends without success. She then walked across the live-weapons firing ranges on Fort Wood, heading west toward Missouri Route 17. She found a house along the highway. The homeowner allowed her to call Mr. Needham for help. The woman also helped her clean up and gave her fresh clothing to wear.

The initial questioning took six or seven minutes. I had the broad outline of the crimes. It was time to take action. Shivering, I walked to my patrol car which contained the radio for critical communications. There were three murdered teens lying in a snowbank somewhere in the woods. *Killed by a military cop?* My throat tightened. Those young people and their families needed me to keep a clear head.

The most immediate problem was that these were not "my" woods. The teenagers' bodies were on the federal reservation known as Fort Leonard Wood. I had no jurisdiction to investigate these crimes. As a Missouri State commissioned officer, I could assist federal officers if they requested, but ultimately the case was theirs. The first issue at hand was to get federal officers headed my way.

My second issue was that the Missouri State Highway Patrol's radio system was not secure. In Pulaski and the surrounding counties, police scanners played in thousands of private homes, gas stations and restaurants 24 hours a day. Every word I might say on the radio to Troop I would be simultaneously broadcast to all of those listeners. And we could not have that in this case. The rumor mill would go nuts. We didn't need gawkers driving by our location to see what they could see. And we didn't need to alert our suspect. The implications presented by my radio traffic were staggering.

At the time it was (and still is) Missouri State Highway Patrol policy that whenever a trooper radios a declaration that he has "rush" traffic, all other radio traffic immediately halts. The trooper in question was the only one allowed to use that frequency. With this crime unfolding in front of me and the other inherent problems I faced, I was nervous. I told them (I remember little of what I actually said to them) that all of my traffic was rush until further notice. I told them to send several MPs, as well as the highest-ranking MP on duty that they could find. I also requested four-wheel drive military vehicles. I told Troop I radio, "Don't ask any questions, just do what I say. Immediately."

I had just started my seventh year as a trooper — and rookie troopers do not tell troop radio dispatchers — or the command staff troop officers standing behind them — not to ask questions. But Troop I was small. Our troopers and radio specialists worked together. As a result, we could almost always tell by the tone of a trooper or radio operator's voice when bad things were happening — no matter how guarded their words. I am certain the mental strain I felt transferred to my voice — and everybody, including citizens in scanner-land, knew something was up. I could only hope my words had not furnished any crucial or confidential details.

With backup alerted, I returned to Miss Deckard and probed for smaller details critical to the coming investigation. She described the man, his clothing, and voice. Unfamiliar with the vehicle he drove, she could only say it was square shaped and was not a Jeep, a car, or a truck. She said it had two bucket seats up front and a single, full-bench seat in the back.

I knew it would turn out to be an International Scout 4WD. The base had a few of them driving around with the MP units and her description fit them perfectly. At that time, I suspected we had a fake military police officer at large.

Roughly one year before, on February 27, 1976, the local law enforcement grapevine circulated a story about a military man who flew into Fort Wood from another base. He overpowered a real MP and left him handcuffed to a tree. Then, he stole MP equipment and — posing as an MP, picked up a payroll officer — and escorted him to a company-area for a payroll distribution. The fake MP made off with $50,000 plus in cash — and left the payroll officer in the trunk of the stolen MP vehicle. The suspect then flew back to Fort Bragg. The CID and FBI broke the case and made the arrest. As a trooper in the local zone, I had heard details of that case. I thought, *Here we go again.*

Miss Deckard described words and phrases that were broadcast over the radio in the MP vehicle. She described the MP's badge. She provided details including a number stenciled on the left front side of the MP's vehicle. She thought the number was 327.

Because of my travels around Fort Wood, I knew real MP vehicles had a number displayed near that location. The Missouri State Highway Patrol used a similar identification system on our cars. But the fact that a traumatized victim, who had been through hell, remembered a number displayed on the vehicle in that specific location was significant. Deckard described a real MP vehicle with a high degree of probability. How did the suspect get his hands on it? I knew that question would be a critical lead to follow in the upcoming investigation. However, as she continued with her detailed responses to my questions, the totality of information in her answers overwhelmed me. This was not a fake MP. This was a real live one gone rogue.

And I had just asked for MP backup!

Oh, my God! My heart discovered the bottom of my stomach.

The black cloud of horror and terror that had surrounded Miss Deckard when I first arrived at Mr. Needham's car, enveloped me. I struggled to control my emotions — and failed epically.

Later on in my law enforcement career, I earned a reputation for being a cool, calm officer. I used clear, concise thinking, facing adversity in situations involving death, destruction, mayhem, and chaos with a high degree of professional competence. I became one of a small number of troopers awarded the Medal of Valor by the Missouri State Highway Patrol, receiving it for my actions while facing a gunman in a 'shots fired' situation. But that was many years into the future. That Thursday — right there, right then — my professional competence and emotional control was several feet below the level of a blabbering idiot.

But then, another complication arrived. Two cars loaded with friends and relatives of the missing kids showed up. Their intention was to follow Miss Deckard's footprints in the snow back to the murder scene.

Regaining my composure, I told them, "No."

That was no easy thing to do as fear and worry were etched on their faces. In their shoes, I'd want to do the same thing. But I also knew a major criminal investigation was coming.

Law enforcement didn't need worried civilians altering the crime scene in the woods. We needed every clue we could find to identify and convict the unknown lone suspect.

For the next several minutes, I was locked in a stalemate with these people. Tempers flared, voices raised, and things, in general, got ugly. After a while, I persuaded Mr. Needham and one of the newcomers to take Miss Deckard to the hospital so her wounds could be treated.

After they left the roadside scene, I blocked the remaining friends and family members, until two carloads of military men arrived. They appeared to be a mix of MPs and CID agents. Captain Raymond Beck, 208th Military Police Company and the current Command Duty Officer for the day shift introduced himself and asked me to fill him in on the situation.

As I briefed Beck on the facts I had, he made written notes and everybody else crowded around, listening to his questions and my answers. After a few minutes, Beck stopped me — and we walked over to another military vehicle that had just arrived. Beck introduced me to Sergeant Jensen, from the game warden detail. Jensen was assigned to take the CID team down to the crime scene, so Beck wanted him to hear the briefing. I repeated the facts from the beginning.

As I was talking, I noticed Jensen leaning against an International Scout 4WD vehicle. When I got to the part where Miss Deckard described the suspect's vehicle and its identifying number, I glanced down at the Scout next to Jensen. It was vehicle X37.

My mouth went dry. This was our suspect's vehicle!

The people who know me best will tell you I never shut up. But, like Lot's wife, I turned into a pillar of salt dressed in blue. I don't know just how long I remained dumbstruck. They all looked at me and asked what was wrong, but I could not respond.

Beck must have realized what I was looking at. I had already given him the number. He turned to Jensen and asked him who last drove the vehicle.

Jensen named two MPs, one of whom was Thornton. Jensen's mouth dropped open.

"Thornton said he shot some dogs last night!"

And just that damn quick, we went from an unknown suspect in Pulaski County Missouri's 'Crime of the Century' to red-hot-murder-suspect number one.

Beck said he needed a phone.

I came out of my trance and told him I knew a man who lived a few miles away. I offered to take him there. When we arrived at my friend's house, Beck called MP command and ordered them to grab Thornton and the other MP Jensen named, read them their rights, put them in a room under guard, and ask them no questions.

A minute or so later, Beck was told Thornton had been in the building and heard the news about a survivor of the shooting. He then checked out a military .45 pistol and several magazines of ammunition from the armory. He left the building at roughly 3:13 p.m. in order to "go to work early."

Just 58 minutes after I started my interview with Juanita Deckard, we had a suspect — and the manhunt was on!

I called Troop I on my friend's telephone and was, at last, able to fully explain the situation to them. At the end of my briefing, my commander told me to do whatever the MPs requested. By the time I got Beck back to the roadside scene, they had decided to put special armed joint checkpoints at all four of the exits from Fort Wood. Since I was the closest trooper to the back gate of Fort Wood, they sent me there.

The south exit or back gate (as it was usually referred) lies just inside Pulaski County on Missouri Route AW. From the back gate of Fort Wood to the Texas County Line, the distance is only 2.25 miles. After that, you're in Texas County, which is part of Troop G, with headquarters at Willow Springs, Missouri. Troop G Highway Patrol troopers were sent to back me up. We stopped every car leaving Fort Wood. We looked for a slender white male, about six-feet tall, weighing about 165 pounds, with brown hair — Specialist Fourth Class, Johnny Lee Thornton of the 463rd MP Company — our murder suspect. A dangerous and violent suspect with police and military combat training who was well-armed and reported to be an excellent shot.

Police officers deal with people having bad days — sometimes very bad days. As troopers, we saw vehicle accident victims every day. As a general rule, we tend to identify with victims of the incidents we see. These people, their questions, and their raw emotions eventually take a toll on an officer. We have to effectively deal with our reactions or the job will eat us alive. It's a never-ending mental struggle. So far this day, I'd lost ground.

As I stopped cars at the back gate at gunpoint, I struggled with what had been one hell of a disturbing day. However, we were looking for an extremely dangerous man. My brain was back in gear and working. Then, fate intervened one more time and kicked me square in the teeth.

I stopped a car with a single occupant — an older, white male — and after ensuring he was alone, I waved him on. But the man didn't budge. Instead, he leaned forward and asked me if the roadblock had anything to do with the missing kids.

"Why do you ask?" His question set me on edge.

"One of the missing kids is my son."

Oh, God! Now what do I do?

The easy course of action would've been to deflect his question and send him on his way. But I had information he'd want to know and I felt the humane thing to do would be to talk to him. I asked him to pull to the side of the road.

We talked. My emotional distress returned full force so I don't remember all I told him. I recall giving him a broad outline of the day. Based on what little information I had, I told him his chances of hearing traumatic news before the day was over were good. I advised he had better brace himself.

As the man drove off, I wondered if I had done the right thing by talking to him. I still wonder today.

Then I was back to stopping cars, looking for Thornton. Shortly after darkness fell and a light, freezing rain began to fall, MP command notified us that Thornton was in custody and we could discontinue the checkpoints. With no other assignments pending and many hours past my normal shift end, I headed home. Before I signed off the air for the day, I was told to report to the MP command building bright and early the next morning for a briefing.

Relaxing that night was hard. In the quiet darkness, ugly images of dead teenagers tormented me. I cried myself to sleep.

When I reported to the MP headquarters the next morning, I was back into full police-action mode. I vowed to do anything and everything in my power to help with this case. But I also wondered why I was there, since the crime was strictly a federal jurisdiction. As I looked around the meeting room, I saw a larger group of men than I expected. I realized they were additional FBI agents brought in overnight, virtually all of the CID officers assigned to Fort Wood, and many MPs. There were several platoons of army engineers outside in the parking lot armed with shovels, tools, and mine detectors. It appeared the federal government was going into full-investigative mode and I would not be needed.

While I mingled with the many federal officers, I learned Thornton had been the first man to report another abandoned car several months before, which had been occupied by two other teens — now listed as missing.

I learned that after I drove off with Captain Beck to make the telephone call, the other officers and agents who'd listened to our verbal exchanges went to the body scene in vehicle X37. While en route, they examined it more closely. They found blood on and around the back seat along with a hole made by a bullet exiting out the unit's rear tailgate.

After I sent Miss Deckard to the local hospital, a team of CID agents had interviewed her there. They obtained the same information I had, plus some additional details. Since the suspect was still at large, they left agents to guard her in the hospital. Her chest bullet wound had probably been made as she was turning and was not considered serious. Her major medical problems were caused by the cold weather as she walked many hours in the snow, looking for help. Of course, she was suffering emotional trauma from her ordeal.

A brother of one of the male victims accompanied Mr. Needham on Route 17. The young man had followed Miss

Deckard's footprints in the snow back to the body site before my arrival at the roadside scene.

I learned the reason the checkpoints had been discontinued was because the Fort Wood Provost Marshal (military chief of police), Colonel Perry B. Elder, along with FBI Special Agent William Castleberry and MP Sergeant First Class Richard Jensen had arrested Thornton, without injury, the evening before. And I learned I had another small job to complete.

The FBI agents said the United States Federal District Court Judge in Springfield, Missouri, wanted Thornton in his official presence as soon as possible for potential court action. Two FBI agents prepared to load Thornton into a vehicle and drive him there. But there had been death threats phoned in to Fort Wood during the night. The caller warned Thornton would not reach Springfield alive. The FBI agents wanted fully-marked, Missouri State Highway Patrol cars to escort the agents' car while they transported the suspect to Springfield.

I made arrangements for the relay. I took the first lap west through Pulaski County into Laclede County, where another trooper took over. I'm not sure how necessary we were because as soon as the agents started west on the interstate, they boosted their speed up to about 90 miles-an-hour. Thornton made it to Springfield safe and sound. And with that task done, my active part in the investigation of Johnny Lee Thornton's unspeakable crimes came to an end.

A few weeks later, Prosecution asked me to write a detailed narrative as to what I could testify to in court. However, I was never called. I can only assume when they compared my possible testimony against that of the CID team who'd first interviewed Miss Deckard in the hospital — and knowing Miss Deckard was available to testify, I was not needed.

Author's note: Throughout this book, recent statements, comments, and observations made by people involved in this case in the 1977 time-frame are included. These statements were compiled for inclusion in this narrative. Since I was the first officer to enter the case when I made contact with Juanita Deckard roadside, my comments appear first.

* * *

Trooper J. B. King, Missouri State Highway Patrol:

This case made a permanent impression on me. I was stationed in Pulaski County during what we referred to here as the "pimp wars." This was when criminal mob factions from St. Louis and Memphis fought for control of vice and other illegal practices in the Fort Leonard Wood area. I'd seen my share of gunshot victims and violence. However, those cases involved members of criminal factions engaged in illicit activity at the time they were shot or murdered.

The Thornton case was something new. Four innocent kids, laughing and cutting up, minding their own business, struck down in a heartbeat. I found it tragic and emotionally devastating. One of the reasons I agreed to write this book for Red Engine Press was the hope that if I immersed myself in the details of this case for long enough, my revelations would be cathartic. The therapeutic writing might allow me to achieve a peace-of-mind.

Another compelling reason to participate is my off-duty hobby — History. Like it or not, the Thornton case is now a part of this region's history. This story must be told accurately and completely so generations to come won't have to rely on the rumor mill.

I've always been proud of my contribution to the Thornton case. While the investigation belonged to the federal government and the federal officers who worked the case, that first golden hour I played a critical and pivotal role. My questioning of Juanita Deckard roadside led to an accurate description of the suspect vehicle and its identifying number. Over the years, I took pride in the fact I helped unmask Johnny Lee Thornton. And then, during research for this book, I discovered the facts on which I'd based my pride were a little off-center.

As we perused hundreds of documents about this case, I learned that on January 12, 1977, the entire military police command on Fort Leonard Wood had a grand total of three International Scouts assigned to their motor pool. And on January 12, 1977, two of those Scouts were in the garage for extensive repairs. The clear description Juanita gave me of the International Scout was sufficient for the military police command staff on Fort Leonard Wood to zero in on the one specific vehicle that had been in operation during the night. The fact Juanita Deckard gave me a possible number off the side of the vehicle was merely extra icing on the probable-cause cake.

Furthermore, the time line of the crimes Juanita provided me and I relayed to the MP command staff, focused their attention on the only person to have had control of that specific Scout during the overnight shift — Johnny Lee Thornton. And so, as recounted in this chapter, 58 minutes after I began my roadside interview with Juanita Deckard, the MP command staff began their search for him. Under the unique circumstances of this case, that time lapse is not a bad record for identifying the lone suspect.

Secondly, I'd like to set the record straight on another issue. Above, I wrote about meeting the father of one of the murdered boys at the back gate. I didn't identify him, then, but I'll now tell you that man was Leroy Bates, father of victim Tony Bates. Mr. Bates currently resides in Alabama. Luck was with me during my research, as I met with him during a visit he made to his daughter in Texas County, Missouri. Our conversation lasted well over an hour.

Mr. Bates told me he was grateful I filled him in on the events of the day. He said I did indeed tell him his son was dead, which I don't remember doing. He was gracious and thanked me several times for my work at the back gate. I no longer wonder if I did the right thing by telling him the news before I knew for a fact it was completely true.

I now have some peace of mind regarding that decision.

* * *

Leroy Bates, father of victim Tony Bates:

When it began, I worked on Fort Leonard Wood. I was at work and Donna, my oldest daughter, called me and she said, "Daddy, I don't know what's wrong — but Tony didn't come home last night. His car is sitting out by the airport." When I questioned her, she said, "I don't know anything other than there's nothing around the car." I said, "Okay. I'll see what I can find out."

The first thing I did was call the Provost Marshal's office to see if they knew anything. They didn't. I then called the Pulaski County Sheriff's office to see if they knew anything. They didn't know anything. I got ahold of the state highway patrol and they said they hadn't stopped them or anything like that. I was at a loss for what to do. So, I went out past their car. I saw an ambulance from the hospital going out that way. I followed the ambulance out the back gate to Highway 17. I lost the ambulance, so I turned around and came back on post.

As far as the time that morning, I'm just guessing because I don't know how much time I spent on the phone trying to get information. All I know is whenever [my daughter] initially told me [the kids] were missing, I started trying to find out from authorities if anybody knew anything. I really don't know how long it took. And then, I spoke to you at the back gate. I'll tell you this much — and I'll say it from the bottom of my heart — it relieved me to know at least what the situation was. I wanted to know. And then I had to react from that. But at that point, I had no idea what had happened. Yes. Yes, I needed to know that. I didn't know what had happened to them. That was my first awareness of what was going on — that they were missing like that.

After I left the back gate, I went back to my office and called my wife and told her what had happened. At that point in time, I was driving a van from Lebanon to Fort Wood. I hauled several people with me, so I couldn't just haul off and go home. I had to wait until everybody was off work. Because they would've had no ride home. So, I had to wait for that."

JB: When did the military officially notify you?

Leroy Bates: I don't know that the military ever did, officially. I don't remember it. But they may have. I know somewhere along the line I found out Thornton was over on the west side of post and they were over there trying to get him to surrender. The Provost Marshal himself was over there. Somehow or another, I found out they got him and they had him in jail then. But I don't really recall just exactly how that played out.

Leroy Bates: I will say this, and it's not very Christian-like, but if I could've gotten ahold of the man, I would've killed him. That's what was in my heart. But I

18

knew there was no way I could do it once he got in jail. I wasn't going to try and be foolish. Man, I felt it so strong. I wanted to kill that man so bad. But I've gotten over it, to a point. That's what the Bible tells us we have to do.

J.B: What do you remember about our meeting at the back gate?

Leroy Bates: As I recall, I asked you if you were there because something had happened to those kids on post. As I recall, you said, "Yes. They found them and three of them are dead." And I said, "Was my son one of them?" And you said, "Yes." And that's pretty much the extent of the conversation I remember. I don't remember you reacting in any way but a kind way to me.

4 shot and buried in snow; woman walks 12 hours to get help

3

THE INVESTIGATION

WITHIN HOURS OF THE DISCOVERY of Johnny Lee Thornton's crimes, the experienced federal officers working the case came to the conclusion it would be challenging. They'd have to prove Thornton committed the crimes. From the start, they knew that would require a detailed and extensive investigation. First indications were that the crime was notable for the multiple, major felonies, complicated by the numerous crime scenes and number of witnesses. Within those first hours, investigators secured several items of direct evidence (firearm-related). But best of all, they had a survivor who could talk and point directly at Thornton.

The downside, as several of the experienced investigators suspected, Thornton's possible criminal defense strategy might be an insanity plea. The officers had to prove premeditation and state of mind. They had to show that Thornton's voluntary actions were not insane — and that he had schemed and plotted to commit the perfect crime. To demonstrate all this, they needed detailed facts to present in court. Even so, it wouldn't be easy.

Within hours, the federal agents realized they were up against countless obstacles. As soon as the conference on Route 17 with Trooper King ended, a team of CID agents entered MP vehicle X37 and drove toward the scene of the crimes. They literally followed the footprints of Special Agent Robert Oster, the CID agent who "caught" the case. Oster had left the roadside conference and headed to the scene on foot. By the time the other agents arrived, he had the crime scene perimeter set and a list of work assignments for the first wave of arriving agents.

The other agents had also been busy while driving to the scene. CID Agent Thomas Byrd observed blood in the back seat of the Scout, and what appeared to be a bullet hole in the rear portion of the vehicle. Byrd had the rest of the occupants of the vehicle move away from the blood stains. After arriving at the scene, the agents commenced an investigation, racing against the clock and the coming darkness.

The known special agents on this first trip were George T. Matthews, Thomas W. Byrd, and Roy E. Black.

* * *

George T. Matthews, CID Special Agent:

At the time of the Thornton case, Special Agent George T. Matthews was on his first field assignment as part of the CID detachment at Fort Wood. He was one of the first agents to arrive at the body site and he immediately went to work. The CID detachment on Fort Wood at the time of the Thornton murders was familiar with homicide.

George T. Matthews, CID Special Agent
Photo Courtesy of George Matthews

In my four years with the twelve-man CID office at Fort Leonard Wood, Missouri, from early 1975 to early 1979, we successfully investigated seven homicides which involved eleven deaths and resulted in confinement totaling nine lifetimes plus ninety-six years for six convicted murderers. Two of the crimes were infanticides. Two resulted in the perpetrators killing themselves. One was a triple murder by an on-duty MP. One was the murder of a guard by a fellow guard. And one was a crime for profit.

Each was unique in-and-of itself. Some had complicated crime scenes — indoors and out, in bad weather and good, while others had relatively simple crime scenes. One resulted in a manhunt. One in a hostage situation. And one resulted in the perpetrator accidentally killing himself while drawing his gun on the MPs attempting to apprehend him.

Some were a matter of documenting what happened and why it happened. Some had to be vigorously fought in court. And one — the most difficult — took two years before the case could be closed, with four subjects and four confessions.

* * *

The three agents were accompanied by MPs, Tyus[1] and SFC Richard (Dick) Jensen. As these officers approached the body dump scene, they found Douglas Hawkins walking away from the scene. They quickly interviewed him and he led the agents to the location of two bodies — his brother, Wesley Hawkins and Linda Needham. He'd been unable to find Tony Bates.

It was getting dark and the local weather forecast predicted four more inches of snow. The few agents on the scene had to take enough pictures of the crime scene, complete several crime scene sketches, and arrange for the bodies to be removed. They lacked enough equipment to accomplish these tasks, but knowing time was of the essence, they jumped in and did the necessary work. Early on, the FBI decided to take control of the case for federal court prosecution since the victims were civilians. But there were no FBI agents on scene.

At roughly 5:00 that evening, Byrd contacted FBI Special Agent Tom E. Den Ouden and advised him of vehicle X37's

---

1   There is no further information on this MP Officer.

condition. Byrd requested instructions on how to handle the situation. The interior of the vehicle had already been unwittingly compromised by the presence of the agents driving from the Fort Wood cantonment area to the rendezvous point on Route 17—and from there to the crime scene. Den Ouden decided the best course of action was for Jensen drive the vehicle back to the main post and place it in a protected area of the motor pool, with an MP on guard. Once this was accomplished, Jensen turned the keys to the vehicle over to Den Ouden.

International Scout X37 used by Johnny Lee Thornton to kidnap teenagers

Federal Court Trial Record

* * *

Thomas E. Den Ouden, FBI Special Agent:

The first FBI agent to arrive at the site of the bodies was Special Agent Thomas E. Den Ouden. Den Ouden had been an FBI agent since July 22, 1968. He'd spent one year in the Houston, Texas, field office and then transferred to the Kansas City Missouri office. He was one of the initial members of the FBI SWAT team.

He wanted to work out of the Springfield Missouri office but there were no openings. When an opening came up at the Fort Leonard

Wood office, he applied for it and was accepted. He was the second agent assigned to Fort Leonard Wood in August of 1976.

Agent Den Ouden lived in Lebanon Missouri which is 30 miles west of Fort Wood. At the time of the Thornton case, Den Ouden's official FBI car contained a radio linked to the Missouri State Highway Patrol radio frequency. The highway patrol dispatched calls to Den Ouden as car 1326.

FBI Special Agent Tom Den Ouden shown with a perfect score target.

Photo courtesy of Tom Den Ouden

It was a dark, dark day when I was contacted on the highway patrol's radio system and told to return to Fort Leonard Wood immediately for a homicide. Upon arrival at Fort Wood, a CID team took me to crime scene number three — the site of the bodies.

I was overwhelmed when I got the call. Then, walking onto the crime scene — and the CID agents there told me, "This is going to be your case." I see all of this yellow tape. Obviously, the bodies are still there — although I can't recollect that now. I'm thinking, *How in the heck am I going to manage this case? It is way beyond my proficiency — my training*. But I didn't have to do it alone. CID had it all laid out — yellow tape everywhere — and had made all the arrangements necessary.

I had never worked a homicide before. The FBI didn't train us to do that. The only time we'd work a homicide was if it was on a government reservation, such as this case. But the outstanding CID agents were taking care of everything. And after we examined the body site, looking at the blood stain evidence (which proved to be monumental at trial), they took me to the game warden's cabin.

We had just started to examine the scene when I got an urgent call on the radio to return to our office at MP headquarters. They specified I should run code to expedite my arrival. It turned out they wanted me to take part in the arrest of Johnny Lee Thornton. But by the time I made it into MP headquarters, the arrest of Thornton had already been accomplished and he was in custody.

* * *

The CID agents on the scene that first afternoon worked quickly and did the best they could under the conditions they had to operate. The eight inches of snow and ice on the ground made everything problematic. The batteries for their flash-lights, radios, and cameras froze and lost power. The agents had limited spare batteries with them. The first afternoon and evening were marked by a combination of chaos and initiative. By roughly 10:00 p.m., the agents had sketched the scenes, taken photographs, and the teens' bodies had been removed.

During this initial part of the investigation, the snow proved to be a blessing for the agents. They found where Thornton had parked the MP vehicle and left it running. Various fluids from the vehicle soaked into the snow. The tracks in the snow leading away from the Scout told their own story. Footprints of the two girls led to the point where Thornton shot them. Deckard's body left blood on the snow where she first was hit and fell. Plainly visible, bloody marks indicated Thornton dragged her limp body deeper into the woods.

The drag marks where Thornton pulled Linda Needham's body into the woods were different. The agents found no blood evidence in the snow there. At the spot where Needham's body was discovered, male boot prints indicated Thornton had, at one point, stood directly over her. The blood and boot evidence at the scene, combined with the autopsy results, showed Needham had been shot one time in the center of her chest. The bullet's travel-angle revealed it was fired from a point directly above her. The only conclusion possible was Thornton's first shot in the dark missed Linda — and she played dead as he dragged her deeper into the woods. It's probable that when Thornton learned Needham was faking her death, he stood over her and fired the fatal shot into her chest. Her body rested there until it was discovered.

The investigators used a mine detector to locate a single .45 bullet buried in the ground directly under where Needham's body lay. The FBI lab forensically matched this bullet to the .45 handgun issued to Thornton for that work shift.

Drag marks leading from the Scout to Wesley Hawkins' body were clear and contained little blood evidence. The autopsy confirmed that Hawkins had been dead for several hours by the time Thornton moved him from the vehicle.

Footprints in the snow revealed Tony Bates was alive when Thornton removed him from the Scout. The evidence indicated that Bates, although wounded by the shot fired in the Scout at the time of the abduction, was upright and mobile. It suggested that Bates broke free from Thornton at one point and ran deeper into the forest. Approximately 50-60 feet later, Bates apparently tripped over a snow-hidden log and fell face-down in the snow. Thornton then came up behind him, stopped approximately 30 feet away, and fired a fatal shot into the back of the boy's head. The autopsy revealed Bates died instantly. Boot tracks in the snow showed Thornton did not approach Bates' body after firing the fatal shot. Instead, he returned to the Scout.

The CID agents arranged for Major Gerald A. Rappe, a military pathologist assigned to the General Leonard Wood Army Community Hospital, (GLWACH), to report to the scene and examine the victims' bodies before they were removed. Major Rappe arrived around 5:45 p.m. and, after an examination of each victim, made the official death pronouncement.

Due to the rough roads leading to the area, a military five-quarter-ton truck removed the bodies. The Fort Wood ambulance sent to retrieve them missed a turn along the way, got stuck and needed a wrecker to extract it.

The victims' bodies, wrapped in blue sheets, were taken to the Fort Wood hospital for autopsy.

With the dawn of January 14, 1977, the chaos and rushed efforts necessary on day one gave way to planning and organization on day two. A case management team was set up to supervise the case work. It consisted of Colonel Perry B. Elder and FBI Agent, William Castleberry, the Special Agent in Charge (SAC) of the resident Fort Wood FBI office.

Castleberry was the lead case agent for the FBI. Special Agent Robert Oster was the on-call duty agent when the crime was discovered, so he automatically became the lead CID case agent. Special Agent Matt Moriarity was the Chief of Operations for CID. This management team reviewed the reports, assigned tasks for work, and generally ensured the investigation stayed on course.

* * *

William "Bill" Castleberry, FBI Special Agent:

At the time of the Thornton case, the Special Agent in Charge (SAC) of the Fort Wood FBI office was 34-year-old William "Bill" Castleberry. Agent Castleberry had been an FBI agent for a little over seven years at that time. However, he'd been in law enforcement since his 21st birthday. His first law enforcement experience was with the Shelby County (Memphis) Tennessee Sheriff's department. Then later, he served four years in command of a security police unit with the United States Air Force. He subsequently joined the FBI and became the Special Agent in Charge of the Fort Leonard Wood office.

Agent Castleberry had been in the Kansas City, Missouri regional FBI headquarters office for a conference on investigations involving Fort Leonard Wood. He was en route back to Fort Leonard Wood when he was notified via his patrol radio that he was urgently needed for a homicide.

The closer I got to Fort Wood, the worse the snow and ice road conditions became. I had to slow down.

Keep in mind, the Thornton case came well before the age of computers and sophisticated case-management software. Therefore, I had to keep up with all of the lead assignments on three-by-five note cards, which I stored in a little wooden box on my desk.

During the chaos of action on the afternoon and evening of January 13th, I quickly realized with a game warden detail member as the lead suspect, we had a crime scene with the potential to cover all of the Fort Wood reservation.

I called the Kansas City district headquarters and briefed them on the crime scene issue. I explained, "Here's what I've got. I've got a crime scene bigger than the whole county. I've got a likely perpetrator on the loose (and I recall some talking in the background that I could hear. There was this person calling off names). It's going to be an unpleasant working situation. Going to be cold and wet and harsh."

I can remember hearing some names I knew being mentioned, and they were really top-flight guys — Don McDonald, Emmet Trammell. And there was a really young agent. I think his name was Jack? Jack Reed, maybe? They started those guys right away.[2]

* * *

The decision to join the FBI and CID agents together as working partners for the investigation was one of the first made. This was done by assigning one FBI special agent and one CID special agent together as a team. They ended up with a total of 14 teams, 28 agents. Each two-man team was able to operate independently or as part of a combined larger team for the bigger crime scenes.

There were a number of reasons for this decision. First, each agency had to complete reports. The men in charge felt it would be better if the agents obtained the information side-by-side, simultaneously, in order to complete more uniform reports for the attorneys to read. Second, leaders felt evidence-collecting training of the CID agents was superior to that of the FBI agents on scene. Since the FBI had already assumed jurisdiction for this case, this practical decision meant any evidence recovered at a scene by a CID agent would promptly be turned over to an FBI agent to ensure a proper chain of

---

2   FBI Agent, Gary W. Reid

custody. Since the agents were working side-by-side, it made the chain of custody transfer much simpler.

Before the case was over, the officers would collect over 250 possible evidence items — of which, 151 were sent to the FBI laboratory for forensic analysis. A proverbial mountain of evidence.

As the days went by in this investigation, the wisdom of the decision to join the two agencies together became more pronounced as a smart move. One of the unspoken things this joint investigation preserved was the ability for both the Federal Bureau of Investigation to pursue a case for federal court and for the United States Army to pursue a court-martial in a military court. The joint cooperation of both sets of agents greatly simplified the investigative process, and later the prosecution process.

The 14, two-man teams were established. The teams jointly assigned to the various crime scenes soon realized they faced many obstacles. Most of the crime scenes were in remote areas of Fort Leonard Wood, accessible only by four-wheel-drive vehicles. The officers working the crime scenes needed tools — such as shovels, rakes, mine detectors, and other special equipment. The First Sergeant of the 463rd MP Company worked overtime to outfit each of the 13-newly-arrived FBI agents, plus agents Tom Den Ouden and William Castleberry from the Fort Wood FBI office, with all of the cold-weather clothing gear they needed to stay on the job.

* * *

George T. Matthews, CID Special Agent:

In a surprise announcement, on the morning of January 14, CID Special Agent George T. Matthews was placed in charge of a combined FBI/CID team that went to the abduction location where the Bates' car was found. From there, the team went to the body dump site.

When Bill Castleberry was making assignments the next morning and announced in front of much more senior CID agents, FBI agents, and MPs that I was in charge of a crime scene team, I

was floored. Never in my wildest dreams did I see this coming...
or wanted it.

I could work the hell out of a complicated crime scene. Or
stick like Super Glue to a suspect until I proved his guilt or
innocence. But to supervise those who I considered much more
qualified than myself left me feeling lacking. I felt — and do to
this day — I let them down. Because of my lack of leadership
experience. I also thought — and still do — the FBI was the
ultimate law enforcement agency.

Author's Note: While Agent Matthews may have had
concerns over his inadequacy to supervise a crime scene
team, in all fairness I should note the other agents
involved in this case — both FBI and CID, who were
interviewed for this book had nothing but praise for the
efforts and leadership of Matthews. The mere fact the
command supervisory team in charge of the case placed
a CID agent in charge of a crime scene team (which
included FBI agents), for the two most important crime
scenes in the case speaks volumes as to the perceived
professionalism and leadership ability of Matthews.

* * *

The training area roads leading to the crime scene were
not real roads in the true sense of the word. They were literal
dirt paths covered in snow and ice, which created problems
for the teams. In order to reach the crime scene, the agents
had to first drive 11 miles south, then four miles west, then
six miles north of the main cantonment area of Fort Wood.

As the number of vehicles assigned to the investigative
effort increased, it became necessary to post guards along the
route to prevent people from getting lost and to ensure a timely
arrival of necessary personnel at the crime scenes. Due to the
cold, snow, and ice, these road guards had to be supplied and
rotated out of duty at regular intervals.

The radio frequencies used by the FBI and CID didn't
mesh with each other nor with the MP radio network. This
created additional problems for the investigation. Agents at
the scene carrying hand-held radios had to arrange for an MP

vehicle to be stationed halfway between the crime scene and the MP command post. This vehicle acted as a relay point on the MP radio frequency.

The vast number of radio messages passing back and forth between the command post and the crime scene proved to be yet another major issue. Large volumes of radio messages going both ways and through the relay point greatly slowed down the flow of information. Additionally, the MPs' daily routine radio traffic around Fort Wood interfered with crime scene transmissions. Within a few days, most of these problems were solved by borrowing tactical radios from military combat units.

Scene of Sexual Activity:
Game Warden Warm Up Shack
Scene where bodies were found

Relation of Game Warden Shack to body dump location.
Federal Court File

The investigators listed at least seven probable crime scenes — all of which required thorough examination and investigation. With the probability from the local weather station forecasting more snow that would severely compromise the crime scenes, investigators knew they had to act quickly. They

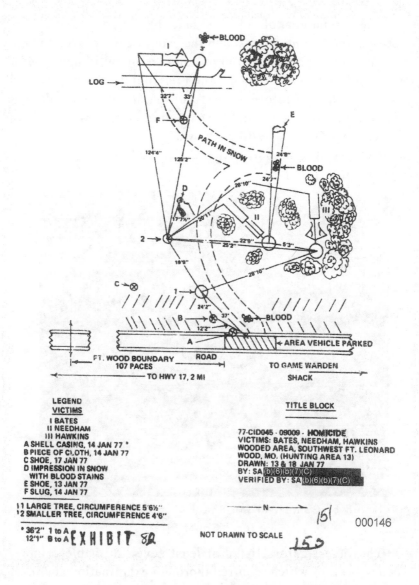

Schematic of the body dump site
Federal Court Trial Record

prioritized the sites by most likely to be destroyed from the impending snowfall.

Therefore, the site where the bodies of Wesley Hawkins, Tony Bates, and Linda Needham were found became a target for more in-depth processing on day two. A second vital area, and the one which took first priority, was the abduction site on the highway south of the Fort Wood airfield. Due to the number of cars passing on the main blacktop road leading to Fort Wood's south gate, the potential for evidence destruction was high. In the early morning hours of January 14, the first team processed it.

In addition to the two aforementioned locations, the military police game wardens' shack, the International Scout, X37, and the borrowed vehicle Johnny Lee Thornton was driving, a 1971 Chevrolet Malibu with Minnesota license plates (which was found parked near the Ballard residence) all needed to be searched, processed, and inventoried.

The acquisition of a warrant to search Johnny Lee Thornton's room at the barracks was a priority.

The autopsy procedures required a witness and a photographer. Many people needed to be interviewed because of their duty association with Thornton or because they were friends with him. One essential interview was with the duty armorer for the 463rd MP Company who had issued Johnny Lee Thornton the military .45 pistol used to commit the murders. The direct forensic evidence related to that specific pistol via serial number would prove to be critical at trial.

* * *

On the morning of January 14, 1977, Colonel Elder supplied the investigators with the basic military biography of Johnny Lee Thornton. Thornton's rank was Specialist Fourth Class (SP4) as of September 1, 1976. He held a Secret security clearance and was sworn into the regular Army for a three-year enlistment, scheduled to end on May 18, 1979. He had a GED diploma. His general testing score was 118. In order to enlist in the Army, he needed a score of 100. The minimum acceptable for the MP Corps was 110 at the time.

According to his file, Thornton enlisted into the US Army on May 19, 1975, at Little Rock, Arkansas. He reported for his initial basic training at Fort Leonard Wood on May 22, 1975, where he was stationed. After basic training ended on July 14, 1975, he reported to the MP school at Fort McClellan, Alabama, for his specialty training. On September 5, 1975, Thornton departed Fort McClellan en route back to his first duty station — Fort Leonard Wood. Thornton arrived at Fort Wood on September 22, 1975, and had been stationed there since.

Thornton's duty specialty was military police but his internal designation within the military police was correctional specialist. He listed no religious preferences on his enlistment paperwork. His marital status was given as married with three dependents — his wife and two children. According to Thornton's record, he'd been charged with breaking and entering in 1971 at Concordia, California. The charges were later dismissed. His last known local, off-post residence was Hickory Hills Trailer Court, #4, Saint Robert, Missouri.

* * *

By the afternoon of January 14, 1977, the stage for the investigation was set. The 14 teams worked on their missions to search a crime scene or to interview a witness. Upon completion of their mission, each team filed a comprehensive report detailing their findings. These individual reports formed the building blocks for Prosecution.

In some instances, a search took several days or had to be repeated. Some sites had to be reprocessed after the snow melted — over a month later. Some witnesses were interviewed a second or even a third time. But as the weeks passed and Prosecution examined the completed reports, the case moved forward. Evidence against Thornton continued to stack up.

* * *

James S. Reist, Military Police Game Warden:

In order to give the reader a sense of the intense effort on the first day of the case, consider the words of former MP, James S. Reist, 463rd MP Company.

> During my tour of duty at Fort Leonard Wood, I worked as a senior patrolman, shift supervisor, desk sergeant, and as a game warden with Johnny Lee Thornton. I remember him as a knowledgeable, professional, and personable individual who was going through either a divorce or separation at the time.
>
> Johnny knew the Fort Leonard Wood military reservation like the back of his hand and was an individual of few words outside of law enforcement duties. We searched for poachers, ran road block operations, tracked suspects and cited/arrested many violators. [Thornton] never gave any indicators of what was to come.

James Reist former MP and Waynesville City Police
Officer 1977

Photo Courtesy James Reist

> The following is an account of events which occurred on January 13, 1977, while I was working as the on-duty game warden at Fort Leonard Wood, Missouri.
>
> I was on patrol when all of Johnny's actions came to light and the radio dispatcher from the MP desk contacted me with instructions to return to the Provost Marshal's office (PMO). When

I arrived at the PMO, I went back to the game warden section, where I was linked-up with a CID agent. We were tasked, along with another MP road patrol, to proceed to the MP barracks, building #1687 to look for Johnny Lee Thornton. And to search for and recover any and all evidence found at that location

We checked Johnny's barracks room and secured the scene by posting an MP at the door, pending further processing. We then went outside to the dumpster, which I climbed into in order to search for any possible items of evidentiary value. We recovered what we believed to be some blood-stained items and bagged and tagged them.

Then we went across the dirt road to the orderly room to talk with the commander and first sergeant. At the end of that building was the arms room, which was our next stop. The CID agent talked with the armorer and collected his statement on Johnny's activities, sign-in and sign-out logs, and accountability of weapons, ammunition, and handcuffs issued, along with any comments he might have heard Johnny make. We gathered-up what we had collected and returned to the PMO for marking, preserving, and securing the evidence.

I then returned to my duty section. We pored over post topographic maps and plotted-out points of concern to this investigation. I went back on patrol for a short time to check some areas. When I returned to the PMO, there was a swarm of FBI agents arriving in their unmarked sedans. There must have been at least a dozen agents who followed me into the PMO, which is where our office for the FBI (on post) was located.

I was back in the game warden section when the telephone rang. A couple of us picked-up the phone, at which time we heard Johnny's voice asking to talk with the section chief. Hand signals went up, and the FBI came rushing in to the section, along with our section supervisor, picked up telephones to listen to what Johnny had to say. Johnny simply stated (as a question) "I hear you're looking for me?" The section chief replied, "We were." And then he asked Johnny where he was.

After a short pause, Johnny asked the section chief if he knew where the yellow farm house on Highway 17, southwest of post was. The section chief replied he knew the location. And then, Johnny said he would remain there. The section emptied out

as all of the FBI agents and our section chief went to apprehend Johnny.

After Johnny was taken into custody, we still had a lot of things
to do in relation to this case. I stayed on shift as the on-duty
game warden.

It started getting dark when the Deputy Provost Marshal and
some CID agents told me they needed to go out to a primary crime scene [the game warden shack/cabin]. However, they
didn't know how to get out there. And they couldn't access the
area with regular vehicles. I agreed the only access to that area
would have to be in four-wheel drive vehicles, like my patrol
vehicle. And I agreed to take them out to the site. The weather
was cold. We had knee-deep snow in that particular area and
there was a mild breeze blowing when we arrived.

As we got closer to the game warden shack, we stopped short so
as not to enter the actual crime scene and disturb any evidence
in the area. The cabin was on our right. And as we looked to
the left, we could see the light sets were turned on to illuminate
the area where the victims were located.

I waited for what must have been an hour and assisted in any
way required to process and prep the bodies for transport to
GLWACH. We had called for a military ambulance — A Cracker
Box, as we called them — and after an hour or so, we contacted
them again...only to learn that they had passed the turn-off
and gone down another road to turn around, only to get stuck.
The decision was made to take one of the military's M880,
three-quarter-ton pick-up trucks, and to load the bodies into
the truck bed.

Three of us wrapped the bodies, one-by-one, in sterile blue
sheets, taking care as to preserve any evidence left behind. We
placed each onto a military litter [stretcher] and carried them to
the waiting truck. We slid two of the litters straight into the bed
of the truck, length-wise. The third litter was placed across the
truck bed and secured. An MP was assigned to ride in the back
of the truck to escort the bodies to the morgue and to maintain
the chain of evidence.

The officials who accompanied me to the crime scene, the Assistant PM [Deputy Provost Marshal] and the CID agents, opted

to catch another ride back from the crime scene. I was tasked to follow the truck transporting the bodies back to post.

The three-quarter-ton truck made its way back up the road until it got to Highway 17, turned left and went back through the south gate, and then continued on to its final destination — the GLWACH morgue.

I followed the truck back to the hospital. And all I could see in my headlights were those three litters and the MP guard in the rear of the vehicle. I remember thinking, What a waste... Three young lives cut short and the terrible ordeal they must have endured while in captivity.

I ended my tour of duty later that night but I have never forgotten the events of that day.

* * *

Frank Jung, Military Police Dog Handler:

A second look at the day of the crime comes from former MP dog handler, Frank Jung of the 208th MP Company.

Okay, my memory of this is... I was on duty the night of the shooting. And, I didn't learn about the shooting until after I got off duty. If I recall correctly, I got off around ten p.m.

This is what I recall the night of the shooting: I was in the MP station. And, I saw Johnny Lee. And, we struck up a conversation. And at that time, I went off duty. I remember the next day they were calling us all back in because the girl got to the road and reported it. And so, they called everybody back in at that time. But I never saw Johnny Lee after I was aware of the shooting. I do not recall ever talking to Johnny Lee after I knew about the girl and the shooting. So, that would not have been me who told him about the survivors.

It was getting close to the end of my shift and, as I normally do, I would stop by the MP station. I drove in there and checked to see if anything was going on before I put my dog away. Johnny Lee was standing there. I asked how it was going. And he said everything was okay. Johnny was quiet. He was not one who would strike up a big conversation with you. I checked with the radio operator to see what was going on. He said, "No, it's pretty quiet." And I said, "I'm gonna go put my dog up and call it a night."

I don't recall the time. I know it was close to the end of my shift. But I don't know what kind of a shift Johnny was working. I do know he liked to work nights looking for poachers. Johnny was always saying, "I'm going to go look for poachers."

I was in the 208 MP Company, and what happened was, when I first came to Fort Leonard Wood, I was in the 463 MP Company. Then they sent me to a dog handler school down at Lackland Air Force Base. When I returned to Fort Leonard Wood, they reassigned me to the 208 MP Company because the 208th was a TRADOC [Training and Doctrine Command] unit instead of a FORSCOM [Forces Command] unit. So, the MPs in the 208 were mainly at the stockade, MPI unit, and the dog handlers. As a TRADOC unit you would never get deployed anywhere.

The 463 MP Company and the 208 MP Company were housed at different locations on Fort Leonard Wood. The only time I ever ran into Johnny Lee was if we were working the same shift. He, as a game warden, and me, as a dog handler. Our acquaintance was casual. We knew each other from working details. We had two dog handlers on duty per shift.

When they called us in that day, they told me I didn't need my dog. They just needed me. They posted me south of the airfield to check every vehicle leaving post for Johnny Lee, in case he tried to get out through another vehicle.

I was by myself and I was not all the way to the south gate. I was actually just past the airport. Another thing I recall is, it was pretty interesting because they would not issue any of us .45s due to the fact they had locked down the armory. I had to use my shotgun to stop the cars. What they did was, they shut down the armory to do an inventory of the weapons. They were trying to determine if Johnny had turned in his weapon — his .45. And so, they weren't issuing any .45s. And so, the rest of us coming in, who had been called in, the duty armorer told us, "I can't issue any .45s to you. I'm issuing M-16s and shotguns." So yes, they were doing an inventory of the weapons. We had an armorer on duty twenty-four hours a day at the MP station.

I remember when they flew the FBI in to take over the investigation. The MPs were really kinda livid because it was like, "Hey, this is our guy accused of this crime and you're telling us to stand down so you can take control of the case?" There was a lot of tension in the air. We wanted to bring him in to account for the crime.

MP Patrol Dog Warning at gate to Fort Leonard Wood
Courtesy of James Reist

4

THE ARREST

AT APPROXIMATELY 6:30 P.M. ON January 13, 1977, Johnny Lee Thornton called into the MP command post and asked to speak to SFC Richard Jensen of the 463rd MP Company. Jensen was Thornton's immediate noncommissioned supervisor on the game warden unit and he had developed a rapport with Thornton. Also present in the command room at the time was Colonel Perry B. Elder. Elder got on an extension and three of them (Jensen, Thornton, and Elder) discussed a meeting with Thornton for a possible surrender. Thornton wanted Elder and Jensen to come to the rendezvous point, unarmed.

Colonel Perry B. Elder, Provost Marshall
Ft. Leonard Wood 1977
Photo Courtesy of Eric Foster

Thornton said, "I want to talk to you about something."

Elder and Jensen agreed to meet him and Thornton specified the location would be the driveway leading to the Ballard
residence, just off of FLW 8 on Fort Leonard Wood.

* * *

According to the CID case files, on January 14, 1977, Mrs.
[name redacted] was interviewed. She stated that at about
6:15 p.m. on January 13, 1977, a Caucasian male came to her
residence and asked her whether he could use her telephone.
She related the individual entered her home and contacted
Sergeant [name redacted]. She stated the individual started
the phone conversation with, "This is Specialist Four John..."
She didn't overhear the full conversation.

She described the individual as approximately 68 to 70
inches in height and weighing approximately 140 to 150 pounds.
He had light-colored hair, possibly light brown. He wore a plaid
jacket, greenish in color. She related the individual ended his
conversation with the statement he would meet [name redact-
ed] at the point where Ballard Road meets the highway. She
stated the individual had told her his car had gotten stuck on
a hill and this was the reason why he had to use her telephone.

After the individual left the residence, she observed he
was walking and there was no vehicle in sight.

* * *

Unnamed Source:

The CID case file contained another entry dated January 13, 1977.
The CID agent in question stated he interviewed Sergeant First
Class (SFC) [name redacted] who was the NCO/Chief Game War-
den Division Officer of the Provost Marshal's office, Fort Leonard
Wood, Missouri. This, of course, could only have been SFC Richard
Jensen. His written statement to CID follows.

[Name redacted] related the following information regarding
Thornton. He stated Thornton currently resides in the barracks
area of the 463rd Military Police Company. He further stated

[Thornton] was living with a WAC sergeant in the quarters adjacent to 11 Indiana Ave, Fort Leonard Wood, Missouri, some time ago. He was unable to provide the name of the WAC sergeant. He stated he was aware Thornton had problems with his wife and had subsequently gone into debt, but to his knowledge was working everything out and there were no problems as of this date.

He further related the last he saw Thornton at six a.m. on January 13, 1977, as Thornton was completing his tour of duty as game warden. He related the game warden vehicle utilized belongs the 208th Military Police Company and has the bumper sticker X37. [Name redacted] related that at approximately four p.m., while he was on a mission along with the CID special agents, he observed what appeared to be blood on the rear seat of X37, and further examination of the vehicle disclosed what appeared to be a bullet hole in the rear of the vehicle.

[Name redacted] stated at the time he talked with Thornton on January 13, 1977, he observed nothing unusual. He further described Thornton as a thorough investigator. He related Thornton had told him he was unable to clean the jeep after his tour of duty at six a.m. on January 13, 1977, as he was unable to wash it due to the cold weather conditions.

At six twenty p.m., [name redacted] was advised there was a telephone call for him on extension 8-3177, military police extension in the game warden division. [Name redacted] was further advised by personnel that Thornton was on the line at this time. He picked up the telephone and joined the conversation between COL [name redacted], and Thornton. Thornton requested COL [name redacted] and SFC [name redacted] come to get him, as he was at and off-post address.

Thornton stated, "Don't bring anything. There is no need. There is nothing to worry about."

The telephone conversation terminated at six twenty-seven p.m.

Agent's Note: After listening to the telephone conversation, aforementioned, it is the opinion of this agent that Thornton appeared to be disturbed and extremely worried. His voice was shaking.

* * *

Eric Lynn Foster, son-in-law of Colonel Perry Elder:

[Perry Elder] told me one of the things Thornton said over the phone was they would have to come unarmed. Perry told me it was recommended to him, "Colonel, you absolutely should not do this. It is not a good idea." But [Elder] said, "You know, I think we need to do this. I need to do this as part of maybe getting him to surrender." So, Perry told me he went in a vehicle with a couple of others and he wore a bulletproof vest.

* * *

The plan for the meeting with Thornton was simple. Elder and Jensen would talk to him but they would have backup from Special Agent William Castleberry. Castleberry was to hide in the back of the vehicle with a Remington 870 pump .12-gauge shotgun. Several carloads of MPs and CID agents in other vehicles would park about a mile away from the meeting site. In addition, Elder and Jensen both hid snub nose .38 caliber revolvers in their pockets so they would appear to be unarmed.

When they arrived at the specified location, things didn't start out well. Initially, there was a herd of cattle in the road where Thornton's car was supposed to be parked. They maneuvered around the cows and drove approximately 150 more yards. There they found Thornton's car parked near a wooded area.

Elder and Jensen positioned their vehicle headlights illuminating the woods so they could see Thornton. Thornton had said he would come out of the woods into the lights. Both officers got out of the vehicle, called for Thornton to come out and talk to them. After approximately 10 minutes of yelling, they were startled by a voice behind them which said, "I am here."

The officers turned around and saw Thornton had outflanked them. Instead of Thornton being illuminated by the headlights of the vehicle, the officers were silhouetted by the headlights of the vehicle. Even worse, Castleberry was hidden in the back seat of the car with the shotgun, between the officers and Thornton.

Elder and Jensen initiated communication with Thornton.

Early on, Thornton made it clear he did not wish to relinquish his weapon. In fact, as he stood in the darkness, the officers saw the .45 pistol Thornton held in his right hand. The gun was pointed down, alongside Thornton's leg. This caused deep consternation to Elder and Jensen.

Thornton admitted he'd been hiding a way down the road and followed behind them on foot to their present location. He wanted to ensure the officers hadn't set a trap for him. Thornton said he was out of breath and would need a moment or two to recover.

When Thornton finally spoke, the first thing he said was, "I know I did something bad but I can't remember what it was." He admitted to stopping a vehicle with two boys and two girls. He revealed the teens didn't say anything to make him mad. He said he sometimes got bad headaches and that when he got the headaches, he couldn't remember things. These headaches had been going on for quite some time. In fact, his head was beginning to hurt again. He needed to sit down and rest.

With that, Thornton sat down on top of a snow mound near the side of the road. Elder and Jensen edged closer, but they couldn't make out any details of his face, only his body outline. Thornton repeated that he knew he had "done something real bad" but just couldn't remember what that was.

Realizing that he and Jensen had been out of radio touch with the command post for quite some time, Elder told Thornton they needed to call in on the radio and let dispatch know everything was okay.

Thornton said he understood.

Elder entered the vehicle to use the radio. While inside he told Castleberry that things were going okay and he and Jensen were going to continue with the negotiation. Then he made the radio call and returned to talk with Thornton.

During the discussion, Thornton made a number of statements:

"What have I done? Don't you know I can't remember what happened to the people?"

At that point, the officers told Thornton that three of the teens were dead but one was still alive. Elder assured Thornton that one of them surviving was a good thing.

"I'm sorry I did this to your police force," Thornton repeated several times over the next few minutes.

Elder told him not to worry. He and Jensen were there to help. During this negotiation, both Elder and Jensen asked Thornton to surrender his weapon several times. He refused.

Thornton said he'd wandered through the brush for some time that afternoon. On three or four occasions, he sat down and tried to shoot himself but couldn't do it. When Webster called for a ride to work, he'd told him that the authorities were looking for some missing kids. At that point, Thornton explained, he realized he'd done something bad.

The conversation took an odd and disjointed turn. Thornton told them that he'd had trouble with his wife and that she'd left him. However, they'd worked out their problems and were getting back together. Thornton said he was concerned about his wife and his two boys because he loved them very much.

Elder repeated his request for Thornton to lay down his weapon. Thornton refused to do so. Then, he stated he had three conditions which would have to be met before he'd lay down the weapon. The first was that he wanted to talk to his wife. The second was, he didn't want to be handcuffed. The third was, he didn't want to be seen by any of his fellow MPs when he got to the MP station. He apologized for what he had done to the MPs.

Elder said he'd have to submit Thornton's demands to the FBI over the radio. Elder returned to the officers' vehicle, where he once again briefed Castleberry on the situation and relayed Thornton's demands.

Elder returned, and the negotiations continued for several more minutes. Thornton made more statements like, "Don't you know? I can't remember,"—and other similar remarks.

Finally, the officers heard Thornton's weapon's magazine eject. Thornton held the gun toward Elder. Elder again asked him to put his weapon down.

"Wait, there's a round in the chamber," Thornton said.

Elder told Thornton to lay down the weapon and he or Jensen would remove the live round from the weapon's chamber. The suspect refused to lay down the gun. The officers then heard the slide racking backward. Thornton said the weapon was empty and he laid it on the ground in the middle of the dirt road.

Jensen stepped forward and picked up the unloaded weapon, the magazine, and the loose round. After patting Thornton down for additional weapons, he took him by the arm and helped him toward the officers' vehicle.

When they got Thornton into the vehicle, they introduced him to Agent Castleberry. Castleberry formally identified himself as an FBI agent and informed Thornton he was under arrest for murder. Castleberry told Thornton he would be taken to the MP station for further questioning.

And so, after a little over 30 minutes of armed standoff and intense face-to-face negotiation, Johnny Lee Thornton surrendered without incident, ending the short, but tense, manhunt.

While they were en route to the MP station, Thornton complained about the bright lights bothering him and said his head ached. During the trip, Castleberry advised Thornton not to make any statements.

* * *

Although it had taken more than 30 minutes to accomplish the arrest of Thornton, this was a major advantage for Prosecution. Thornton made the self-incriminating statements during the negotiation process and not while in police custody. Therefore, his statements didn't require a Miranda warning to be admissible in court. And in fact, his statements were later admitted into evidence during the trial.

In addition, a knife was taken from Thornton at the time of his arrest. Later, this knife was forensically linked by the FBI crime lab to the flat tire on the Bates' vehicle. This evidence confirmed Juanita Deckard's statements and showed proof of premeditation on Thornton's part.

* * *

FBI Agent William Castleberry's memories:

When Johnny Lee Thornton checked in after his shift, he claimed he'd expended rounds on wild dogs. This comment, combined with other evidence, made him a suspect in the murders. Colonel Perry Elder told me that Thornton refused to come in for questioning and that they were looking for him.

Later, Colonel Elder approached me and said that the suspect had been in touch again. Johnny Lee Thornton was ready to turn himself in. He requested that his boss, Sergeant Jensen, come to the meeting with Colonel Elder — but no one else. As they were preparing to meet the suspect, I became concerned about security and said, "I'm going with you. I'll secrete myself but you've got to have some backup.

We believed Thornton was armed. That the meeting point was somewhat remote increased the risks of a violent encounter. However, Thornton's relationship with Sergeant Jensen made that scenario less likely. I said, "I'll get down in the back seat with my Remington 870. If he starts shooting, you just hit the ground and I'll take care of him."

When we reached the meeting point, the suspect wasn't visible. Colonel Elder said, "Well, he's not here. He was supposed to come out into the headlights."

Then one of them said, "I think I see him in the rear view mirror. He's behind us."

Feeling at a disadvantage, Elder and Jensen exited the vehicle, leaving me concealed in the backseat. I repositioned myself so I could see what was going on. It didn't look like a confrontation to me, but it did seem to last awhile.

Colonel Elder and Sergeant Jensen spoke with Thornton and after a few minutes the three of them returned to the vehicle. I opened the car door and told Thornton, "Now you know. The reason I'm here is just standard procedure."

Johnny Lee Thornton nodded. He got into the car and I patted him down. He wasn't concealing a weapon but there were papers in his shirt pockets. I didn't take anything off of him.

Sergeant Jensen started to say something but I interrupted, "I think it would be best if we just kept quiet until we get back to headquarters."

We remained quiet until we pulled up to the base and I said, "Would it be possible to get a medical doctor over here for a medical examination?"

* * *

Johnny Lee Thornton being escorted into the Springfield Federal Court building by FBI agent George Scruggs on the left and George Adams on the right.

(Associated Press Wire Photo, January 16, 1977)

5

FBI INTERVIEW

AFTER HIS ARRIVAL AT THE MP building, Colonel Robert Mosebar MD, the Commander of GLWACH gave Thornton a thorough examination and pronounced him fit for questioning. Following the doctor's report, William Castleberry and Tom Den Ouden conducted Johnny Lee Thornton's first official interview.

Fort Leonard Wood Front Gate, 1977
Courtesy of James Reist

At the start of questioning, they advised Thornton of his Miranda rights. Thornton stated he understood those rights and signed the FBI rights-waiver form. He told the agents he wanted to talk to the FBI because he wanted to know what he had done. He requested his first-line supervisor, Jensen, remain in the interview room with them during questioning. His request was granted.

Thornton told the officers he'd been having bad headaches since high school. He didn't know why he had the headaches nor how long they typically lasted or what caused them. When he had a headache episode, he couldn't remember what he'd done and he had many questions.

He was on duty from 10:00 p.m. on January 12, 1977, until 6:00 a.m. on January 13, 1977. He confirmed he'd operated the game warden vehicle unit number X37 — a four-wheel-drive, International Scout. He remembered being on patrol on the south gate road and that he stopped one or two vehicles for excessive speed, but he didn't issue any traffic tickets. He simply warned the people to slow down. He recalled stopping his vehicle several times to watch the road at Range 34 or possibly Ranges 25, 51, and 52 — the ranges adjacent to the south gate road.

After a lengthy pause, Thornton asked for something to drink. The agents gave him a sandwich and soft drink. When Thornton resumed the interview, he recalled stopping a car with some kids in it. He said the kids were 'real nice' but one of the boys said something to him. Thornton said he couldn't remember what it was, exactly, but it didn't make him angry.

After another lengthy pause, he acknowledged seeing the car and putting on his red lights. He couldn't remember what happened next. He stated he wanted to talk to someone and wanted someone to understand. He said he'd thought earlier he'd want to talk to his wife but he didn't want to talk to her at this time.

He recalled approaching the kids' vehicle — but could not say what kind of a car it was or how many kids were in it. As he approached them, his thoughts were on his mother and his head ached.

"I love my mother but I also hate her." Johnny paused for a bit, then continued with details of that evening.

"I drove down some roads, but I don't recall much that night. I remember driving by Penn's Pond..." Johnny looked up from his folded hands. "What did I do?"

The agents gave Thornton a brief description of his crimes.

Johnny looked from one agent to another. "I know I must've done it but I don't see how I could've done it. I should have done it, and I should have done it out there."

"What should you have done, Johnny?"

"I should've done it to spare my wife the grief. I should do it. I have already hurt her enough. I will just hurt her more now.

"Johnny, are you talking about killing yourself? That you should have killed yourself?"

"Yes." Then, Thornton repeated, "I know I must've done it. I don't think it was because I needed a woman."

"I have a headache again." After another long pause, he added, "I don't remember anything else, I can't tell you anything else."

At the conclusion of the interview, Castleberry searched Thornton's pockets and pulled out a handful of papers — notes that Thornton had written. The notes were revealing, and are as follows, including his misspelled words and bad grammar:

> *"My love I once said if I ever hurt you again I wouldn't be able to live. Now I know it's true. I didn't mean to hurt you or the boys, I love all of you more than life, even more than that but I can't put it into words."*

*

> *"There were so many nights I cried after you left. I was so lonely so hurt, so lost, I know you did the right thing by leaving me. I really know it was right."*

*

> *"Everything seemed to be going so good, after you said you would come back. The feeling you gave me just knowing you still love me. I wish I could say it."*

*

> *"I hope you can forgive me for hurting you and the boys if you can don't let them find out. They're be hurt enough growing up without of father."*

*

"I hate leaving you with two boys and possibly a girl on the way. But I'll only cause you more hurt if I stay alive."

*

"It wasn't you that cause my mind to finally snap. You're the only thing that ever held me together, even when we were apart your memories were enough to keep me together."

*

"What did it, I think was being with Betty, the way she treats her son, always with different men always hurting him. I think it made me remember my mother and the way she used to do me. I am sorry for mentioning her and my mother in this letter to you I just want you to understand."

*

"I love you more then ever, more every day till the end of time. Please don't blame yourself. Give the boys my love. Love always forever John."

*

"P.S. Don't forget the income tax and saving bonds. You'll need the money it's all I have left to give you except my love please forgive me that's all I'll ask of you please."

*

"Please forgive me. That's all I'll ask of you please... [turn] over."

*

"Patti, I need to talk to you some more. Am not scare of dying only losing you. But maybe now I'll always have you. I never meant to hurt you or anyone else."

*

"Remember I told you I sometime got headaches. I tried to hide them from you, because they scared me. Those headaches made me foreget, they changed me or something I still don't understand."

"I wish I could see you an love you one more time. God I need to be held by you right now. I'd turn my sef in if I could

only hold you one more time. But I know it would only hurt you more."

*

"Please don't blame yourself. It's not your fault it would have happen along time ago I guess. But you held me together you were my beath in life. You were my life. I wish things could've been more different for us."

*

"If you do remarry make sure he loves the boys and our little girl to be don't let them get hurt."

*

"An giving you my full power of attorney, so you can take care of every thing. An sorry for putting you threw this. I do love you very much. Well I just heard then drive up by Paul's car. I better do what I have to do."

*

"Please forgive me. I hope God will. Please believe me I do love you. I always will. Take good care of the children. Love forever John."

*

"P.S. I may sound funny but I save this little toy for Michael."

*

"I just stop walking again. I need to talk you again. I don't feel afarid of dying. I'll be at peace no more hurting you or the boys."

*

"I wish I could have controlled what happen to me. I was so happy knowing you were coming back to me. But my mind went blank. I've been trying to remember what I did. An not even sure I can remember why I'm here right now. If I could only hold you now. Continue on the next page."

*

"I've decided to do it hear so you won't have to carry my body to far. I left Paul's at 5 mins till 4:00."

*

"The time now is 5:30 pm."

*

"This is for your reports."

*

"The car is by H highway."

*

"I wish you and the boys all the best. Please don't let then find out if you can."

*

"If it wouldn't hurt you to much, I'd like for us to be buried next to each other if its possible."

*

"I wish I hadn't hurt you again. I wanted you back so bad."

*

"I keep trying to tell myself thats its a dream. I can't understand how I did what I did."

*

"You're going to call in about one hour & 15 mins. I wish I could tell you I love you. God only knows how much I love you."

*

"Please Patti foregive me. I didn't mean to hurt you. I really love you. Love always John."

* * *

That first interview was a solid gold win for the FBI and the federal prosecutors for a few reasons. First, a doctor examined Thornton and pronounced him fit for the interview. This move countered any claims of diminished mental capacity, or exhausted state of body and mind, or claims of alcohol or drug impairment during the interview.

Second, Thornton waved his Miranda rights prior to interview. All his verbal responses were available for Prosecution to use at trial.

Third, the same Miranda waver rendered the handful of notes from Thornton's shirt pocket available to Prosecution. However, agents suspected Thornton wrote the notes in an attempt to establish an insanity defense.

* * *

FBI Agent Thomas Den Ouden:

Whenever we pushed Thornton with strong questions, he'd lean his head back, close his eyes, and say something like, "I don't remember that." or "I can't remember, I have a headache." I quickly formed the opinion that Thornton was feigning his responses and the interview was pretty much bullshit.

* * *

FBI Agent Castleberry:

I had asked for a doctor to examine Thornton. I will tell you, the reason I did that was because I felt like if we had as much physical evidence as we did, it was probably going to be some kind of a mental incapacity defense. I don't know what Perry did — he left. I took Thornton into the little FBI room that they had there at headquarters just for us. It was real small, just room for a desk and a couple of chairs.

The doctor came in and examined Thornton. Afterwards, he said, "There's nothing physically wrong with him." I went into the room and chatted with Thornton — not advising his rights yet. Something struck me almost immediately. He had absolutely no expression. He didn't make eye contact at any point in the interview or any time later.

I was struck by how stoic he was. I mean, absolutely no expression whatsoever. We went through the whole interview. He wasn't going to say anything and he wouldn't answer direct questions. I tried to get a rise out of him. I knew the interview was going to be over. So, I moved a little bit to the side to where it would be more eye-to-eye with him — and he moved his eyes. But he still wouldn't look me in the eye.

He'd talk to me, but not much. He's answers were short. Then he'd look off at about a forty-five-degree angle. I reached into his pockets and pulled out all of his belongings — including the writings — and put them on the desk. The notes were an admission against his interest. I'm sorry I can't remember the wording. It was excusing himself—the letters he had written. I got the impression he'd contemplated suicide. Later, I got a chance to talk to the psychiatrist at the federal medical center for prisoners in Springfield, about why Thornton might have thought about it but he wouldn't have done it.

Thornton didn't change his expression either. I said, "You know, Johnny..." I called him Johnny throughout the entire interview. I said, "Johnny, you know it's really, really, a good thing one of those girls you shot is alive and talking." I only said that to get a rise out of him. He never changed his expression. I thought to myself, This guy's psychotic. He's functional. And he's going to be found sane. But he is psychotic. Absolutely no remorse. I couldn't get him to even change his expression.

* * *

Shortly before midnight on January 13, 1977, CID Agent Michael A. Caldwell escorted Johnny Lee Thornton to GLWACH's emergency room. A doctor conducted a second exam on Thornton—to include testing for sexually transmitted diseases.

The hospital staff took fingernail scrapings for blood analysis and combed Thornton's pubic area, searching for foreign pubic hairs and other evidence. Once these items of evidence were collected, the hospital turned the evidence over to Caldwell.

At a later time, Caldwell turned this evidence over to the FBI. At the conclusion of this more thorough forensic examination, he returned Thornton to the military police command building. Agents housed Thornton for the evening in the temporary detention cell located inside the building. Later that morning, two FBI agents drove him to Springfield, Missouri, where he was temporarily housed at the Greene County Jail pending his first appearance in federal court.

6

WITNESSES

Interview with Douglas Hawkins:

At approximately 3:35 p.m. on January 13, 1977, Special Agent Roy E. Black of the United States Army CID interviewed Douglas B. Hawkins, brother of the deceased victim Wesley Hawkins, at the body location site in the remote hunting Area 13 on Fort Leonard Wood.

I got a call from Juanita Deckard about twelve thirty p.m. asking me to come and get her. Juanita told me I wouldn't believe what she was going to say — they had been shot and needed help. I asked for her location and she said she didn't know. She handed the phone to a person who identified herself as Mrs. Echelberry. Mrs. Echelberry told me where to find Juanita.

While I was en route to pick up Juanita, I stopped for Hershel Needham, Linda's father. The two of us proceeded to the Echelberry residence on Highway 17.

When we got to the Echelberry residence, I asked Juanita what happened. She told us she had been with Linda Needham, Tony Bates, and Wesley Hawkins in Bates' 1971, two-toned, blue, special edition Dodge Charger. They were stopped near the Fort Leonard Wood Airport by a military police vehicle. The military policeman said he'd stopped them for speeding. Juanita thought they'd only been driving forty miles-per-hour in a forty-five mile-per-hour zone.

Juanita said the MP told them he'd have to arrest them and that he was taking them to the station. The MP then placed handcuffs on the two boys, telling them to get into the back of the MP's vehicle. The two girls also got in. The MP shot the two boys seated in the backseat. After being shot, Wesley didn't move but Tony moaned and moved his head around.

The MP drove to a small cabin in a wooded area where he took the girls' eye glasses, purses, and billfolds. He then drove to another area where the MP shot the two girls and covered all four of them with snow. Juanita told me she'd laid still until the MP left. Then she got up and walked out of the woods. She managed to get to the Echelberry residence and called me. Juanita added that at the Fort Leonard Wood Airport — where they had been initially stopped — the MP caused a tire on the Tony's vehicle to go flat. She didn't say how he did that.

After a few minutes of listening to Juanita, the three of us left the Echelberry residence and drove to the location where she said she'd emerged from the woods and onto Highway 17. While Hershel and Juanita waited for the highway patrol, I followed Juanita's tracks in the snow back to the body site. Once there, I found the bodies of my brother, Wesley and Linda. I couldn't find Tony's body.

Author's Note: Agent Black said that during the interview, Douglas Hawkins was distraught and had difficulty remembering exactly what Juanita Deckard had said to him. Since he'd just left the site of his brother's body in the woods, his emotional state of mind was understandable.

* * *

Janice Echelberry, Richland, Missouri:

On January 13, 1977, Janice Echelberry was 29 years old. She was supposed to have gone to work that day — however, she managed to get her car stuck in the deep snow and ice in her yard. She couldn't go anywhere. Janice was forced to stay at home with her 7-year-old daughter and her 4-year-old son. She decided to make the best of a bad situation. Later that day she had a chance to watch her favorite soap opera, *As the World Turns*.

The TV show had just started the opening credits at twelve-thirty p.m. Just as the big round world began to spin on the TV screen, there was a knock on my door. I answered it and found a young lady, shaking with cold, standing on my doorstep. I thought she was fourteen or fifteen years old. She was half frozen and could barely talk. I brought her into the living room where the wood stove was, and she began to thaw out.

As the young lady warmed up, she told me about her dead friends in the woods and that she'd been raped. She also said she'd been shot. I didn't know what to think about all that but I realized she was severely cold. I got some of my clothing for her to wear. As I was helping her undress, I saw that snow was packed underneath the pant legs of her jeans — all the way up to her knees.

As I helped her remove a sock from her foot, a ring fell out of the sock and rolled across the floor. She looked at the ring and said, "That's my boyfriend's ring. He's dead in the woods."

At that point, I didn't know what to think or what had happened. This was a scary situation since I was home alone with my two young children. While helping her change clothing, I saw two bullet wounds on Juanita's body. That made the situation even scarier. I didn't even think about calling the Highway Patrol for assistance. I just continued helping her change clothing.

As she got warmer, her story began making more sense. She told of being stopped on post and of being transported to a cabin on the river after her boyfriend was shot. She told me the man made her and her friend perform sexual acts on each other and then on him. And then the man shot her and buried her in a snowbank.

Once Juanita got warmer and more coherent, she asked me if she could call some friends for help. Sometime later, these friends arrived at my place on Highway 17.

When she looked out the door and saw them, she said, "Don't let them in." After knocking on the door without an answer, the men turned to walk away.

I asked her who the men were. She said they were the father of her girlfriend and the brother of her boyfriend. So, I ran to the front door and called the men back to my trailer. The men came into my home, where they talked with Juanita for some time. The older man asked me if he could use my telephone to call the highway patrol. I told him to make the call.

I'd not checked on my children for a long time while I was helping Juanita, so while the three of them talked, I went to the far end of my house to check on my children. When I came back to the front room, the three of them left. They went south on Highway 17 to wait for the Missouri State Highway Patrol to respond.

Later that evening, two federal agents came to my door and collected all of the clothing Juanita left behind and removed it from my residence. Approximately one week later, Juanita Deckard's parents came to my home and gave back the clothing I'd loaned her that day.

Author's Note: Janice Echelberry was subpoenaed for the trial in Council Bluffs, Iowa. This deeply concerned her because she had two young children and didn't like the idea of going out of state with them for a long trial. In the end, she wasn't summoned to the trial. And for her, the Thornton case came to an end.

* * *

CID interview of Juanita Deckard at the Pulaski County Memorial Hospital:

At approximately 2:45 p.m. on January 13, 1977, CID special agents Michael A. Caldwell and Alexander Kerekes drove to the Pulaski County Memorial Hospital to interview the victim, Juanita Deckard. The agents found Miss Deckard to be alert and coherent during the interview.

At around fifteen minutes after midnight on January 13, 1977, on the main paved road near the airport on Fort Leonard Wood, Missouri, I was riding in an automobile with three friends. A military policeman driving a military vehicle pulled us over with his red light. The MP told us that the Southgate Texaco station had just been robbed and we were suspects.

The MP said he was going to have to take us in. He handcuffed Wesley and Tony — and slit a tire on our vehicle, causing it to go flat.

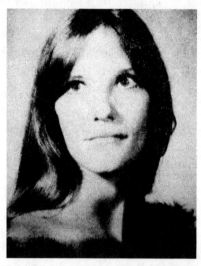

The Sole Survivor –Juanita Deckard
Courtesy Gatehouse Media, Daily Guide

Author's Note: At this point, Miss Deckard experienced some confusion as to what happened next. She believed the MP placed the boys in the Scout and then shot each of the males one time. With the two males in the rear seat of the vehicle, the two females were ordered to get into the front seat.

He drove quite some distance to a cabin structure in the woods. The MP left the boys in the Scout and took Linda and me inside the cabin. He made a fire in a cast iron stove for warmth. He talked to us for a while and told us he wasn't really an MP.

He made us undress at gunpoint and raped us. He made us get dressed and then took us outside. He made us face the front of the vehicle. And while he stood at the rear of the vehicle, he shot Linda. Then he dragged her body to the side of the road and covered it with snow. Then, he shot me. After I fell onto the ground, he dragged me to the side of the road and covered me with snow.

Game Warden Cabin Crime Scene
Federal Trial Record

I heard several more shots. A short time later, another body was placed near me. After a time, it grew quiet. I waited until the MP had driven off before I dug myself out. I checked on Linda and Wesley. Both their hearts were beating, but I couldn't get them to respond.

I started walking and finally arrived at a house and a lady there called the police.

Deckard provided a description of the suspect and stated she could identify him. At approximately 4:25 p.m., Caldwell concluded the interview and instructed Kerekes to remain at the hospital as a security guard for Miss Deckard since the suspect was not yet in custody.

* * *

Another guard for Juanita that afternoon in the hospital was Doyle T. Wright.

Doyle T. Wright, 463rd MP company assigned to the Military Police Investigation unit:

My only recollection from my time spent at the hospital was speaking to Juanita Deckard's distraught parents. They didn't yet know that Johnny was the assailant. They questioned me about how someone could get an MP badge, brassard and a Scout with a red light and all the markings of a legitimate MP vehicle. Of course, I couldn't tell them the tragic truth. I don't recall the CID agent who was at the hospital, or if there was one there when I was. CID Special Agent "Tweety" Byrd was the guy we worked with and knew best.

Author's Note: The game wardens who patrolled Fort Leonard Wood were a part of the Provost Marshal's office and were responsible for the enforcement of hunting and fishing regulations on the military reservation. Their vehicles were radio-equipped. However, at the time of the Thornton case, there were many radio dead-spots around Fort Wood. Radio contact wasn't always possible. It wasn't unusual for a lone game warden to be out of radio contact with his base for several hours. The shack Thornton drove to was known as the game warden's shack and was used as a warm-up shack during extended periods in the field. It was furnished with a potbellied stove and two sets of bunk beds. At the time of the murders, there were no mattresses on the beds.

* * *

In 1977, Penny D. Moats was a young clerk-typist working for the United States Army Criminal Investigation Command at Fort Leonard Wood. Moats and the other members of the clerical office pool first met Johnny Lee Thornton when the MP game warden section supervisor brought him into the clerical staff area and introduced him to the support staff.

Moats recalled several of the single girls in the pool thought he was cute.

Later, when the murder case investigation began, Moats found herself typing a transcript of the audio recording made by the CID agents who interviewed Juanita Deckard at the Pulaski County hospital. The entire recording of the criminal acts and especially the explicit details of the sexual assaults gave her nightmares.

"It was like a big shadow came at me. I jumped straight up in bed and landed on my husband."

The nightmares bothered Ms. Moats for a long time.

* * *

FBI interview of Juanita Deckard, Pulaski County Memorial Hospital:

Special Agent Paul A. Van Someren conducted a second interview of Juanita Deckard at the Pulaski County Memorial Hospital on January 14, 1977. At this point in time, Thornton was in custody. The agents didn't have to rush to obtain information. They had no time restrictions. This allowed them to probe for small details. Thus, this interview was more detailed and covered a wider scope than the previous CID interview at the same hospital (while Thornton was still on the loose).

According to Miss Deckard, on the evening of Wednesday, January 12, 1977, she and her boyfriend, Wesley Hawkins traveled to the residence of Anthony "Tony" Bates in Evening Shade, Missouri. It was around nine-thirty p.m. Upon arrival, they found Bates had company — another friend of theirs, Linda Sue Needham. The four of them stayed at the Bates' residence until about eleven-thirty p.m. About that time, Tony Bates said that he needed gasoline for his vehicle. The four of them then drove to the small city of Success, Missouri. However, they could not find an open gas station. They decided to drive to St. Robert, Missouri to fill the vehicle. The shortest route to St. Robert cuts across Fort Leonard Wood.

Deckard told the FBI agents that as they were driving across Fort Wood, they noticed a military police vehicle parked on the side of the road. After they passed the MP vehicle, it pulled out and followed them. The MP then turned on his red lights and stopped them. The MP came up to the side of the vehicle and asked Tony Bates for his driver's license. The MP also inquired if any of the occupants of the vehicle were military dependents. When Hawkins stated he was a military dependent, the MP asked to see his identification card. The MP then requested identification from everybody inside Bates' vehicle.

Tony Bates' Dodge Charger.
Federal Court Trial Record

At the MP's request, Anthony Bates and Wesley Hawkins got out of the car and walked back to the MP's vehicle. Deckard heard them talking about a robbery at the Southgate Texaco station and that the Bates' vehicle met the description of the robber's car. After that, the MP told all four of them to leave their vehicle. He would transport them to the MP headquarters.

At some point in the process, the MP instructed Tony Bates to pull his automobile off of the south gate road onto a smaller gravel offshoot, known as Friendship Cemetery Road. It led to several firing range areas. There, the MP had the kids take their personal belongings with them. After telling Bates to lock his car, he handcuffed the boys and placed them in the back seat of the MP vehicle. He ordered Linda Needham to sit between the two boys. Finally, he opened the front right jeep door and told Deckard to sit in the passenger seat.

Juanita Deckard

When the MP closed [the passenger] door, he walked around and opened up the driver-side door. I saw he had a gun in his hand. Without warning, he shot both Tony and Wesley as they sat in the back seat. Then he told Linda to "leave them alone." He said to me, "Don't look back." I could see Tony doubled over and I heard him say, "Oh that hurts."

Author's Note: The autopsy examination revealed Thornton shot Bates one time in the lower chest. After impact, Bates doubled over in the seat. The .45 bullet passed through his body, having nicked his kidney, exited through his back and grazed one of his handcuffed hands. The coroner determined this initial shot as a non-fatal wound. The bullet passed through Wesley Hawkins' heart, killing him instantly. The FBI lab technicians found both of the initial impact bullets lodged in the back seat of the International Scout. These were forensically matched to the .45 pistol issued to Thornton that night. This information (the fatal and non-fatal impacts) became a key factor at trial time as it pinpointed the exact geographical locations where the boys were shot, thus giving the federal court jurisdiction for two criminal charges.

Juanita Deckard:

The MP got in and started the vehicle. He drove a short distance down Cemetery Road. Then, he turned around drove back to Tony's car. He told us, "Don't move and you won't get hurt." He got out of the vehicle and left the engine running. While he was gone, I heard air being let out one of the tires on Tony's car. If I or Linda knew how to operate a clutch-type vehicle, we could've driven off but we're unable to.

After approximately one minute, the MP returned and again told Deckard not to look back. They drove down Cemetery Road and away from the main paved road.

Juanita Deckard:

We traveled for almost ten minutes at speeds of between thirty and forty-miles-per hour. We came to a small cabin in the woods, around one o'clock the next morning.

The MP told us to get out of his vehicle and go into the cabin. He warned us not to attempt to escape because he could run faster than we could. He said he'd also be able to track us in the snow. He faced his vehicle and told Tony and Wesley not to "try any funny business because I know Fort Leonard Wood like the back of my hand."

The MP had a flashlight. After we entered the cabin, he told us to face the wall while he built a fire in the stove. There was no wood in the cabin, so he said he had to go outside and gather some. He was gone a couple minutes and then came back into the cabin with the wood.

While he built a fire in the stove, the MP told us, "If you do everything I tell you, you won't get hurt." As the fire warmed up the cabin, he ordered us to remove everything from our pockets. He also wanted Linda's rings. We complied and gave him everything we had. He told us he wanted us to talk to him.

He said, "I suppose you're wondering why I am doing this." He said he wasn't really a military policeman. He was trying to get out of the Army, but he had to change his plans. He said he'd been in the United States Army for one year and had been stationed at Fort Wood for three months and seven days "as of today."

I asked him why he shot the boys. He said, "So they won't be rowdy." I became confused and somehow interpreted his remark to mean that he hadn't actually shot the boys, but somehow had sedated them.

He said he intended to leave Fort Leonard Wood Friday morning. He was going to Canada. I asked him how he thought he could do that without being caught. He said, "They don't even have bed checks or roll calls anymore."

After about twenty or thirty minutes, the MP said it was warm enough in the cabin and we should take off our coats and stand facing the wall again. He then ordered us to take off each other's clothing, except for our socks. While we undressed, I took my boyfriend, Wesley's ring off and slipped it into my sock. I wanted to keep the ring.

Once we had undressed, the MP pointed his gun at us and forced us to commit sexual acts on each other and then later on him. He committed a series of sexual assaults on us, which continued for a long time. At the conclusion of the sexual assaults, the MP ordered us to get dressed again.

After dressing, the MP told us he was going to handcuff us together in the cabin and we'd be found two or three days later. I asked him what he was going to do with the boys. He said, "Don't ask about the boys again." I was confused at this point because two times during the time of the assaults, the MP had left the cabin to get more firewood. I thought I heard him speak to the boys during those trips.

A short time later, the MP said, "It's four-twenty a.m. I'm behind schedule." He ordered us to go to his vehicle. When we got back to his vehicle, he told us we'd both have to ride up in the front seat. I saw Tony sitting up and he was conscious. I heard him groan. Wesley was slumped over and made no sound.

Dump site 3 and 4 where the bodies of Wesley Hawkins and Linda Needham were found.
Courtesy Gatehouse Media, Daily Guide

I sat on Linda's lap as he slowly drove away from the cabin. He said he was looking for a little road. He had a spotlight turned out in an attempt to find this road. Then he stopped the vehicle and backed up. He said he'd found the road. He ordered Linda and me to get out of the vehicle and told us to walk down this little road. As we walked down this road, we only got about fifteen or twenty feet from the vehicle when he told us to stop and turn around. As we turned around, he fired two shots at us. We both fell to the ground. I didn't lose consciousness. I saw him drag Linda by the arm thirty or forty feet to a pine tree and lay her down near the tree.

The MP came back to me and dragged me to the same area as Linda. He kicked snow over me. Then, I heard Linda scream and maybe heard another shot. I heard Linda groaning. The MP returned to the vehicle and said, "You boys get out." I saw Tony walking and then heard two more shots. I didn't see Wesley. A little bit later, the MP came back to where I was and pushed my body over with his boot. Then he kicked more snow over me. I think he remained in the area, walking around for twenty to thirty minutes before he returned to his vehicle. I think he sat in the vehicle for another twenty to thirty minutes. I heard the engine running. When I heard the vehicle finally leave the area, I remained under the snow for about five more minutes.

Dump site 1 where searchers found Tony Bates' body covered with snow.

Courtesy Gatehouse Media, Daily Guide

After I was positive he was gone, I got up. I felt someone near me. I uncovered them, and realized it was Wesley. I attempted to give him mouth-to-mouth resuscitation but he didn't revive. I called out for Linda. When I didn't hear an answer, I looked for her. When I found Linda, she was lying near Wesley. I tried to give Linda mouth-to-mouth resuscitation also but I couldn't revive her. I looked for Tony but couldn't find him.

A short time later, Deckard walked across the firing ranges on Fort Leonard Wood. She came out on Route 17, near the residence of a Mrs. Echelberry, around 12:30 p.m. on Thursday, January 13, 1977. Deckard asked to use Echelberry's phone.

She immediately called Douglas Hawkins, Wesley's brother, and asked him to come and pick her up at the Echelberry home.

Douglas Hawkins and Hershel Needham drove to the Echelberry trailer and picked Juanita up. They drove back down to the point on Route 17 where Juanita said she had walked out of the woods.

Juanita said she was positive she could identify the MP and gave the FBI a detailed description of the man and his vehicle.

Juanita Deckard's statements to the FBI proved critical at trial. First and foremost, Deckard detailed the actions of Johnny Lee Thornton. This allowed Prosecution to present the required specific elements of each of Thornton's crimes. In addition, her statements as to the locations of these crimes enabled Prosecution to specifically state that the crimes occurred on a section of Fort Leonard Wood covered by the federal jurisdiction.

Dump site 2 where Johnny Lee Thornton left Juanita Decker in the snow with the bodies of her friends nearby.
Courtesy Gatehouse Media, Daily Guide.

* * *

A mountain of physical evidence secured by the investigation teams supported Juanita Deckard's statement. These corroborating details proved that Johnny Lee Thornton planned the attack. Deckard's story also showed that Johnny Lee Thornton sought to deceive or mislead his victims — further proof of premeditation.

The biggest plus for Prosecution was Juanita Deckard's statement that she could positively identify her attacker. Since she had been within an arm's length of him for several hours during the evening, and within mere inches of his uncovered face during the actual rapes and assaults, Prosecution felt her statement was a valid one.

During a criminal investigation, a police agency will often try a live lineup with the suspect appearing with other men who resemble him. Or they might opt for a photographic lineup using an image of the suspect alongside pictures of people with similar characteristics similar to each other and the accused. These procedures determine whether the victim can positively identify the person in question as their attacker. In this case, Prosecution was confident that Deckard could identify Thornton. They told the investigating officers to refrain from doing any type of lineup involving Thornton.

This decision was important during the trial. Prosecution effectively pointed out to the jury that the last time Juanita Deckard saw Johnny Lee Thornton was when he dragged her into the woods, dumped her near a tree, and kicked snow over what he thought was her dead body. This tactic also allowed Prosecution to rebut any hint by the defense team that Juanita Deckard had been coached. So, at the end of over 90 minutes' worth of testimony, when Juanita Deckard stood up in front of the jury and pointed at Thornton, identifying him as her attacker, no one doubted her certainty. Johnny Lee Thornton was the guy.

* * *

FBI Agent William Castleberry:

I would sit there and I would write out leads and a bunch of [my notes] would be for me to do this, do this, and do this.

A lot of my efforts were ... okay... I had to send an agent to do task A, B, C, and D. We had autopsies. We had interviews — all the military policeman, all of his friends, and all the people he had contact with, and his girlfriend. The list seemed endless but we had the evidence collecting well under way.

I remember that we sealed the Scout. Not only did the evidence confirm that X37 was the vehicle Thornton used in the commission of this crime, it also provided bullet trajectories in support of Deckard's eyewitness testimony.

Now, we did take apart his personal vehicle as far as the inside, the front seat compartment, the rug, and the seat. And one of the interesting things the lab found was, one of the victim's pubic hairs was in the front seat of his personal car. And she had never been in the vehicle. And we could prove that. One of the girls from the four. Well, what we discovered was, he masturbated almost continuously to the point where he rubbed his penis raw. Most likely after all of this, when he got back into his vehicle, he masturbated in the front seat.

The amount of physical evidence was so overwhelming that Defense ultimately decided they were not going to challenge it. Of course, I didn't know for sure that Defense would argue that Johnny Lee Thornton was crazy — complete with a good Johnny and a bad Johnny. But given Thornton's claims of headaches and memory loss, it seemed a good bet. So my team focused on collecting evidence. We took possession of and examined Thornton's military vehicle, his sleeping quarters, his bed, personal car, his weapon, the spent cartridges at the murder site, and, of course, the bodies. On top of all that, we knew that Juanita herself was key to the trial and we prioritized recording and confirming her testimony.

We decided — and when I say we, I'm talking about Perry and Matt and myself — that we'd put a CID guy who was familiar with the military and with the post with an FBI agent. We would not send out two FBI agents to do something or two CID agents to do something else. We would combine the agents together to make two-man teams. If there was anything other than that, I never heard about it.

We worked eighteen-to-twenty-hour days, three or four days in a row. By this point, we had secured a mountain of evidence. And it was all under control and properly documented. I believe the man who took control of the evidence and made the proper submission documents was Don McDonald, an outstanding FBI agent. He and Emmet Trammell — who was another outstanding agent — did the evidence. When I saw the outline, the first draft, I remember thinking, Man, that was a great choice by the supervisor in Kansas City who sent him down here.

An older agent, George Scruggs, filed the initial complaint. I don't remember if I met him or talked to him over the phone... or if he drove down here and I gave him everything. I just can't remember.

I do remember the first trip I took to Springfield was to interview the psychiatrist. From the very beginning, I was concerned we would have a mental incapacitation defense we couldn't beat. Because by then we had seen the mountain and we knew we had the case locked in. But it was so horrendous and the impact of it had hit so many of the guys so hard. And you could see when we were talking about the case, the look on their face would be like the-deer-in-the-headlights look and my thought was, *We can't lose this. This is not one we can lose.*

And I remember this thought — since we were not having any luck finding the bodies of the first two kids, *If we hit this son of a bitch hard enough, if we get him enough time, if he's doing life, why wouldn't he tell us?* I don't know if you know this but after he was convicted, we did take a run at Thornton for that. After he had been inside for a while. And the only thing he said was, "You guys are barking up the wrong tree."

I was not part of that post-conviction interview. I was advised by the behavioral science unit we should send another guy to do it who was familiar with the case and not send me. And so, I think Tom Den Ouden did that.

The most difficult task of the case was interviewing Juanita and her family. And the other victims' families. I didn't know we got all of it at first from Juanita so I went back several times.

You know when you're in an evidence-collecting mode in an investigation, you have to turn off your emotions and your feelings so you can do the job. And during this whole case I did the best I could to stay unemotional. It's almost like you were acting like a mechanical person.

* * *

Sergeant David Paul Cogswell:

The supervisor for the evening shift was one of the first people the CID interviewed. Sergeant David Paul Cogswell of the 463rd Military Police Company had been working as the shift supervisor for the 1:00 to 9:00 a.m. time-period on January 13, 1977.

Nothing unusual happened during the shift until about five-minutes-after six a.m. on January 13th. At that time, Thornton came to me and handed me a signed, sworn statement. I read the statement. It was Thornton's account of having expended six rounds of ammunition for the purpose of disposing of three dogs in hunting Area 20 on Fort Leonard Wood. The statement said Thornton had disposed of the canines at the Fort Leonard Wood stump dump. I read the statement and then showed it to Master Sergeant James D. Morrow of the 463rd MP Company. Morrow was scheduled to be the next shift supervisor. I had a Military Police journal entry made for Thornton's shots fired report.

At approximately eight-ten a.m., the MP desk received a call from Mr. Leroy Bates in reference to Bates' daughter seeing his son's car parked on the side of the road on Fort Leonard Wood. Mr. Bates stated his son, Tony Bates and three other young teens had not been heard from since the previous evening and Mr. Bates was concerned. The radio operator on duty told me that Thornton had called in about the same vehicle around five or six that morning. Thornton stated a tire was low or flat on the vehicle. At eight-twenty a.m., I dispatched a different patrol unit to the vehicle's location to obtain further information.

During the time period from eight-forty-five a.m. to one p.m. on the 13th, Military Police Investigators [MPI] were sent off post to obtain information on the missing persons and to prepare a dispatch for statewide dissemination to all law enforcement

75

agencies. At approximately one-eighteen p.m., the Missouri State Highway Patrol notified the military police radio operator that Mr. Needham had called in stating Juanita Deckard had been found, shot — and Mr. Needham knew where the other missing teens' bodies were.

At approximately two-thirty p.m., the radio operator received the initial notification from the state highway patrol that Deckard had been located and had been shot, and the bodies of the other three missing teens were on the Fort Leonard Wood reservation. The suspect was named as a possible AWOL soldier dressed up as an MP.

Author's Note: This interview with Cogswell was critically important for Prosecution's case because Thornton had not only completed a sworn statement acknowledging he'd fired six rounds of ammunition but he'd also told Cogswell face-to-face the same story. Thornton retained possession of the sworn statement with the apparent intention of turning it into the unit armorer so the six rounds of ammunition Thornton had expended could be replaced. Prosecution now had a second witness to testify Thornton admitted to firing six rounds of ammunition that night. In addition, after a thorough search of the stump dump (where Thornton said he had dumped the bodies of the three dogs he'd killed) no dog carcasses were located. The sworn statement by Thornton that he had fired six rounds of ammunition the night of January 13, 1977, was later admitted into evidence as a federal court exhibit.

* * *

Sergeant David B. Webster:

At 12:45 p.m. on January 14, 1977, CID agent Larry R. Rodery interviewed Sergeant David B. Webster of the 208th, Military Police Company at Fort Leonard Wood, a friend of Johnny Lee Thornton.

The last time I talked to Thornton was around three-twenty or three-thirty p.m. the afternoon of January 13, 1977.

At about three p.m. that afternoon, Thornton picked me up at my house and gave me a ride to the Provost Marshal's office, prior to going on duty as a game warden. While Thornton was in my home, I mentioned to him that four bodies had been found in a wooded range area on Fort Leonard Wood. Thornton asked me if he should get into his uniform and go to the MP station to go on duty. I told Thornton he should call the office and see if his assistance was required.

Thornton called operations of the Provost Marshal's office and inquired on the identities and locations of the reported bodies. Then we left my house en route to the Provost Marshal's office. We arrived there at about three-twenty or three-thirty. Thornton stopped his vehicle on Iowa Avenue in front of the MP station and told me he had to go down the street to see someone. He said he would be back in just a few minutes. That's the last time I saw Thornton.

> *Agent Rodery:* Was there anything out of the ordinary about Thornton's actions that day?
>
> *Webster:* The only thing I can think of is that Thornton let me out of the car on Iowa Avenue rather than driving into the parking lot adjacent to the MP station. As far as I know, everything was going fine with him. He and his wife had solved their marital problems and they were going to resume living together in the month of February, 1977.

* * *

Sergeant Thomas W. Connors:

Special Agent Donald E. Cagle of the United States Army's CID interviewed Sergeant Thomas W. Connors who was the unit armorer for the 463rd Military Police Company.

I issued a .45 caliber military weapon to Johnny Lee Thornton at about ten p.m. on January 12, 1977. My records indicate the serial number of the weapon in question was 2360549. At the same time, Thornton was issued the weapon, he was also issued two pairs of hand irons. According to my records, the weapon was returned to the arms room at around six-forty a.m. on January 13, 1977. Thornton also returned the hand irons at that time.

It's most unusual for an MP to ask for two sets of hand irons for a duty shift. When I questioned Thornton about the need for two set of hand irons, Thornton said, "I'm going to play super cop tonight."

Author's Note: Sergeant Connors produced the record of the transaction showing where Thornton had signed for the weapon as being issued to him and had signed upon returning the weapon. This was a critical piece of evidence in the case as it identified the specific weapon used to commit the crimes. In addition, the six expended bullets and the five fired shell cases found at the abduction and body dump sites were later forensically matched to the specific firearm issued to Thornton for that shift. Later at trial, Federal Court Exhibit #132 was the weapon's receipt registration form Thornton signed for this weapon.

* * *

Sergeant Philip Edward Marketon:

On January 18, 1977, in a follow-up interview, Special Agent Donald E. Cagle, CID interviewed Sergeant Philip Edward Marketon of the 463rd Military Police Company.

I was an armorer for the 463rd and was present in the arm's room at six-forty a.m. on January 13, 1977, when Johnny Lee Thornton returned a .45 caliber military-issue weapon and two sets of hand irons.

It's extremely unusual for a military policeman to draw two pairs of hand irons. During my assignment as an armorer for the unit, this incident was only the second time I saw an MP draw two sets of hand irons. The other time was on January 11, 1977, when Thornton drew two pairs of hand irons prior to going on shift that day.

7

THE BODY DUMP SITE

THE MORNING OF JANUARY 14, 1977, a team of experienced agents — both FBI and CID — went to the location where the victims' bodies had been found the evening before. The team was led by CID Special Agent, George T. Matthews. Matthews was one of the primary agents who'd responded to the same location the previous evening.

When the agents first arrived at the site on the evening of January 13, the newly-fallen snow Thornton used to cover his victims proved to be both a blessing and a curse for the investigators. Tire tracks left by Thornton's vehicle, footprints where Thornton walked around, and bloody drag marks made by the victims' bodies all told a story. The agents were able to piece together what happened that first night from the disturbed snow. They learned even more during the search on the 14th.

The snow was a curse in that it made tangible evidence such as shell casings and expended bullets difficult to find. The icy conditions played havoc with the metal detectors the investigators brought along. In the final accounting, though, these two detailed searches of the body dump site produced a great deal of evidence presented at trial.

During the first evening search, investigators located a spot where it appeared a parked vehicle sat with its engine running for an extended amount of time. Various fluids leaked from the engine. Tire tracks in the snow ended at that same point where investigators believed the vehicle was parked. Using the parked vehicle location as a starting point, agents began their search.

On the 14th, they revisited each location where the teens' bodies were found. This time they used different models of military anti-personnel mine detectors.

This second search proved to be successful in that investigators found an expended bullet in the ground under the impression in the snow where Linda Needham's body had lain. They found another expended bullet near the footprint trail leading to where Anthony Bates' lifeless body was located. And the agents found empty cartridge casings near the location of the parked vehicle.

Agents seized these items as evidence and the FBI laboratory later forensically linked this evidence to the specific .45 caliber weapon issued to Johnny Lee Thornton the evening of the 12th.

* * *

Postmortem Forensic Examination

In any homicide case one of the legal requirements is that not only do you have to prove the victim is deceased you have to be able to prove exactly how and why the victim became deceased. Thus, the postmortem forensic examination has to take place. In this case the examination was done by Major Gerald Rappe, MD, a pathologist with GLWACH.

Major Rappe conducted the forensic examination on all three of the victims in this case. But one of the victim's examination stood out above the others. During the course of the research for this book several people commented on this and some went so far as to describe it as an eerie feeling. Many of the CID and FBI agents in attendance at this examination were visibly disturbed by the procedure and several of them had to leave the room to regain their composure.

CID Agent George Matthews:

Linda Needham had been a petite girl, 5'2" tall, 90 pounds, with blonde hair and green eyes. The fact she was attractive was apparent even to the investigators who only knew her in death. When she was murdered, Thornton covered her with snow. Even though Deckard had removed most of this when she tried to revive her, some snow remained frozen in her hair and around her eyes. When she was brought to the morgue, the bright lights caused the ice to melt from around her eyes and run like teardrops down her cheeks.

The agents who saw this, even though accustomed to violent death and autopsies, said it would be a long time before they could forget the dead girl's tears.

* * *

Search of the Abduction Site

The morning of January 14, 1977, also saw a team of agents dispatched to the alleged abduction site (Friendship Cemetery Road just off of the south gate road). This particular search was felt to be critical in that large volumes of traffic regularly passed by this scene on the south gate road. If there was any evidence at this scene, investigators needed to find it quickly. Unfortunately, their initial examination revealed nothing but a few tire marks. Agents also conducted a sweep of the same area using metal detectors without results.

On January 15, 1977, FBI agents, CID agents, and enlisted personnel from the 5th Engineer Company searched the abduction area again. Operating seven military mine detectors, they found a .45 caliber shell casing and one expended bullet.

The expended bullet was found approximately 50 feet from where the vehicle had been parked — on the opposite side of the roadway in a snow-covered embankment. At the time, agents thought they found the bullet that traveled through one of the victims and exited the rear of the Scout — accounting for the bullet hole in the vehicle's tailgate. The agents only saw two entry holes in the rear seat back on vehicle X37. However, as they discovered later, they were wrong.

As part of the investigation, agents sent the Scout's rear seat and tailgate to the FBI lab. The laboratory technicians found two expended bullets embedded inside the seat. These bullets had gone through the boys and lodged in the seat cushion. The investigators concluded Johnny Lee Thornton fired a third shot, point blank, somehow missing them completely. That bullet passed through the tailgate and came to rest in the embankment on the opposite side of the road.

All of the bullets and casings located at the abduction site were forensically matched to the .45 caliber pistol issued to Thornton the night of January 12, 1977.

* * *

Examination of MP Vehicle X37

Following the discovery of the blood on the seat and the bullet hole exiting the tailgate of International Scout X37, FBI Agent Tom Den Ouden instructed Sergeant Richard Jensen to drive the vehicle back to the main cantonment area on Fort Leonard Wood. As instructed, Jensen parked the vehicle in a bay at the Transportation Motor Pool (TMP)—and locked up the vehicle. An MP guarded the vehicle until it could be forensically examined. The keys for the vehicle were given to Den Ouden.

On January 15, 1977, vehicle X37 was subjected to a thorough search. As mentioned, the back seat of the vehicle and the tailgate were removed for examination. Everything in the vehicle was inventoried and listed as possible evidence, including possible bloodstains found on the rear seat and the rear floorboard.

* * *

Interview PFC Paul F. Mara, 463rd Military Police Company:

On January 14, 1977, at approximately 6:45 p.m., Special Agent Thomas W Byrd, CID, interviewed PFC Paul Mara of the 463rd MP Company. Mara owned the 1971 Chevrolet Malibu with the Minnesota plates Johnny Lee Thornton was driving at the time of his arrest. Agents located Mara's vehicle near the site of the stop and removed it from the scene as potential evidence.

> *Byrd*: Did you know anything about Thornton's headaches or blackout spells?

Mara: I don't recall a time when Thornton complained of severe headaches or blackout spells or anything of that nature."

Mara signed a 'Consent to Search' form authorizing the CID to process his vehicle.

At approximately 8:05 p.m. that same evening, CID agents used a wire coat hanger to gain access to Mara's vehicle. They found a note on the dashboard which said:

"I got this paper at the riding stables. I found out you knew — when a dog handler told me at the arm's room, they had found one of the girls. And then at Webster's house I called and I heard Lt. Doran talking on the phone to the arm's room about me and someone else checking out our weapons.

"I don't remember doing what I did. Sometimes I get these headaches. I want to die from the pain. I don't want to hurt people (but when?) these headaches come, something snaps in me. I wanted to talk to someone about it because I know [I] am sick, but I was afraid. I don't know what of, just afraid. I guess I was [tired] of the hurting since I was little.

"I don't want to mess up Paul's car, you should be able to follow my footsteps in the snow, I want to write a letter to my wife Patty and pray to God for forgiveness. I really didn't want to hurt anyone. I only remembered after someone, I think it was David, told me there were four missing persons. I've never done this before at least I don't remember doing it. I've only felt this way, I mean really sick, for only a few months.

"I'm sorry maybe God and my wife can understand, because I don't."

Johnny Thornton

"P.S. I hereby give my wife Mrs. Patty J. Thornton my full power of attorney. Please help her, she needs money for the kids. SFC Jensen I want you to tell her. She'll call [at?] Dave's house tonight at 6:30 p.m. I wish I could talk to her."

Johnny Thornton

* * *

Examination of Anthony Bates' Personal Vehicle

At approximately 10:00 a.m. on January 15, 1977, at the Transportation Motor Pool on Fort Leonard Wood, Special Agent Michael A. Caldwell, CID, examined the vehicle owned by Anthony Bates. He described it as a 1972 Dodge Charger Special Edition with a navy-blue top and gray-in-color body. The agent found the left front tire on the vehicle flat. In his report, Caldwell described the flat tire as a Goodyear GT radial, size GR 70–14.

Caldwell seized every non-attached item in the Charger as evidence. He also took the left front tire and wheel to send to the FBI laboratory. But first, he filled the flat tire with air and discovered an apparent knife puncture in the tread. About 5/8 inch in length, the defect forensically-matched a knife taken from Johnny Thornton at the time of his arrest. This evidence corroborated Juanita Deckard's statement that Thornton let air out of the tire before taking them to the game warden's cabin.

* * *

Examination of the Game Warden Cabin

On January 14, 1977, FBI agents Roger D. Browning, David A. Palladino, and Donald R. McDonald (assisted by CID agents) searched the game warden cabin. The agents discovered and seized a large number of items as evidence — including numerous hairs, a stain-like material on a bunk bed in the northwest corner of the cabin, and one bobby pin under that same bunk bed.

CID Agent Alexander Kerekes lifted a number of latent fingerprint impressions from the bunk bed. Additional latent fingerprint lifts were made on and near the cabin's metal stove. At the conclusion of the search, the stove and the bunk bed were seized and sent to the FBI laboratory.

The FBI laboratory later discerned the fingerprints and palm prints found on the bunk bed and the stove were a match to Johnny Lee Thornton and Juanita Deckard. These latent prints proved Deckard had been in the cabin with Thornton and further corroborated her statements of that evening.

Bunkbed inside of the Game Warden Cabin.
Federal Court Record

* * *

SP4 Interior Laloulo, 463rd MP Company:

SP4 Interior Laloulo was the game warden officer who relieved Johnny Lee Thornton at 6:00 a.m. on January 13, 1977. CID Agent Mike Caldwell interviewed Laloulo.

> *Laloulo*: Thornton acted completely normal when we met at shift change. He appeared calm and made no unusual statements. He asked me to wash the vehicle.
>
> *Caldwell*: Did you?
>
> *Laloulo*: No. I didn't.
>
> *Caldwell*: Did you see any blood in the vehicle?
>
> *Laloulo*: There was blood on the back seat and floor. I thought the blood probably came from a dog or a road kill.

85

* * *

Sergeant David L. Edwards 463rd MP Company:

Sergeant David Leroy Edwards was a member of the game warden detail at Fort Leonard Wood. He was interviewed by FBI special agents Thomas E. Den Ouden and Paul A. Van Someren.

> *Edwards:* On January 12, 1977, I was on duty from two p.m. until ten. I drove the International Scout with the marking X37 on the body while on duty.
>
> *Den Ouden*: Did you notice anything unusual about the vehicle that day?
>
> *Edwards*: The Scout was dusty and dirty from normal use but I didn't notice anything unusual about the vehicle.
>
> *Den Ouden*: Did you notice any blood in the back seat or bullet holes in the seat or tailgate?
>
> *Edwards*: No. It's normal procedure to check over a vehicle before going on duty.
>
> *Den Ouden*: Were you required to use your service weapon at all while you were on duty January 12, 1977?
>
> *Edwards*: No.
>
> *Den Ouden*: Did you transport any animals in the vehicle on that date?
>
> *Edwards*: No. If I have to transport road kill, I normally drop the tailgate and place the animal on the tailgate for transportation.
>
> Between nine-thirty and ten p.m. on January 12, 1977, I signed the International Scout X37 vehicle over to Johnny Lee Thornton in the parking lot of the Provost Marshal's office. Thornton went on duty at ten p.m. that evening. I noticed at that time, Thornton had signed out two sets of handcuffs which is not normal. I asked him, "What are you doing with two sets of handcuffs?"
>
> Thornton replied, "I'm playing super cop tonight."
>
> The conversation just dropped at that point.
>
> *Den Ouden*: Did you observe Thornton sign for his service weapon that evening?

Edwards: Yes.

* * *

Interview Hallie Jane Cottingham:

On January 20, 1977, FBI Special Agent Gary W. Reid and CID agent Thomas W. Byrd interviewed a civilian friend of the Thornton family. Hallie Jane Cottingham previously lived in the Hickory Hills Trailer Court.

Around the first of September in 1976, Patti Thornton moved into the Hickory Hills Trailer Court next door to me. Patti and her husband, Johnny Thornton, were separated at the time. Patti had filed for a divorce. The Thorntons later decided to try to work things out, you know, and save the marriage.

Byrd: Was Thornton ever violent?

Cottingham: Patti was afraid of Johnny. I recall an incident where I went to Patti's trailer to take her to the grocery store. When I went in their home, I found Patti lying on the floor. Patti said she had fallen off of the chair, and she couldn't get up. Johnny was in the trailer at that time — and he just sat on the couch and looked at Patti. An ambulance had to be called. Patti was taken to the Fort Leonard Wood hospital. Patti later told me she had asked Johnny to feed their youngest son. Johnny became upset and threw a jar of baby food at Patti. It hit her hard in her stomach.

According to Patti, Johnny had once whipped their oldest boy with a belt so hard it'd bruised the boy.

Byrd: Were their marital relations good?

Cottingham: Patti never mentioned her sex life with Johnny except to say she could not stand for Johnny to touch her. When Johnny spent the night at the trailer, Patti would sleep on the couch with their oldest boy.

Patti was having an affair with Johnny's best friend. I don't know his name but I think the boyfriend is a service member. I think Patti's boyfriend was transferred to a station in Germany.

Patti eventually left Johnny and moved to California sometime around first of October 1976. She told me that Johnny had pleaded with her not to leave him. I think Johnny's friend — with whom Patti was having the affair — was supposed to take leave and meet her in California at a later date.

Byrd: How would you describe Johnny Lee Thornton?

Cottingham: Johnny Lee is a withdrawn person. Patti told me Johnny slept a lot and after she filed for divorce, Johnny started complaining of bad headaches. Johnny once brought a paperback book to the trailer. Patty became upset and called the book 'filthy trash.'

Byrd: When was the last time you saw Thornton?

Cottingham: The last time I saw Johnny was at the Walmart store in St. Robert just before Christmas of 1976. Johnny didn't speak to me at that time.

* * *

Sergeant Elizabeth (Betty) Cochrane:

Special Agent Larry R. Rodery CID interviewed Sergeant Elizabeth Cochrane. Rodery began the interview by telling Cochrane he had been told she was a friend of Thornton's.

Cochrane: Yes, I am three months pregnant by him. He lived with me for several months.

Rodery: Did he ever speak about his wife.

Cochrane: Yes, he talked to me about his wife. The news about him and the murders is hard to believe because he is so level-headed and so super straight.

* * *

Sergeant Elvin Cole:

Sergeant Elvin Cole of the Military Police Investigations unit (MPI) was one of the officers sent to the stump dump to look for the bodies of the dogs Thornton claimed he'd shot the early morning of the 13th. Sergeant Cole reported he was unable to find any dog carcasses at the stump dump.

* * *

Interview Charles Gibbs, Air Traffic Controller:

Agents interviewed Mr. Charles Gibbs, who was an air-traffic controller at Fort Leonard Wood's Forney Airfield. Gibbs told them a man who identified himself as a military game warden called in on the morning of the 13th to inquire if there were going to be any helicopter flights in the area of the game warden cabin or hunting Area 13 on Fort Leonard Wood that day.

* * *

Specialist Lora Woods Motor Pool Supervisor:

Agents interviewed SPC Lora Woods, the Motor Pool Supervisor. Woods told them Johnny Lee Thornton wanted her to wash vehicle X37 when he brought it back to the motor pool on the morning of January 13.

> *Agent*:   That was a strange request — to want to wash the vehicle under the snow and ice conditions existing at that time.
>
> *Woods*:   Yeah. The wash idea was quite odd.

The vehicle was not washed as Thornton requested.

* * *

Sergeant David Carlson:

Sergeant David Carlson, 463rd MP Company was the shift supervisor for the company at the time of the murders and as such the game wardens on duty reported to him. Sergeant Carlson stated the morning of the 13th, Thornton told him he had shot some dogs.

* * *

Thomas Avery, civilian employee:

Agents interviewed Thomas Avery, a civilian employee on Fort Leonard Wood. Avery told the agents he found a tan purse and a blue billfold in a trash dumpster on Fort Leonard Wood. The items contained Linda Needham's identification.

Avery said he turned the purse over to Charles Edward Miller who worked in the motor pool. He said when they realized who owned the purse and the wallet, Miller called the MPs and later turned the items over to an MP. The dumpster in question was in the motor pool area.

* * *

Specialist George D. Brocious, 463rd MP Company:

Specialist George D. Brocious was the MP radio dispatcher during the early morning shift on January 13, 1977.

> *Brocious*: Thornton called in a license plate check on the Bates' vehicle. He said the vehicle appeared to be abandoned and had a flat tire. The time was between five and six a.m. The license information system for Missouri plates was not working correctly that morning so I couldn't access the information.

* * *

Dean Neal, civilian:

> *Neal*: I was driving on the south gate road at approximately ten forty p.m. on January 12th. I was on my way to work after having attended school in Licking, Missouri. The snow on the road reduced my speed.
>
> Approximately three miles into Fort Leonard Wood, a military policeman driving a scout vehicle with one red light on top stopped me. The MP asked for my driver's license and asked me where I had been that night.

After I explained my situation, the MP apologized for stopping me and said they were stopping cars out there that night. No statement was made by the MP that I was driving over the speed limit.

Neal would later identify Johnny Lee Thornton as the MP who stopped him.

The investigating officers' conclusion was, Thornton was hunting for victims when he made this and several other traffic stops.

* * *

Specialist George Palmer:

During their investigation, agents discovered a second vehicle had been stopped by a military police officer that same night. At approximately 11:50 pm., SFC George Palmer was driving north on the south gate road returning to his quarters.

Palmer: I was a short distance past the Bloodland Range Control building when I rounded the curve and saw headlights coming out of the woods. The lights from the vehicle followed me along the south gate road for about three to five minutes.

The vehicle then pulled up close behind me and the driver flashed his lights to high beam and then back down to low beam. The vehicle slowed down and made a U-turn and went back the other direction.

I pulled over to watch the vehicle. The vehicle then turned around again and approached my car — which was stopped on the side of the road. The driver got out and asked me if there was anything wrong. I told him, "no." The MP told me he was checking out my license plate number because the officer was looking for a specific vehicle.

Palmer was unable to identify Johnny Lee Thornton as the officer who'd stopped him.

Palmer: The [MP] was in an Army fatigue uniform. I can't remember if the vehicle had a red light on top but I'm sure it was an International Scout with lettering on the side. The Scout's driver appeared to be very calm.

* * *

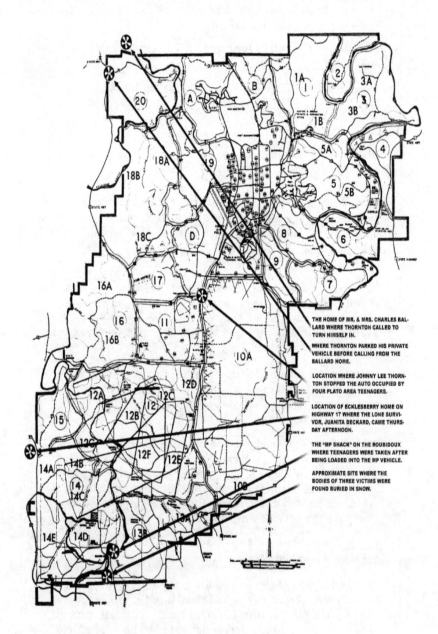

THE HOME OF MR. & MRS. CHARLES BAL-
LARD WHERE THORNTON CALLED TO
TURN HIMSELF IN.

WHERE THORNTON PARKED HIS PRIVATE
VEHICLE BEFORE CALLING FROM THE
BALLARD HOME.

LOCATION WHERE JOHNNY LEE THORN-
TON STOPPED THE AUTO OCCUPIED BY
FOUR PLATO AREA TEENAGERS.

LOCATION OF ECKLESBERRY HOME ON
HIGHWAY 17 WHERE THE LONE SURVI-
VOR, JUANITA DECKARD, CAME THURS-
DAY AFTERNOON.

THE "MP SHACK" ON THE ROUBIDOUX
WHERE TEENAGERS WERE TAKEN AFTER
BEING LOADED INTO THE MP VEHICLE.

APPROXIMATE SITE WHERE THE
BODIES OF THREE VICTIMS WERE
FOUND BURIED IN SNOW.

Thursday, January 20, 1977, Sketch of Crime Scenes
Federal Court Trial Record

Robert L. Hall Jr of Plato, Missouri:

> *Hall*: I was riding to work with my partner, Stanley Handley. We work the midnight to eight thirty a.m. shift at the post commissary. Approximately twenty minutes after midnight on January 13th, an MP driving a Scout stopped us on the south gate road in the vicinity of Range 26.

They were traveling north when they met the MP vehicle, which turned around to stop them.

> *Hall*: The MP asked for identification and shined his flashlight inside Handley's Chevrolet pickup. Handley always carried a shotgun in the truck and I was holding it in my lap.

The MP made no comment about the shotgun. He was looking for a particular person and let them go.

Neither Hall nor Handley could identify Thornton as the man who stopped them but they were sure it was an MP International Scout.

* * *

In addition to the interviews which were cited in this chapter, the FBI sent agents throughout the state of Arkansas and California to interview people who'd played a role in Johnny Lee Thornton's childhood, employment, and hospitalizations.

The FBI interviewed Thornton family friends in Arkansas and California to determine if Johnny Lee Thornton had a history of unusual medical problems. They found that Thornton sought treatment at several medical facilities in California — and the records from each of them were subpoenaed.

The agents interviewed every person they could locate who'd worked with Thornton during his civilian employment — in a number of grocery stores and other jobs in the Arkansas area. They specifically asked about blackout spells, headaches, anger issues, and any other factor that might shed light on Thornton's behavior. The agents didn't find anyone who recalled Thornton having medical or psychiatric problems.

Interviewees remarked about Thornton's shooting ability with various firearms and the fact he was withdrawn. A number of these people were subpoenaed for the criminal trial but never called to testify.

The FBI contacted all local law enforcement agencies in and around the areas where Johnny Lee Thornton grew up. They were looking for evidence of similar unsolved crimes to the one committed at Fort Leonard Wood. They specifically looked for signs Thornton may have had a hidden past as a serial killer. No unsolved or unresolved cases resembling the Fort Wood murders were ever discovered.

8

A NEW COMPLICATION

ON APRIL 30, 1977, AT approximately 6:40 a.m., a turkey hunter walking across Fort Leonard Wood found partial human remains — still clad in military clothing and wearing military boots — scattered across a densely wooded hillside. The hunter, Edward Nelson of St. Robert, Missouri, contacted the Fort Leonard Wood authorities and advised them of his grisly discovery.

Since April 30, 1977, was a Saturday, CID agents were called out to handle this investigation. In a fluke of circumstance, virtually the entire team who'd worked the Thornton case also investigated the John Doe in the woods.

Private Fredrick E. Williams

Persons having information pertaining to the events leading to the death of Private Fredrick E. Williams, or any persons responsible for his death, are asked to contact Special Agents Roy E. Black or Matthew E. Moriarty, Fort Leonard Wood Field Office, US Army Criminal Investigation Command, Fort Leonard Wood, Mo. 65473. Information may be telephoned to (314) 368-3165. All replies to this notice will be treated confidentially. Private Williams, 6 feet 1 inch tall, 165 pounds, was last

Courtesy Gatehouse Media, Daily Guide

Agents found identifying information inside and stenciled on the uniform in several places. The information identified the body as Frederick E. Williams, even though the agents never found his wallet. It didn't take long to determine Frederick E. Williams was listed as Absent Without Leave (AWOL) from his Fort Leonard Wood unit.

At the onset of this case, the investigating agents realized that during the February search of Fort Leonard Wood by the military and FBI agents for two other missing kids, Alfred Marshall and T. C. Gossage, the searchers had marched to within 50 or 60 yards of this body and had not discovered it. The location of Williams' body and its proximity to Thornton's known dumping ground raised questions as to Johnny Lee Thornton's involvement in this case.

The Williams investigation started with attempts to locate the last time Williams was known to be alive. The initial interviews with his unit commander and peers proved to be burdensome. Williams, who had just graduated from basic training, was assigned to a remedial training company. It specialized in correcting training issues for new members of the military who had difficulty in basic training. After completing their specific individual training, these soldiers were assigned to Army bases worldwide.

The military unit in question kept poor records and had little accountability for the men assigned to their command. This complicated the investigation. The supervisory personnel in charge of the company were lax in following existing procedures and policies addressing accountability for Williams' whereabouts.

It didn't take the agents long to determine that a series of assumptions and errors convoluted their case. The company command thought Williams was in the Fort Wood Hospital, yet when members of the company went to visit him, he wasn't there. These fellow company members formed the opinion Williams was being treated in a hospital off-post. Nobody followed up on Williams' whereabouts. After missing several paydays, Authorities declared Williams AWOL and initiated the usual steps of contacting civilian police and family members for information (in an attempt to get him to surrender back to military authority).

Once the Army notified Williams' family members of his death, they accused the military of hiding the cause. They felt it was due to foul play at the hands of "that crazy MP." And so, the stage was set for the next several months. The Williams family gave numerous press interviews accusing the Army of covering up the death of their son and attempting to protect Johnny Lee Thornton. The Williams family contacted their congressional representatives — and as a result of those contacts, those representatives pressured the military and CID agents working the case for transparency.

Meanwhile, the Williams investigation crept forward. The men from his special training company, known locally as the Shirley Temple School, had been transferred all over. CID agents interviewed them at their new duty stations. In addition, interviews with Williams' friends and family members in Kansas City, Missouri, proved to be difficult. Without the Williams family's approval, interviewees refused to answer CID agents' questions. The entire situation delayed the investigation, stifling and frustrating the CID agents working the Williams' case.

Agents eventually determined the last time anyone saw Williams was January 5, 1977. He was seen with several of his friends from his unit at a function on Fort Leonard Wood. No one recalled seeing him after January 6, 1977. During a series of interviews with friends and other members of his unit, a number of contradictory statements gave the investigators a starting point in the criminal case. As the case continued, these contradictions eventually led the agents to scrutinize three members of Williams' company and one military dependent living on Fort Leonard Wood.

The speculation in the newspapers and local rumor mills as to Thornton's probable involvement in other cases on Fort Wood not only continued but increased in number. The CID agents assigned to the Williams murder found themselves in the classic position of being between a rock and a hard place. Since the Thornton trial was approaching, agents could not comment on how it might relate to the Williams case. Such pretrial publicity would be detrimental.

At the same time, with the Williams investigation finally starting to produce possible suspects, agents couldn't discuss it in the press for fear of warning them. And of course, that stance did nothing to control the rampant rumors.

The murder of Private Frederick E. Williams, in January 1977, was eventually proven not to be the work of Johnny Lee Thornton. The CID team located four possible suspects, who were later charged and convicted in federal court. The last appeal in the court process extended the Williams case to January 1981 before it was finally closed. As a result of the long investigation and trial in the Frederick Williams case, many people in the local area still believe that Thornton murdered an AWOL soldier on Fort Wood.

The same basic unit of CID team members who helped convict Johnny Lee Thornton also secured the conviction of the four men who murdered Private Frederick E. Williams. Agent George Matthews was one of the CID officers involved with the case.

George Matthews, CID agent investigating the Freddy Williams case:

> To have had the opportunity to be a part of a murder investigation such as the Freddy Williams case is, in my opinion, the high point of the CID agent's career. To be at the crime scene the first day, suffer the frustration of dead-end leads and contradictions and then find yourself sitting in the courtroom more than two years later to hear a panel of men and women deliver the fates of the killers won't soon be forgotten.
>
> Having been one of the agents who went to Kansas City to talk to Freddy's family, I was well-aware of Mr. Williams' attitude toward the Army, and the fact he never believed, at least during our association, the CID was doing anything more than attempting to cover the circumstances surrounding the death of his son.
>
> Then to be sitting next to him in court on that day, watching the expression on his face as the verdicts were read, knowing full-well he had to realize the effort put forth on behalf of the crime against his son...after seeing representatives of the

military and civilians who came from all parts of the world to testify to their part in the effort to put the killers of his son in jail, knowing that Mr. Williams was seeing what he knew to be justice, was the perfect ending to a classic investigation.[1]

From Left to Right: Agent bending over is CID SA Mike Kremper, with the plaid shirt is Major (Doctor) Gerald Rappe, GLWACH Pathologist, to the rear is CID SA Mike Caldwell, center holding camera is CID SA George Matthews, next with a cigar and writing, is FBI SA William "Bill" Castleberry, and to the far right, CID SA Lee Blasingame. This is an actual crime scene photograph of the first hours of the Private Frederick E. Williams murder case. Photo courtesy of William Castleberry.

The January, 1977, murder case was not the first time CID agents Bob Oster, and George Matthews had a run-in with Johnny Lee Thornton. George Matthews recalls a night when he and Oster were on a surveillance detail at a construction site just outside of Fort Leonard Wood. Multiple thefts of building materials destined for construction on Fort Wood had been reported from this site. The agents were on a stakeout in one of the trailers attempting to catch the thieves.

Matthews said it was an uneventful night until they heard a loud voice telling them to come out of the trailer with their

---

1 If you will look for an interview with PVT Williams' mother that appeared in JET magazine, July 14, 1977, you will get a sense of the dread the family felt while they waited for answers from the CID investigation.

hands up. Matthews looked out the window and there stood the game warden, Johnny Lee Thornton, with legs spread and his .45 leveled in their direction.

Thornton ordered the agents out again. Matthews said he held his badge to the window and identified themselves as CID agents on a stakeout. Simultaneously, Matthews was on the radio with the MP desk telling them to "get this joker called off." When Matthews next looked out the window, he saw Thornton's taillights melting back into the woods.

Matthews said the next day he talked to Thornton about the incident. Matthews could see his words going in one of Thornton's ears and out the other.

Matthews thought nothing about this incident — even after the murders. Many years later, Matthews recalled it when talking to his son about Johnny Lee Thornton and the dead teenagers. At that point, it dawned on him that if he and Oster had come out of the trailer and been taken into Thornton's custody, who knows what would've happened next.

According to Matthews, a better police tactic would have been for Thornton to remain hidden, call in a crime-in-progress, and request backup to surround the trailer before the MP demanded the thugs come out.

George Matthews has often wondered what would've happened that night had they surrendered to Thornton. Or, what would've happened had two, real thieves surrendered to Thornton when Thornton was by himself?

9

THE MISSING KIDS

WITHIN A FEW HOURS AFTER the first details of the January 12-13, 1977, murder case became known to the federal law enforcement officers, they began to suspect Thornton had committed another similar crime on Fort Leonard Wood.

Sometime during the evening/early morning hours of October 9-10, 1976, two other local youths disappeared on Fort Wood. Their car was found abandoned near the vet clinic, which was on the east side of Fort Wood, as opposed the Bates' site, which was on the southwest corner of the Army base. The most alarming fact was, Thornton was reported to have been the first to advise radio dispatch about the parked car. The kids were listed as missing. With nothing to investigate and no real leads to follow, the investigation into the kids' disappearance hit a dead-end right from the start.

Alfred Hofmann Marshall, age 18, and Teresa (TC) Gossage age 17, were the dependent children of active duty military members stationed at Fort Wood. They were on a date and were known to have been driving on Fort Wood during the evening hours of October 9, 1976. They were in the Marshall family car. It was found locked and abandoned on Fort Wood during the early morning hours of October 10th. These few facts were enough for many of the investigating officers to immediately fear the worst about the fate of Marshall and Gossage.

Friends of the two youths, particularly fellow students of Al Marshall at the Waynesville High School, were shocked to hear his cherished high school letter jacket was found inside his vehicle. Marshall was fiercely proud of that jacket and what it stood for. He wore the jacket everywhere. The simple fact Marshall was separated from his jacket and missing filled them with a dread.

In 1977, Julie Emmons was 16 years old and attending Waynesville High School. One of her best friends was Teresa (TC) Gossage. Julie had been TC's friend for about a year and a half. They lived in the same housing area on Fort Leonard Wood. Julie described TC as a free spirit and said TC's parents were strict with her. TC's grades were not the best, so she had mandatory study times at home. Therefore, TC didn't get out of her house much. When she did, TC liked to have fun.

Julie Emmons said that on the day Marshall and TC disappeared, TC and Julie's boyfriend, Mark, had been to a school-sponsored band competition in Columbia, Missouri. Julie and Mark were supposed to join TC and Al for a double date that night. But Julie and Mark had a fight and they canceled on TC and Al.

TC Gossage
Courtesy Gatehouse
Media, Daily Guide

Al Marshall
Courtesy Gatehouse
Media, Daily Guide

Around 1:30 or 2:00 a.m. that morning, Julie's parents got a call from TC's folks wanting to know if Julie was home and if so, if TC was with her. Later that morning, around 4:30 a.m., TC's father came over to Julie's house. Mr. Gossage and her father, Dewey Emmons, questioned her as to where TC and Al might've gone parking. The fathers thought the two missing teens might have fallen asleep or something. Julie's dad and TC's dad went out looking for Al's vehicle. The vehicle was later found parked a short distance from TC's home at the Veterinary Clinic.

For the first few days after TC and Al disappeared, some people thought they had possibly eloped or something like that. Nobody who knew them personally put any emphasis on that. It seemed far-fetched and out of character for TC and Al. The CID officers investigating the case questioned Julie and Mark extensively thinking they might have some inside knowledge of what TC and Al had planned. Julie and Mark didn't have any idea.

Later in January of 1977, on the day when the news about the murders of the other three youths became public knowledge, Julie was babysitting for some folks on Fort Wood. Her father came to the residence and told her about the other kids being killed. At that point, Julie said she and her father "knew" what had happened to TC and Al.

The pace of the investigation frustrated the missing teens' parents. The news media quoted Bill Williams, the FBI special agent in charge of the Kansas City, Missouri office as saying, "After all this time, the only thing we have to go on in that case is the abandoned car and the fact two young people are missing."

Newspapers often quoted Al and TC's parents. Mrs. Helga Marshall, mother of Alfred Marshall said, "They kept telling us [our kids] are runaways."

But Mrs. Marshall didn't buy that theory. After the Bates' killings became public knowledge, Mrs. Marshall was quoted as saying, "I pray and wait and hope. It never goes out of my head. It drives me crazy. He was my only child." Mrs. Marshall feared the kids encountered Thornton — someone they would have trusted, "Because the car was parked and locked, it looked like they would come back later and get it. It was thirty-four degrees that night. And we found Al's jacket in the back of the car. He would never have left his jacket when it was that cold. His hair brush, which he never goes without, was in the console and the car showed no signs of foul play."

Mrs. Marshall also reported her son had in excess of $1000 in the credit union. None of his money had been withdrawn. Al and his father had planned a hunting trip in October. The Marshall family was planning a trip to Germany for Christmas. Al planned to go to college.

"He was a good student, a good kid and [TC] was a good student too." Mrs. Marshall said TC Gossage was a member of the school's band. The band had just won a district contest qualifying her for a state musical competition.

"She was very happy. All I want to know is if they are alive or not."

FBI Agent Tom Den Ouden:

> I don't know much about that case at all because the FBI was not really involved in the case of the missing kids. I had only been there at Fort Wood a couple of months. And we didn't see any FBI jurisdiction because we weren't sure these kids had been abducted. We thought they may have eloped. We were trying to find some evidence of that but of course it looked sketchy.

> Thornton's name didn't come up. He was not a suspect in that case until much later. And you know what happened then. Investigators went back and reviewed the records. Thornton had written down an excuse for expending shells similar to what he did in the Bates case.

> I've not seen that document but I've been told that. We got that information from the CID. They're the ones who went back and checked. I was just told by the CID, you know, the night that couple was missing, Thornton came back and did the same thing — he wrote a similar report with regard to having to use shells. Because that was protocol. MPs had to do that.

* * *

The issue of the missing kids became an immediate media sensation — particularly in the local papers. The Pulaski County Democrat Newspaper, which was published in Waynesville, Missouri, inserted a rather large box with a heavy black border, in one of their early issues that covered the Thornton case:

Will More Bodies be Found?

"Where does the story begin or end that was brought to light on Thursday when a young woman stumbled, exhausted, cold and wounded, to relate one of the most sordid and shameful stories of the abduction and murder ever recorded in this entire area of Missouri?

"All persons, regardless of their station in life, are asking over and over, is this it? Is this all? Could more unknown victims have met similar fates and just how far could this type of murder have gone had it not been for the determination to live of Miss Juanita Deckard? Does the vast uninhabited area of southwest Fort Wood contain stories yet unrevealed?

"Could Johnny Lee Thornton be responsible and hold the key to the knowledge surrounding the mysterious disappearance of two popular Fort Wood teenagers on October 9? Their abandoned auto was discovered locked on Fort Wood in the general area of the abduction of the Plato teenagers on October 10. Their whereabouts are yet unknown.

"Unconfirmed reports are that their abandoned auto was discovered by none other than Johnny Lee Thornton on this date, while on routine duties as an MP (Military Police) acting in the capacity of a game warden there.

"Is there more—much more—to be revealed of the actions of Specialist fourth Thornton?"

* * *

In a desperate attempt to minimize what could only be described as horrendous publicity for the United States Army, military authorities on Fort Leonard Wood adopted an open policy toward the press. Reporters were allowed access to the various crime scenes involved in the case.

Members of the Press were escorted around post and given daily briefings by both the Fort Wood public information office and the FBI headquarters command in Kansas City, Missouri. As a result, numerous articles in papers throughout Missouri

and the rest of the nation carried the Thornton murder story —
along with photographs inside and out of the game warden
cabin and of searchers marching through the woods looking
for the missing kids. Photographs of all the victims — both
known and suspected — flashed across the nation. And, the
media interest in Johnny Lee Thornton continued for quite
some time.

The United States Army focused on minimizing the bad
press and protecting the criminal investigation from improper information leaks. A delicate balance was required. The
months of media coverage might taint the potential jury pool
for Thornton's upcoming trial in the western district of Missouri Federal Court.

In addition, the case of the two missing kids presented
legal challenges for the FBI and CID. The FBI couldn't determine if the pair had been kidnapped or if there any other
legal grounds that would allow them to enter the case. And
the CID agents were in the same boat — they couldn't develop
any preliminary information to support a criminal case either.

* * *

FBI Agent Bill Castleberry:

Initially, [TC and Al's] disappearance could only be classified
as a missing person's case with no evidence of a criminal act.
All that could be done at that point was a NCIC missing person's
entry. When Thornton happened, it was almost immediately
apparent to Matt [Moriarty], Perry [Elder], and me that the
teens had most likely been kidnapped and killed by Thornton.
After the initiation of the Thornton case, I remember briefing
the SAC [Bill Williams] that we had a responsibility to include
their disappearance in our investigation, and he agreed. I remember when we had the wide area search teams brought in,
the SAC briefed the press we were looking for bodies and not
just evidence from the Bates case. You should probably have
that quote in a newspaper article.

And, this is the part where I really am struggling to remember.
I recall about three or four days, and I can't remember the exact

number, where there was Matt Moriarty, Perry Elder, and myself trying to coordinate all the agents, the FBI agents who came down and the CID agents who were outstanding...they did an outstanding job, and the military police. We were convinced that if Thornton killed those other two teenagers, their bodies were out there somewhere. And that was one of our primary focuses from the very beginning.

I recall looking (with Matt and Perry) at the activity logs and reports of Thornton. For one reason, we were trying to figure out where Thornton was at the time of [Al and TC's] disappearance. Since I looked at all of the logs and reports, I probably saw the report by Thornton of shots fired. But since we had already assumed he was the responsible party, it would just have served as further justification of our belief. We eventually used all of the activity logs and reports to try and narrow our searches to no avail. We then went back and tried to find a pattern to his activities and used that for searches also to no avail.

It was then that I called Bill Williams and asked him to send down some agents — preferably some of the guys who were there for the initial investigation because they would likely be more familiar with the area — and the CID agents they had been working with to assist in a wide area search.

I specifically remember being frustrated with our inability to locate the bodies and the lack of anything we could rely on which pinpointed where Thornton was on any given day. He pretty much had an area of responsibility (as game warden) for any of the less used parts of the base because of his assignment. I remember an agreement by Matt, Perry, and myself — we couldn't even assume the activity logs were accurate. I remember day after day of driving to remote locations and walking into areas he might have used. I remember a lot of caves.

They waited until February 14, 1977 — after the snow melted — to begin the hunt. Approximately 300-350 military personnel and thirteen FBI agents gathered on Fort Wood on that day. Many of these men were the same ones who responded the night the of Bates crime. They were familiar with the case — and somewhat familiar with Fort Wood.

Starting on February 14th, these men walked within arm's length of each other. They looked at or turned over every object in their paths. The head of the FBI's Kansas City regional field office, Agent Bill Williams, was on the scene and briefed the media on a daily basis. The press was even allowed access to the search area. Pictures of the searchers in action filled the newspapers.

Kansas City Regional Field Office Agent Bill Williams
Courtesy Gatehouse Media, Daily Guide

Agent Williams was quoted several times with regard to the case. When asked about efforts near public roads, he indicated spectators would be discouraged.

> *Agent Bill Williams*: Certainly, we would expect people to respect the area being searched.

In another session, when reporters pressed Agent Williams to be more specific about what the FBI was trying to find, Williams acknowledged that, "Sure. There's no question about it. We are looking for bodies." He also indicated Army officials knew the search might be lengthy. "We will stay until we're satisfied."

The Fort Leonard Wood Public Information Office also responded to media requests. The Public Information Officer, Major Lyle Ten Eyke said, "It's a tremendous effort." Ten Eyke also said that the operation was being fully funded by the government, with the FBI providing assistance and specialized equipment.

FBI Agents and a Fort Leonard Wood soldier
search for traces of Al Marshall and TC Gossage in
the woods.

Courtesy Gate House Media,Daily Guide

Each day, the team covered a new section of land. They
marked out an elaborate grid that they could replicate and track
on paper — however, the results were dismal. This large-scale
effort went on day after day until February 22, 1977, but they
found no trace of Al Marshall or TC Gossage.

The searches were not failed attempts though. Three expended cartridge casings and two fired bullets were later linked
to the Bates' vehicle stop. A brief mention in the newspapers
indicated the discovery of a possible human pelvic bone. The
media reported nothing more about It. However, the CID case
file provided more information regarding this intriguing tidbit.

The CID file documents this in more detail. On February
16, 1977, investigators conducted a search in a wooded area
identified as Hunting Area 4, which can be reached from Hale
Cemetery Road. During the course of this operation, they found
a bone in the vicinity of grid coordinates 842769. The searchers
photographed it and the FBI collected it for evaluation. The

evidence was then transported to the pathology laboratory in GLWACH. The bone was examined and determined to be that of a human. The sex of the victim could not be determined. However, they could tell that it was from the right side of the pelvic structure. The bone was then forwarded to the Armed Forces Institute of Pathology for the further analysis.

The CID report went on to say, "It should be noted the bone in question may be related to the bone remains of a murdered female which was investigated by this office under CID case number 74–CID 045–01629. It should also be mentioned the pelvic pertaining to the aforementioned body was never located during the 1974 crime scene search and therefore, may not be related to this present investigation."

No additional information about the discovery of this bone was located.

* * *

FBI Agent Bill Castleberry:

After all the things with the Thornton case settled down, we still had leads to follow. Almost all of them had to do with the two missing kids' case. And that's what I focused on. It was like a month later, and we were going to have a couple of hundred soldiers at our disposal. I told headquarters I needed a large team sent down again. So, they sent down the same guys as before. The same team could accompany the soldiers because we were going search this damn base. The SAC [Bill Williams] himself came down with them.

We had to wait until the snow was gone and the ground thawed out a little bit. We went on both sides of the road — with military and FBI agents and CID — along the entire route Thornton had to have driven. Obviously, the little hut was part of the attack which occurred and we pretty much dismantled that place.

I remember being in a Jeep with Perry Elder, the SAC, and the driver of the Jeep, and we were going up an incline that was still in the shade under the canopy of trees. The sun had not yet hit [this area] directly. Therefore, there was still ice on the trail and the jeep started sliding backwards. The kid driving the Jeep looked over at Colonel Elder and said, "Sir, I've never driven on ice before."

You talk about bailing out. We got out of that Jeep real quick and the driver was left all by himself.

We spent a lot of time out there. They put up tents — for coffee and everything — for people to warm up. But we didn't find what we were looking for. The only benefit I saw coming out of that, was I knew where I didn't have to search again. That went on for months and I just focused in on that.

* * *

Betty Elder, wife of deceased Provost Marshal Colonel Perry Elder:

Perry didn't bring work home to the house. Whenever he was off-duty, he basically was off-duty. [Perry] was astounded Thornton did this, of course. Everybody was. He was totally disappointed he and the other MPs were never able to solve this, were never able to find those kids. That was one of the biggest regrets in his life, in his military career.

* * *

After 40 years separating fact from fiction, or just trying to understand an issue that has been in limbo for that long, information can be confusing. At the time the Deckard investigation started in January of 1977, suspicion about Al Marshall's parked vehicle being linked to Johnny Lee Thornton was regarded as solid. I personally heard that at the briefing on January 14, 1977. At that time, the information was supposed to have come from the MP radio operator who said Thornton was the first to report a parked automobile, asking him for a Missouri license check on the plates. As part of the research for this book, I discovered a second way the radio operator would have known Thornton was at Al Marshall's vehicle and placed that information in the radio log.

* * *

Sergeant William Moredock:

On October 10, 1976, Sergeant William Moredock of the 463rd MP Company was the acting supervisor for the patrol units working on Fort Wood. Moredock recalls an APB alert broadcast for Al Marshall's vehicle. Moredock and his driver were part of the team searching Fort Wood for the car.

I decided to look in the not-so-usual places for the car. I found it almost immediately — near the lot of the animal control building (post veterinary clinic) across the railroad tracks on the east gate road and up to the right on top of the little knoll.

I advised the radio operator of my find, and told the operator "Moredock will be out of his patrol unit investigating."

Johnny Lee Thornton then arrived at the scene of the parked car probably within about, I'm going to guess, two or three minutes or something like that. I was still looking the car over when Thornton arrived in his game warden vehicle — almost out of breath, almost paranoid, and demanded to know what I knew. I, of course, didn't associate him with anything else. But I told him, "Look, I just found this vehicle. I'm conducting a little inquiry here and I would appreciate it if you went back to your business." He was not really supposed to mess with patrol business. I was the patrol supervisor at the time.

The fact Thornton was at the car site, well, that's a detail I and the radio operator at the time would have known. Yes, I instructed him to leave — ordered him to leave. He had no business there. Because of the way he was acting, you understand what I am saying? Now if he had acted like he was supposed to and had offered to help — look around the area or something, I would have let him do that. But all he wanted to do was know what I knew. And he was really exasperated. And he was upset, you know? He wasn't acting right. I stood by the car until the MP investigators arrived on scene and took over.

Later, when I got back to the station — almost at the end of the shift — [Thornton] came up to me again and wanted to know if I knew anything more about what happened to the kids, and if I had found anything around the car or anything. I told him it was an open investigation at that time and that's all I told him. I didn't give him any other information.

* * *

FBI Agent William Castleberry:

One of the major parts of the case was trying to figure out where those other two kids could be buried. What we found out when we started looking through his activity logs, was he had complete free reign and access to the entire base as a game warden and military policeman. It was interesting. As I said, [Thornton] had just won the title of Military Policeman of the Year for Fort Leonard Wood.

I specifically recall talking later to the behavioral science people — I think it may have been Bud Teten or maybe Roy Hazelwood, but I'm not sure. Whoever it was told me if they were Thornton's first victims, he would have done a thorough job of disposing of the bodies. The victims would have likely been transported away from the initial crime scene [the kid's vehicle]. That also fit with what we knew about what happened with the victims in the Bates case — being removed from the area where their car was found.

* * *

As time went by, the Marshall/Gossage case grew colder. The FBI could not enter the case, and the CID agents did not come up with enough evidence to open a proper criminal inquiry.

The facts of the case were still the same. The car was found parked on Fort Wood and the kids were missing. There was literally nothing to investigate. The Bates case reopened the investigation but it stalled again because Thornton was in the Federal Medical Center for Inmates, being tested for mental illness. He could not be questioned by investigators without the permission of his attorneys. And so, the case didn't move forward at all. The suspicion that Thornton killed the two kids grew stronger with time.

The large-scale search efforts on Fort Leonard Wood involved significant manpower, many man-hours, and covered a vast territory. The toll on the searchers was mostly physical, but there was at least one member of the searching party who had a different perspective of the search.

* * *

Scott Markley, Company D, 5th Engineers:

In 1977, Scott Markley was stationed on Ft Leonard Wood. He was also a 1976 graduate of Waynesville High School and personally knew Al Marshall and TC Gossage. And then on a snowy day in January of 1977, his two worlds collided and left him with painful memories.

We had an emergency fallout of the barracks. We fell out in formation and our commander was there, and instructed us that there had been a crime on the installation. They were going to take us out. We were going to search for skeletal remains or anything. At that time, I went with Lieutenant Ramirez, Sergeant First Class Blakely, and I believe it was Larry Thomas — and we got into one of those old five-quarters we called them. (The Humvee took the place of the Five-quarters.) It was bitterly cold that morning, too. I remember it was snowing and cold. I know it was in January, '77. It was a regular work day, I know. As for what day it actually was, I don't recall.

From our unit, we went out towards the woods, out there. I remember it was a long way out. Then we went down a road that took us down by the river, and there was a cabin there. There were uniformed officers there and military officers — regular Army was there. We went into the cabin where Johnny Lee Thornton assaulted the girls. And it was the crime scene.

Then we went out, and we were able to visually see where he had buried the young teenagers in the snow. That's always had somewhat of an impact on me, especially as we learned of the young lady who dug herself out and the struggles she went through to get some help. That was very powerful. Then again, I still remember to this day how bitterly cold it was. And to think about her, no clothing on, to be gravely wounded and to have seen her friends murdered in front of her... and to experience the assault against her whole being. She went through what it must have been like that in the dark — trying to get to where she could get help. I remember just as a young boy — I was eighteen-years old — it was crushing.

Then we got into formation and they told us. I had known Al and TC disappeared, but no one ever said anything. Some people said they eloped but those of us who knew Al and TC knew that they wouldn't do that. They were good kids. They were brought up right. And, they had their heads on their shoulders. So, when [the authorities] talked to us, they told us our company was going to go out into an area in the woods where Johnny Lee Thornton had patrolled. And the reason being was that they had found Al's car out there parked in the woods.

That was heavy on me because you're looking at a crime scene which was brutal and sadistic — almost made you think an animal did it — and then you're thinking your two friends — who had disappeared with no trace on the face of the earth ever again — may have fallen prey to [Thornton].

They took us way, way, out in the woods to the area where they had found Al's car. I believe we spent two days, at times in the snow on our hands and knees, brushing everything aside, looking for everything. Trying to find any evidence of skeletal remains, any type of clothing, any type of personal belongings. Again, it was sad knowing you were looking for your friend. And at that point, all this talk and everything, we fully believed they had fallen ill at the hands of Johnny Lee Thornton. We never did find anything. Nothing at all.

I think it was after a couple of days, they had called the search off. Then you heard all kinds of different things. But over the years, it bothered me that somewhere out there in those woods, Al and TC's remains are. For all these years, Johnny Lee Thornton has been such a coward and such a deceptive cruel despot, he would not even give Al and TC's family the peace of heart and mind where they could gather up whatever remains were left and do a decent burial for them and grieve properly.

It burdened my heart the young lady who survived. I can't recall her name but I am friends with a cousin of hers. He has told me over the years of the mental anguish and the psychological deep depression she has gone into at times. The struggles she has encountered, it is just…what Mr. Thornton did that day continues on to this day. He may be locked up in prison behind bars and probably relishing at times. No one knows where Al and TC's bodies are but him. He probably goes back and revels in that. But what he did affected Juanita from the moment he interacted with her till the day she passes away. And he put an end to families and generations which could have come from Al and TC. And he has, like a sinister being, left a web of pain through so many hearts by what he has done.

It ended in 1977, physically, in that capsule of time — but it has lived on in a wake of pain and agony. Not only did he bring great discredit on the United States military, not only did he bring shame on his own personal family but the heartache and the wickedness he drove through the hearts of the families who lost their loved ones that day. There's something, over all these years, that I have hoped. That sometime you [will] read that Johnny Lee Thornton confesses to Al Marshall and TC Gossage's murders and lets the families know where their bodies are.

Scott Markley still has vivid memories of that search — and those memories are hard to endure at times:

There's this cabin sitting in the woods alone. There are the graves the young people had been in. It was so bitterly cold and the snow...you could almost sense, like, these icy fingernails of evil all through that area, you know? And the sad thing is, at that time, Johnny Lee Thornton was a beast. And like a predator coming out of the woods, attacked and assaulted those kids. And, for his own sick, sadistic, twisted purposes, snuffed their lives out. And with no regard for their humanity, walked away from them.

Searching for TC and Al.
Courtesy Gatehouse Media, Daily Guide

* * *

Frank Marshall, the father of Al Marshall:

Al was my stepson. His real name was Alfred Elmar Hoffman but he went by Marshall. He had left the house in his mother's car — which was an Oldsmobile Cutlass — and had not been gone long when he returned to get something he'd forgotten. Well, I was a drill sergeant at the time, and I worked extremely long hours, seven days a week, for months on end. It was not too often I even got to see him except when he was asleep.

But he left on a date with Teresa — and about eleven p.m., or so, he was not home. I was in bed asleep. About one a.m., Al's mother woke me up and said, "Al's not home."

I said, "Well, I don't know what to do. I'll just sit here and wait a little bit." I can't remember how much longer, might've been two or one-thirty a.m.—something like that. Teresa's dad called me and he had found the car. He told me where it was and I went over there. And the first thing I did was feel the hood of the car. It was cold.

It was parked in a secluded area near the veterinary clinic on Fort Leonard Wood — in a wooded area. I'm not even sure I could take you there now, it's all grown over. But knowing him and knowing all the kids he ran with, his idea of parking was the main PX parking lot. It was not in the woods.

The boy was in the *Who's Who* — both his junior and senior year — with the American Honor Society. He was a smart man. Very smart. I raised that boy from six years old until he was eighteen. When I married his mother, he didn't speak a single word of English. He could not understand English. Nothing. He spoke German.

One of the classes I taught was minefield computation — computing the number of mines you needed for a minefield — and I had officers and high-ranking enlisted men who had a hell of a time with it. And I would bring [Al] in there and let him do the math on the chalkboard and embarrass them. Then they would get a grasp. I mean, you have a six-year-old child drawing on a chalkboard and figuring up the math. And if you can't do it, you've got a problem.

I think he had somewhere in the neighborhood of two grand in a savings account at the credit union. And then, after so many years, his mother had him pronounced dead because of no contact and she took the money.

Al didn't do anything without thinking it through. He was a smart kid, had a lot of common sense and he respected authority.

10

THE LEGAL PROCESS

THE AFTERNOON AND EVENING HOURS of January 13, 1977, were a logistical nightmare for Special Agent William Castleberry. First, he had to drive back from his meeting in Kansas City to arrive at Fort Wood safely while driving as fast as possible in the snow and icy road conditions. Then, he had to sit down to a briefing by Provost Marshal, Perry B. Elder and CID agents as to the known details on the crime. Once briefed on the case, Castleberry took action.

He placed a call to his command headquarters in Kansas City, outlining the crime details they had at the time. Castleberry's fear was his crime scene could literally be as large as the Fort Leonard Wood installation — some 70,000 plus acres of land could be involved. The FBI headquarters responded by ordering 13 additional FBI agents to leave their homes immediately and report to Fort Leonard Wood for an extended tour of duty.

Castleberry's second job for the evening was to interview Johnny Lee Thornton. Following the interview, Castleberry's next task was to start the legal process required to hold Thornton in custody.

During the late evening hours of January 13 and early morning hours of January 14, 1977, Castleberry struggled to put together a criminal complaint sufficient to hold Thornton in custody. He had to confer with the United States Attorney in Kansas City and brief him on the nature and facts of the complaint he'd drawn up. After the United States Attorney in Kansas City approved Castleberry's complaint, Castleberry sent the details of it to the Springfield, Missouri, FBI office, addressed to Agent George C. Scruggs Jr.

Considering the short period of time they'd been able to work the investigation, the complaint drawn up by Castleberry and Scruggs was a well-written document — a marvel of speed and accuracy.

The original complaint was based on the information the investigators were able to determine the evening of January 13, 1977, and was presented before the United States Magistrate in Springfield, Missouri the morning of January 14, 1977. The investigators had little time to prepare this original charging complaint but it was a legal necessity to allow the government to hold Johnny Lee Thornton in custody. The main portions of the complaint are as follows:

United States District Court for the Western District of Missouri

United States of America versus Johnny Lee Thornton, a complaint for violation of the United States Code, Title 18, Section 1111 (a) (b). The complaint was placed before the Hon. James C. England, United States Magistrate Judge located in Springfield, Missouri.

The undersigned complainant being duly sworn states that on or about January 12, 1977, at Fort Leonard Wood, Missouri, in the Western District of Missouri, on land within the maritime and territorial jurisdiction of the United States, Johnny Lee Thornton did with premeditation and malice aforethought, and by means of shooting, unlawfully kill Anthony Lee Bates, all in violation of title 18 United States code section 1111 (a) (b) and the complainant states that this complaint is based on information furnished to Special Agent George C. Scruggs Jr. See the attached affidavit. And the complainant further states that he believes that;

1. James B King, Missouri Highway Patrol, Troop I, Waynesville, Missouri

2. Alex Kerekes, CID agent, Fort Leonard Wood, Missouri

3. Paul VanSomeren, Special Agent, FBI

4. William Castleberry, Special Agent, FBI

5. Col. Perry B. Elder, Provost Marshal, Fort Leonard Wood, Missouri

6. Robert E. Lee, military policeman, Fort Leonard Wood, Missouri

7. David Cogswell, military policeman, Fort Leonard Wood, Missouri

8. Dr. Gerald Rappe, M.D., Fort Leonard Wood, Missouri

9. Juanita Deckard, Plato, Missouri

10. George Matthews, CID agent, Fort Leonard Wood, Missouri

11. Brooks Black, Special Agent, FBI

12. Philip E. Marketon, military policeman, Fort Leonard Wood, Missouri

13. David Leroy Edwards, military policeman, Fort Leonard Wood, Missouri

14. Interior Laloulo, military policeman, Fort Leonard Wood, Missouri

Are material witnesses in relation to this charge.

George C. Scruggs Jr., Special Agent, FBI

Sworn to before me, and subscribed in my presence January 14, 1977

James C. England, United States Magistrate

* * *

Affidavit of Special Agent George C. Scruggs, Jr., Federal Bureau of Investigation in complaint entitled United States of America v. Johnny Lee Thornton:

"On January 13, 1977, Juanita Deckard advised Missouri State Highway Patrol Trooper James B. King, and CID Investigator Alex Kerekes, and on January 14, 1977, advised Special Agent Paul Van Someren of the Federal Bureau of Investigation, she and her three companions, Linda Needham, Anthony Lee Bates, and Wesley Hawkins, were stopped on Southgate Road on the Fort Leonard Wood reservation by a military policeman in military uniform and driving a four-wheel drive military vehicle bearing red emergency lights and containing a military police radio which was on. She further advised the military vehicle was believed to bear the numbers 327.

Ms. Deckard further related the vehicle operated by her and her companions was stopped by a person in a military uniform identifying himself as a military policeman for the reasons stated by the military policeman, that the car occupied was similar to one used in an armed robbery. Ms. Deckard further reported the military policeman removed Anthony Lee Bates from the automobile and placed him in the military police vehicle and at that time she observed the military policeman shoot, with a large handgun, the above-named Anthony Lee Bates. Johnny Lee Thornton was the only military policeman on duty during the night hours of January 12, 1977, and the morning hours of January 13, 1977, who was driving a four-wheel drive military vehicle, the number of which was X37.

David Leroy Edwards, a military policeman at Fort Leonard Wood, Missouri, reported that Thornton received from him at approximately 10:00 p.m. on January 12, 1977, a four-wheel drive military vehicle, to wit, an international Scout military police vehicle designated X37. Interior Laloulo, a military policeman at Fort Leonard Wood, Missouri, reported Thornton turned over to him at 6:00 a.m. on January 13, 1977, a four-wheel drive military vehicle, to wit, an International Scout military police vehicle designated X37. Subject vehicle is the only military police vehicle bearing the designation X37. At the time Thornton picked up the subject vehicle and turned it back in he was in full military uniform.

Thornton, upon completion of his term of duty at 6:00a.m. on January 13, 1977, surrendered his weapon back to Sergeant Philip E. Marketon, military police control, and executed a sworn statement that he had expended six (6) cartridges from his weapon while killing dogs which he reported he had dumped at the Fort Leonard Wood dump. The executed statement was delivered to David Cogswell, a military policeman at Fort Leonard Wood. Thereafter Robert E. Lee, military policeman, 463rd Military Police Company, conducted an investigation at the Fort Leonard Wood dump and was unable to locate any dead dogs. Ms. Deckard further provided a description of the subject which generally fits that of Johnny Lee Thornton.

During the afternoon of January 13, 1977, Thornton contacted the Provost Marshal Col. Perry B Elder at Fort Leonard Wood, indicating he had heard a serious crime was under investigation and his, Thornton's, services were required. Elder instructed Thornton to appear for duty but Thornton failed to ever make an appearance. On January 13, 1977, in a 1971 Chevrolet bearing Minnesota license JY4-278, being utilized by Thornton at Fort Leonard Wood, Special Agent Paul VanSomeren and of the FBI, located a letter signed by Johnny Lee Thornton addressed to his wife which read as follows:

"I don't remember doing what I did. Sometimes I get these headaches, I want to die from the pain. I don't want to hurt people, but when these headaches come something snaps in me I have never done this before, at least I don't remember it. I've only felt this way, I mean really sick, for a few months."

On January 14, 1977, a search by Special Agent George Matthews, CID, Fort Leonard Wood, Missouri, and special agent Brooks Black of the FBI, of the military vehicle X37 revealed a bullet hole and a substance which, on preliminary examination, appeared to be blood. The military vehicle carrying the designation X37 was operated by Johnny Lee Thornton during the night hours of January 12, 1977, and the morning hours of January 13, 1977. Miss Deckard further reported she was taken by the subject to a cabin in an isolated area of Fort Leonard Wood. The cabin is known on Fort Leonard Wood as the game wardens refuge. Thornton's assignment as a military policeman was presently that of a game warden. Gerald Rappe, M.D., pathologist, Major, AMC, Gen. Leonard Wood Army Hospital, Fort Leonard Wood, Missouri, pronounced Anthony Lee Bates dead on January 13, 1977. On January 14, 1977, Gerald Rappe, M.D., determined the cause of death as gunshot wounds.

Signed, George C. Scruggs Jr., Special Agent, FBI

Sworn to before me, and subscribed in my presence, January 14, 1977.

Signed, James C. England, United States Magistrate

* * *

The morning of January 14, 1977, FBI agents drove Johnny Lee Thornton to Springfield, Missouri. Members of the Missouri State Highway Patrol escorted them. Thornton appeared before the United States Magistrate Judge, James C. England who committed him to the Medical Center for Federal Prisoners, Springfield, Missouri in lieu of a $150,000 secured bond. Judge England set a preliminary hearing date for January 24, 1977.

On January 18, 1977, the United States Attorney, Bert Hurn announced his intention to send the case before a federal grand jury. Hurn also announced his number one assistant,

Mr. J. Whitfield Moody would be responsible for obtaining an indictment against Johnny Lee Thornton. One of Moody's first requests was for Juanita Deckard to be available for testimony before the federal grand jury as soon as possible. However, Dr. Harvey E. Nickels, Deckard's personal physician at the Pulaski County Memorial Hospital in Waynesville, Missouri, stated she would not be able to travel or testify before February 8, 1977. Dr. Nickels furnished the federal government with a notarized statement to that effect.

The next step in the legal proceeding was to impanel a federal grand jury in Kansas City, Missouri. This grand jury heard testimony in closed hearings and, after their deliberations on January 27, 1977, returned a true bill four-count indictment against Thornton.

Count one was for murdering Wesley Hawkins. Count two for assaulting Anthony Bates on the installation with intent to murder. Count three was for committing rape against Linda Needham. And count four was for unlawfully kidnapping Linda Needham, Juanita Deckard, Anthony Bates, and Wesley Hawkins for the purpose of committing rape.

The single previous charge for the murder of Tony Bates on which Thornton was being held in custody was replaced by the grand jury indictment. The murder charge related to Bates was dismissed.

Thornton was then scheduled to appear before the United States Magistrate in Springfield, Missouri on January 31, 1977, for the official reading of the indictment. During the wait for the reading of the indictment, Thornton continued to be housed at the United States Medical Center for Federal Prisoners in Springfield. The appearance bond for Thornton was continued in the amount of $150,000, fully secured — and Johnny Lee Thornton was unable to post that bond to obtain his freedom.

Following the court hearing on the indictment, on January 27, 1977, a request for a warrant of arrest and an accompanying order authorizing a warrant for arrest were filed with the court. The warrant was then delivered to the United States Marshal's office. This made the United States Marshal Service legally responsible for the custody and transport of Johnny

IN MEMORY OF
ANTHONY LEE BATES

BORN
SEPTEMBER 29, 1958

PASSED AWAY
JANUARY 13, 1977

SERVICES FROM
PLATO HIGH SCHOOL GYMNASIUM
2:00 P. M., MONDAY, JANUARY 17, 1977

MINISTERS
REV. WESLEY WALLACE
REV. DALLAS WELLS
REV. EWELL GROVES

MUSIC
Community Churches

RESTING PLACE
STARK CEMETERY

ESCORTS

Bill Wilson	Eddie Kimery
Bob Hall	Ronald Aiken
Mike Lane	Junior Vaughan

COLONIAL FUNERAL CHAPEL
T. J. & DeLores Shadel

Funeral Card Courtesy of the Bates Family

Lee Thornton to all of his trial hearings. On January 28, 1977, an information was filed to determine bail. Also, on January 28, an affidavit of financial status for Johnny Lee Thornton was filed.

On January 28, 1977, Johnny Lee Thornton's counsel was appointed as the Federal Public Defender in his case. The first request from the public defender's office was for assistance. Therefore, on February 7, 1977, the court order appointed Homer D. Wampler III of Springfield, Missouri as Johnny Lee Thornton's second representing attorney. Federal law authorizes the use of two defense attorneys in any case involving a capital charge. Also under federal law, both murder and rape can be a death penalty case. Thornton's case had both charges and there were no objections to the second attorney being appointed.

One of the first legal moves made by the Federal Public Defender came on February 1, 1977, when he filed a motion for a psychiatric examination, with suggestions in support of that motion with the court. This motion was granted and the defendant was subjected to psychiatric evaluations at the Medical Center for Federal Prisoners. On March 4, the Federal Public Defender filed a motion to enlarge the time period for the filing of pretrial motions with suggestions for the court on behalf of the defendant. On March 7th, that order was approved and copies were issued to all parties.

Defense was not the only side busy filing motions before the court. On March 25, 1977, Prosecution filed a motion for a court order to compel the defendant to permit the taking of blood, saliva samples, and body hairs for evidentiary purposes. From this day forward, Defense and Prosecution fought each other tooth and nail with motions and counter motions on every phase of the Thornton pretrial legal maneuvering.

Defense filed motions to suppress statements and admissions made by Johnny Lee Thornton in the early stages of the case. Defense also filed a motion for transcripts of the grand jury testimony. Defense then filed a motion to limit the testimony of the sexual offenses that could be produced at trial. The defendant's attorneys also filed a motion to sever counts three and four of the indictment, and filed a motion for a separate trial for these particular offenses. Naturally, Prosecution filed a motion to object to every motion filed by Defense.

In the midst of the bewildering barrage of motions and counter-motions, on May 25, 1977, the court filed an order with a copy to all parties, announcing its decision to set a hearing on the defendant's Motion for Judicial Determination of Mental Competency, under the provisions of title 18 USC § 4244. That hearing was to be held on at 9:30 a.m. on June 2, 1977. Subpoenas were issued and served to all parties required to testify.

The first persons to receive subpoenas were:

- Sergeant First Class, Richard Jensen of the 463 MP Company;
- Colonel Perry Elder, Fort Leonard Wood Provost Marshal;
- Colonel Robert Mosebar (GLWACH medical doctor who examined Thornton just after his arrest);
- William Castleberry, FBI agent in charge of the Fort Leonard Wood office;
- Dr. Charles D. Ottensmeyer (a psychiatrist who had examined Thornton);
- Paul VanSomeren of the FBI (who had participated in part of the initial day's investigation of the case).

They were all ordered to appear June 2, 1977, at the United States courthouse in Springfield, Missouri, to give their testimony.

On June 2, 1977, the competency hearing began. Represented by David Freeman of the Federal Public Defender's office, Philip Moomaw, an Assistant Federal Public Defender, and Homer Wampler, the civilian attorney appointed by the court, Johnny Lee Thornton appeared in court. Representing the United States government was J. Whitfield Moody, the Assistant United States Attorney.

The competency hearing was held in open court — and was well-attended by the media. As a result, the first glimpses of the case began to appear in the public eye. During this proceeding, five people testified. Dr. Charles D. Ottensmeyer,

FBI Agent William "Bill" Castleberry, Dr. Robert Mosebar, Colonel Perry B. Elder, and Sergeant Richard Jensen, 463rd MP Company. The transcript of their testimony runs 131 pages.

The testimony of the four officers reflected much of the same information contained in the chapter detailing the investigation, and further amplified within the chapter on the actual trial. The testimony of Dr. Charles Ottensmeyer is the only testimony covered in this chapter and the coverage is brief because he also testified at the trial.

During the mental competency part of the hearing, federal prosecutors presented only one witness — Dr. Charles D. Ottensmeyer, a psychiatrist at the medical center for federal prisoners where Thornton had been held for psychiatric examination. Dr. Ottensmeyer testified that the people who participated in the 60-day evaluation of Johnny Lee Thornton included doctors, correctional officers, Thornton's case worker, and his counselor.

Dr. Ottensmeyer final opinion: "I believe [Thornton] is able to understand the nature of the proceedings. I believe he is able to assist his counsel in his own defense."

During cross-examination by Federal Public Defender, David Freeman, Dr. Ottensmeyer testified Thornton had undergone several electroencephalogram (EEG) examinations to test his brain waves. Defense attorneys asked Dr. Ottensmeyer if a person who suffered from severe headaches could experience some type of interference with the EEG results. Dr. Ottensmeyer said such a condition "may or may not" change EEG results. Dr. Ottensmeyer further testified one of the physicians at the Medical Center had noted an abnormal reading on one EEG test and had requested it to be repeated. Additional brain tests done on Johnny Lee Thornton showed "no more abnormalities."

During the competency hearing, the defense team attempted to show Judge Collinson that Thornton was physically and emotionally exhausted at the time of the FBI questioned him. They argued Thornton had been on duty from 10:00 p.m. January 12 until 6:00 a.m. on January 13. He was then arrested about 7:00 p.m. on January 13. The defense team argued Thornton had little, if any sleep, was exhausted during questioning — and didn't know what he was saying.

At the conclusion of the competency hearing, Judge Collinson denied Defense's Motion to Suppress Thornton's Comments to the FBI at the time of his arrest. Judge Collinson also ruled Thornton was mentally competent to assist his attorneys with his defense and therefore the case could proceed to trial.

However, he did grant Defense's Motion for Change of Venue. The judge ruled the adverse pretrial publicity would preclude any chance of a fair trial for Johnny Lee Thornton in Springfield, Missouri.

Judge Collinson set the trial for June 13, 1977, at the federal courthouse in St. Joseph, Missouri. Under the provisions of the federal speedy trial act, Thornton's trial had to start before August 1, 1977.

On Monday, June 13, 1977, a jury panel consisting of 93 persons reported to the federal courthouse in St. Joseph, Missouri for possible jury duty. Following an extensive voir dire, approximately 60 prospective jurors were selected for additional individual questioning in the judge's chambers.

A number of the prospective jurors remembered reading about the bodies of the three teens being buried in a snowbank. Others recalled the fourth victim had survived by playing dead and then walking several miles for assistance. Some remembered Thornton's name as being the one accused of this incident — and said that Defense would have to present evidence showing he was innocent before they would be convinced of his innocence.

Judge Collinson was quoted as saying, "A person who feels that way can't be a fair juror. I thought if we came up to St. Joseph that situation wouldn't exist."

Judge Collinson granted a second Defense Motion of Adverse Pretrial Publicity. A new change of venue sent the case to Council Bluffs, Iowa. The trial in Council Bluffs, Iowa was set to begin on July 18, 1977 — again with the provisions of the speedy trial act in mind.

* * *

FBI Agent William "Bill" Castleberry:

When we got ready for trial, I knew there was going to be a mental defense. But we also knew there was going to be a change of venue. At one of the hearings, there was a change of venue request. The judge granted it and we ended up in St. Joseph, Missouri. We were in the St. Joseph courtroom ready for trial—with all the guys from the lab and all of the evidence—we were ready to go. It was during the opening *voir dire*...and the first thing the judge does during *voir dire* is introduce everybody—the defense lawyers, agents, defendant, prosecution members, and anybody who was sitting at the front prosecution table. I was sitting there.

The judge would call out our names and we would stand up and his question to the *voir dire* jury panel was, "Do you know or do you have any knowledge of this man or have any connection with any of these men?" A woman raises her hand and stands up and says, "Yes, I know that FBI agent. And if he says something, I'll believe it because he's been in my home before. He knows my husband who is a police officer."

The entire courtroom went silent. Defense looks over at us and then looks up at the judge and says, "Your Honor, we declare this panel has been tainted." And the Judge says, "Yes, it is." We ended up in Council Bluffs Iowa.

11

THE TRIAL

Part One:
The Prosecution Begins

THE CRIMINAL TRIAL OF JOHNNY Lee Thornton began on Monday, July 18, 1977, in the United States Federal District Court at Council Bluffs, Iowa. One of the people in the courtroom that morning was Marjorie Bates, mother of murder victim Anthony "Tony" Lee Bates.

As Marjorie Bates sat in the courtroom that morning, she noted the arrival of the attorneys on both sides and the 99 potential jurors who had been assembled for the jury panel. The official proceeding started at 10:00 a.m. United States District Court Judge William R. Collinson began with the introduction of the prosecution attorneys and the defense attorneys to the courtroom spectators and to the prospective jury pool.

The attorneys for the United States were, First Assistant United States Attorney, J. Whitfield Moody of Kansas City, Missouri and Assistant United States Attorney, David H. Jones. The attorneys for Defense were Federal Public Defender, David R. Freeman of Kansas City, Missouri, Assistant Federal Public Defender, Phillip Moomaw of Kansas City, and Homer Dee Wampler III of Springfield, Missouri.

Following the introduction of the attorneys, guards escorted the accused into the courtroom. Marjorie Bates described Johnny Lee Thornton as "pale and quiet." He appeared to know what was going on. At the same time, he was trying to look unconcerned. "He just sits and looks down at the middle of the table. And it looks like he's clamping his jaws together real tight."

The first order of business (following the introduction of the opposing legal members) was the questioning of the jury panel to determine their suitability. The potential jurors were asked if they knew anyone present in the court room, or if they had read or heard about this case in the news. They were asked if they had ever been the victim of a violent crime as well as many other questions.

Following the questioning of the jurors, a clerk read the list of possible witnesses in the case to the courtroom. Court was adjourned to allow both the defense and prosecution teams to assemble a list of jurors for the trial. Each team could strike 20 members off the jury panel without question. Any remaining jurors dismissed by either side would have to be for cause.

At 2:00 p.m., when the court was back in session, Judge Collinson announced they had a jury panel. The names of the 12 jurors — eight women, four men, and two alternates — were read aloud and the jury panel was seated. Judge Collinson announced there would be no court on Friday, July 22, of the first week. He stated court would begin at 9:00 a.m. each morning and continue until 5:00 p.m. each evening. Then he instructed the United States Marshals in the courtroom to escort the selected jury panel members to their homes to obtain clothing and other necessities for their sequestered trial.

* * *

Prosecution's Opening Statement on Tuesday, July 19, 1977:

According to Prosecution, the day of the crime began at 10:00 p.m. on January 12, 1977. It was cold and snowing when Johnny Lee Thornton went on duty as a Fort Leonard Wood game warden. Thornton filled out and signed a form to get his weapon — a .45 caliber semiautomatic pistol. He also signed for 15 rounds of ammunition. Thornton had a .45 pistol he normally used but, on this date, that specific firearm was down for maintenance so he received a different pistol.

Thornton also requested two pairs of handcuffs that evening which was unusual for a single shift. When a fellow MP asked Thornton about it, Thornton replied he was going to "play super cop that night."

Thornton was assigned a vehicle, identification number X37, an International Scout four-wheel-drive vehicle, to drive for the evening.

At approximately 12:15 or 12:30 a.m. on the morning of January 13, 1977, Tony Bates, Juanita Deckard, Wesley Hawkins, and Linda Needham left Plato in Tony's 1972 Dodge Charger. They headed to St. Robert, Missouri, to purchase gasoline for the car. They were driving on the south gate road, within the boundary lines of Fort Leonard Wood, when a military police vehicle stopped them.

The lone MP spoke with them for a minute and requested their identification papers. Then, he arrested the two boys for an armed robbery that had supposedly occurred at the Southgate Texaco station, off post. Ordering them to take their personal belongings with them, the MP placed all four young people into his vehicle.

As the MP got into the vehicle, he drew his .45 pistol and shot Wesley Hawkins and Tony Bates — one time each — as they sat handcuffed in the back seat of the police vehicle. Wesley slumped over immediately, but Tony said, "That hurt." And he continued to moan and make other sounds for some time. In fact, he was still alive many hours later.

The MP drove the four teens to a secluded cabin on the Roubidoux River on Fort Leonard Wood, where he parked the vehicle and ordered the two girls to accompany him into a small shack at that location. Wesley Hawkins and Tony Bates remained in the military police vehicle.

Prosecution told the jury there would be testimony to show that once inside the shack, the MP built a fire in a small potbellied stove and talked to the two girls while he built that fire. When the interior of the shack was warm, he ordered the girls to undress and forced them to perform sex acts. Following the sex acts, he ordered the girls to dress and returned them to his vehicle.

He drove down the road approximately one-and-a-half miles from the cabin before he parked the International Scout. He ordered the young girls out and told them to start walking down a path in front of him. He fired two shots at their backs. Both girls fell to the ground.

Juanita Deckard watched as the MP took Linda Needham by the arm and dragged her into the woods. Deckard heard a scream and another shot followed by moans. The MP returned to where Juanita Deckard lay on the ground, playing dead, and dragged her into the woods. There, he covered her with snow. The MP returned to his vehicle and ordered the boys out. Only Tony Bates was able to move. Bates attempted to escape from his captor — running several yards into the woods until he tripped over a log and fell. The MP came up behind Bates and shot him in the back of the head. This second wound was instantly fatal.

Prosecution informed the jury the testimony would show that after the MP drove from the scene, Juanita Deckard searched for and found her friends, Wesley Hawkins and Linda Needham, buried in the snow. She was unable to get a response from them. Then Juanita Deckard walked five or six miles across the snow-covered hills. Deckard arrived at a farmhouse at approximately 12:30 p.m. on January 13, 1977. Deckard called Douglas Hawkins, brother of Wesley Hawkins, and asked him to come pick her up.

Douglas Hawkins, along with Hershel Needham, father of Linda Needham, picked Deckard up and drove her to the spot where her footprints in the snow came out of the woods. While Hershel Needham and Juanita Deckard waited for the highway patrol to arrive, Douglas Hawkins followed her tracks back to the murder scene. There, Douglas found the bodies of his brother, Wesley, and Linda Needham. Douglas was unable to find Tony Bates' body.

Prosecution stated the testimony would show that on the morning of the 13th, when Johnny Lee Thornton got off duty, he turned in his .45 caliber pistol and stated he'd expended six rounds of ammunition killing some stray dogs in a hunting area. Thornton reported he had buried the dogs at the stump dump. Prosecution stated testimony would also show Thornton had called the Fort Leonard Wood airfield and inquired if there would be any helicopter flights over the specific area in the southwest corner of Fort Leonard Wood where the bodies were buried in the snow.

Prosecution stated Johnny Lee Thornton knew right from wrong, and attempted to cover his tracks. For example, when Thornton turned in vehicle X37, he requested that it be washed because there was blood in it. He also called in a radio check on Tony Bates' 1972 Dodge Charger — that same morning, claiming he found it abandoned on the south gate road.

Prosecution told the jury members they would hear later that morning that relatives of the four young people called MP headquarters and reported the teens missing. When they found the 1972 Dodge Charger, the Military Police began an investigation. As the day went on, they called in numerous off-duty MPs to assist in the search. Thornton reported to the MP headquarters building where he was issued a weapon and more ammunition. Then, Johnny Lee Thornton disappeared.

Later in the day, after he became a suspect in the disappearance of the youths and the shooting of Juanita Deckard, an active search for Thornton began. Prosecution told the jury they would hear testimony from other military police officers and an FBI agent about the telephone call at MP headquarters they received from Thornton. These officers would testify that they went into a remote area of the woods to meet with — and eventually — arrest him.

Prosecution told the jury that following Thornton's arrest, he made numerous incriminating statements to the FBI and MPs. The jury heard about the shell casings and expended bullets found near the teens' bodies — and Thornton's and Deckard's fingerprints inside the shack. Prosecution told the jury they would hear testimony Linda Needham's billfold and purse were found in a trash container near the MP motor pool.

At the conclusion of Prosecution's opening statement, the court ordered a 15-minute recess. All attorneys were directed to the Judge's chambers. At approximately 10:20 a.m., the court resumed and Judge Collinson dropped a bombshell.

Thornton's defense team was not contesting Prosecution's opening statement. They stipulated that all of the facts Prosecution related did, in fact, occur. Wesley Hawkins was killed. Linda Needham was killed. Tony Bates was shot and killed. And Juanita Deckard was raped. However, the defense team did not stipulate to the four counts of kidnapping. In a statement to the news media later that day, Defense Attorney David Freeman said, "We wanted to get down to the real issue in this case: the sanity issue."

* * *

Testimony of Douglas Hawkins:

Hawkins told the jury Juanita Deckard called his home at approximately 12:30 or 12:45 p.m. that day. He picked up Hershel Needham and drove to the Echelberry residence to make contact with Deckard.

At approximately 1:15 p.m., Hawkins followed Deckard's footprints in the snow back to where the kids' bodies lay. He walked or ran most of the way — and when he got there, he found Linda and Wesley partially covered with snow. He couldn't find Tony Bates.

When asked by Prosecution in what condition he found the teens, Hawkins stated that they were dead.

Hawkins testified he then walked back up toward the road where he met two other friends of the family coming down the trail. The three of them went back to the scene. They found Tony Bates. When asked what Tony Bates' condition was, Hawkins said that Bates was dead.

Douglas Hawkins identified pictures of Wesley Hawkins, Linda Needham, and Tony Bates. Following his identification, the Prosecution placed the photographs into evidence as exhibits.

Defense chose not to cross-examine Douglas Hawkins — and the judge dismissed him from the witness chair.

* * *

Juanita Deckard's Testimony:

Judge Collinson ordered all parents of the victims to leave the courtroom. Once the parents were gone, the bailiff swore in Deckard who then took the witness chair. News reporters in the courtroom described her as calm, poised, and soft-spoken. They noted she wore tinted glasses and a matching blue skirt and blouse.

Responding to questions from Prosecution, Juanita Deckard told the jury she knew the other three victims since grade school. Deckard and Wesley Hawkins were a couple — and Linda Needham was Tony Bates' date for the evening. She described the events of January 13, 1977. They were in Plato playing cards together when Tony said he needed gasoline (for his vehicle). The four of them got into Bates' Dodge Charger — and headed for Waynesville, Missouri, since the gas stations in the Plato area were closed at that hour.

Deckard said that as they were crossing Fort Leonard Wood, a military police vehicle came up behind them and turned on the red lights. Tony pulled over to the side of the road. The military policeman came up to the door and asked Bates for his driver's license.

The MP ordered the boys out of the car and over to the Scout telling them that the Charger matched one used in a local gas station robbery. Deckard said the MP then came back to Bates' car and ordered the girls out with all their personal belongings. He handcuffed the boys' hands behind their backs and placed them in the backseat of the MP vehicle. He made Linda Needham sit between the two boys — and told Deckard to sit in the front passenger seat.

> *Deckard*: He kind of acted like he was going to get in and then I saw the gun go off. Thornton said nothing before firing the gun. Wesley got hit and doubled over. And Tony said, "Oh that hurts." [Thornton] told me not to look back and told Linda to do and say nothing.

At that point, she said Thornton — who had driven the Scout a short distance down the road — turned around and drove back to the Bates' car. He got out and slashed a tire, leaving the vehicle running. Deckard explained that she had limited

137

experience driving a stick-shift vehicle — so she didn't think to try and drive away.

> *Deckard*: Thornton drove for about ten minutes until we came to a cabin somewhere in the woods. [Thornton] left the boys in the backseat. He ordered us girls into the cabin where he began to build a fire in a stove in the center of the room. He ordered both of us to take off our clothing and to perform sex acts on each other and then on him. He then forced sodomy and sexual intercourse with both of us. I can't recall much conversation except a comment made by Thornton. He said he was not really an MP but was a soldier and was deserting and leaving for Canada the next day.

Deckard described how Thornton held a .45 caliber pistol in his hand throughout the long ordeal in the cabin.

> *Deckard*: After the sexual assaults finally ceased, Thornton told us to get dressed and then ordered us back to his vehicle. Thornton said, "It's four-twenty a.m. and I'm behind schedule.
>
> Thornton drove all four of us to a snowy clearing some distance away. He ordered Linda and me, at gunpoint, to get out of the Scout and face the other way. I heard a shot. I felt dizzy and faint. I was wounded in the side of the arm and in the chest. Linda fell to the ground. He was behind Linda, picking up her shoulders. He started to drag her back and into the woods. I heard her scream and I think I heard a shot. He came back and started dragging me. Then he started kicking snow over me. He kicked me with his boot and then kicked more snow on me.
>
> [Thornton] went back to the Scout and ordered Tony out and told him to walk. A moment later, there was another shot. He remained in the area for about thirty more minutes before he finally drove away.
>
> I waited until I couldn't hear the vehicle anymore. Then I called for the others by name. None of them answered. It was dark and snowing. Then, I felt someone lying behind me. It was Wesley. I uncovered his face and tried to get him to talk to me. Then I called for Linda and she didn't answer. So, I got up and looked for her. She was a few steps away and she wouldn't answer. I called for Tony. I couldn't find him. I tried mouth-to-mouth resuscitation on Linda and Wesley but.... I tried to pull their coats

over their faces so it wouldn't snow on them and then I started to walk.

At the end of her testimony, Deckard identified the military policeman who stopped the Bates vehicle on the south gate road on January 13, 1977. She stood at the witness chair and with a trembling hand pointed out Thornton, who sat between the Defense attorneys.

Author's Note: According to the newspaper accounts from 1977, Juanita Deckard testified for 90 minutes. The information found in the newspaper articles of the day and from Marjorie Bates' notes don't equal 90 minutes' worth of testimony. There was a good deal more to Juanita Deckard's testimony at the trial than we're able to share. Since the main trial recording was never transcribed, we don't have access to complete question-and-answer responses from each person who testified.

* * *

FBI Agent Tom Den Ouden:

For some reason, they only allowed one agent to be in the courtroom. That was Bill Castleberry. He sat at the council table and I was kind of the go-to guy — get stuff, bring it in to the courtroom. We need this. We need that. I was also on assignment to protect Juanita from the press, from the media, from all of those kinds of things, and I did that. I got her to the courtroom and I stayed outside until she was finished. And then, I made sure she got back to her motel room okay. I tried to avoid the media as much as possible. The testimony was tough on her but [Prosecution] was satisfied and pleased with her testimony. They thought she did really well.

* * *

FBI Agent Bill Castleberry:

Johnny Lee Thornton was the first real case-agent homicide I worked. What I was involved in during that phase was presenting the details of the case to the prosecutor — and we had a great prosecutor. I would come in and lay the case out. They were almost overwhelmed by the volume of the case, and it took a lot of effort on their part just to keep up with it.

It was during the start of the trial. One of the things the prosecutor asked me to help out with was the scheduling of the witnesses and staying with that person to assist them. So, I had to leave the courtroom to get Juanita and she was like, almost catatonic. So, I spent a couple minutes with her. And then, I walked her into the courtroom. Then something happened I hated — and everyone on the prosecution team hated — but it happened. It actually ended up helping the case. When she got on the stand and she was asked the question, "Can you tell us what happened on that occasion?" She started telling the story.

We had told her — because she didn't want to talk about the sex acts Thornton had made her perform — we told her, "You don't have to say that. Skip over that part and just talk about him shooting you and the others and making you perform sex acts. But you don't have to go into any detail."

But she did. It was like she was reliving the night and, in telling the story, she lost her composure. The judge called a recess. I went up to her and it was like she could not move from the witness stand. I helped her back into the witness room. Juanita then told me, "I thought I wouldn't have to say that." And I said, "Well, you really didn't have to." And Juanita said, "But, I did."

All of a sudden, she relaxed as she realized it was over with. The only thing she said to me at that point was, "You know, my family doesn't know anything about this. I haven't told any of the details to anybody but you all."

Afterward, she just sat there. She had calmed down. She said, "You know, my brothers, this is the first they've heard of that." She looked up at me with a look on her face that said, "You all need to make sure my brothers don't do anything stupid."

That was before metal detectors. So, I got with one of the court bailiffs and told him what we were going to need to do when the jury comes in. That was to be standing very close to where the family was sitting. They agreed to do that. And, they brought in extra deputies for the verdict.

* * *

Testimony of Criminal Investigation Command Special Agent, George Matthews:

After Matthews was sworn in as a witness, Prosecution questioned him.

> *Prosecution*: Describe the scene where the bodies were found.

> *Matthews*: I arrived at that location at approximately two thirty-five p.m. on January 13, 1977. I found three persons and they were all deceased. Tony Bates was one hundred and fifty feet from the road, lying face down with his hands behind his back and covered in snow. The only part of Bates' body not covered with snow was part of his hands.

> *Prosecution*: Agent Matthews. Please examine photographs of the grove of trees by Wesley Hawkins' body and Exhibit 21 [a picture of Tony Bates].

> *Matthews*: Wesley Hawkins also had his hands behind his back and was lying on his back.

> *Prosecution*: Agent Matthews, please identify these pictures of the scene.

The photos showed bloodstains and the positions of the bodies. Agent Matthews testified that several shoes were found at the scene of the crime. Also, two shell casings were near the bodies. Following Agent Matthews' testimony, the photographs were admitted into evidence. The court went into a brief recess to permit the jury time to examine and discuss the photographs in the privacy of the jury room.

* * *

When court resumed, the next witness to testify was not identified in any news articles or Marjorie Bates' notes — but this person testified that fingerprints at the game warden cabin belonged to Johnny Lee Thornton and Juanita Deckard. One would presume this was one of the six members of the FBI crime lab or one of the six FBI agents all from Washington, DC, who were subpoenaed for the trial. The two most probable persons were Robert C. Bartley, who was a latent fingerprint examiner at the crime lab, or Special Agent Thomas Cummere, who was listed as a fingerprint examiner.

* * *

Captain Robert DeWitt, Criminal Investigation Command Unit Commander:

Captain Robert DeWitt was stationed at Fort Leonard Wood, Missouri. DeWitt told the jury he was on duty on January 13, 1977. He stated that at approximately 9:00 a.m., the Criminal Investigation Command unit learned Bates' vehicle was parked roadside. DeWitt arrived at the scene at 10:00 a.m. He identified a series of pictures of the automobile in question — a 1972 light-colored, Dodge Charger.

> *Prosecution:* Did you examine the vehicle?
>
> *DeWitt:* I did. I noticed the right front tire was flat. I examined the tire but didn't find a slice or a nail in it.

DeWitt also identified photographs of Friendship Cemetery Road, showing the location where the Dodge Charger was parked — on the north part of the road headed west four-and-a-half to five feet from a sign, and about one foot from the snow bank. DeWitt declared the car a possible crime scene. This ensured that it would not be removed or touched until crime technicians could process it.

*

Defense Cross-Examination:

> *Defense:* Are you acquainted with Johnny Lee Thornton?
>
> *DeWitt:* Yes. I've known him about six months.

Defense: Have you ever complimented Johnny Lee on his work?

DeWitt: I don't recall ever doing that. Thornton performed his duties fairly well.

*

Prosecution Redirect of DeWitt:

Under Prosecution redirect, DeWitt testified Thornton was reprimanded once. He had made an illegal search in a marijuana case and was regarded as "too enthusiastic." DeWitt said Thornton wanted to be a policeman.

*

Defense Re-Cross-Examination:

Under Defense cross-examination, DeWitt stated it appeared Thornton learned from the reprimand.

DeWitt: Thornton was a good MP but I can't make any statements as to his dedication to the job.

* * *

Testimony of SFC Richard Jensen, noncommissioned officer in charge of the Fort Leonard Wood game warden detail:

In response to questions from Prosecution, Jensen testified he supervised nine men.

Jensen: On the night of the crime, Thornton was assigned to drive a 1972 Scout four-wheel-drive vehicle, identification number of x-ray 37. The vehicle is a standard shift and is to be used for military duties only. The vehicle is equipped with a red light and a spotlight.

Jensen identified pictures of the Scout. When asked if he observed the vehicle later, Jensen said he did.

Jensen: I found it had a hole through the tailgate, which appeared to be a shot fired from inside the vehicle.

Prosecution: Did Colonel Elder assist in any way with the investigation on January 13th?

143

Jensen: I don't know the answer to that question.

Prosecution: Sergeant Jensen, were you present at the scene of the crime?

Jensen: I was.

Prosecution entered an exhibit into the court record.

Prosecution: Sergeant Jensen, do you recognize this map?

Jensen: It's a map of Fort Leonard Wood.

Prosecution: Sergeant Jensen, can you point to the location on this map where Tony Bates' vehicle was located?

Jensen: Yes, sir.

Jensen indicated the location for the jury.

Prosecution: Can you tell the jury on what road Tony Bates' vehicle was found?

Jensen: Tony Bates' vehicle was found on Cemetery Road.

Prosecution then asked Jensen a series of questions about the game warden's cabin. Jensen stated he was familiar with the cabin. Jensen was shown a few pictures and was asked if he recognized the scene. Jensen testified picture #34 was the cabin he knew as the game warden's cabin down by the Roubidoux River. Jensen further stated there was no electricity to the cabin. It had two beds welded together and a potbellied stove. Jensen testified the cabin was about one or one-and-a-half miles away from the location where the kids' bodies were found.

Jensen testified he had known Thornton for a year.

Jensen: Later that evening, about six p.m., Thornton called me at the MP command headquarters. He wanted to talk to me and Colonel Elder. I asked Thornton where he was. He told me he was near the Ballard farm. So, we agreed to go out there and talk to him. Thornton knew the military police were looking for him, and he wanted to talk to us. He wanted us to come to the scene unarmed and for us to come alone.

I drove Colonel Elder and Special Agent Castleberry of the FBI to the meeting location near the Ballard farm. The night was clear and cold and all three of us were armed. Once we arrived at the location, Thornton came up from behind us and called out to us. At first, Thornton didn't have a firearm visible but after a moment I asked Thornton if he was armed. Thornton said, "It's in my right hand." Colonel Elder and I talked to Thornton for fifteen or twenty minutes trying to get him to give up his weapon and surrender.

Thornton wanted to know what we wanted him for. He talked about his wife and kids and several other topics.

After approximately 30 minutes of testimony, SFC Jensen identified Exhibit #1–a United States Army .45 caliber pistol from rack #171, with the serial number of 1092358. The gun was shown as not loaded to the courtroom. The knife taken from Johnny Lee Thornton at the time of his arrest was identified and entered into evidence as Exhibit #7. Jensen identified Thornton's weapons card and it was also entered into evidence.

*

Defense cross-examination:

Defense: Did you ever have occasion to review Johnny Lee Thornton service records?

Jensen: No, sir. He was a good soldier who performed his duties in a good way. I had not had an occasion to review his service records.

Defense then asked Jensen to look at Thornton's service records and find an evaluation sheet on him. He asked Jensen how often he prepared an evaluation sheet on each soldier.

Jensen: Once a year.

Jensen looked through the records.

Jensen: I can't find the evaluation sheet in the file.

When asked if he recalled the evaluation report, Jensen testified he believed it was a favorable report giving Thornton a 123-point score out of a possible 125 points.

Jensen: I am surprised Thornton did this [crime].

*

Prosecution's redirect examination:

> *Prosecution*: To the best of your knowledge, did [Thornton] know how to use a .45 pistol?
>
> *Jensen*: Yes. I know he knows how to use one but I've never seen him use one.
>
> *Prosecution*: Was there anything unusual about Thornton's behavior or conversation that night?
>
> *Jensen*: No.

*

Defense's re-cross-examination:

> *Defense*: If you recall, what was Thornton's state of mind at the time of his arrest?
>
> *Jensen*: He seemed scared.
>
> *Defense*: Had Thornton indicated he was distressed?
>
> *Jensen*: Thornton said he was tired and exhausted. He didn't give us that answer. Thornton wasn't distressed when he was captured but later in the evening, he exhibited signs he was distressed.

SFC Jensen was excused from the witness stand.

* * *

Testimony of Colonel Perry B. Elder Jr., the Provost Marshal of Fort Leonard Wood Missouri:

> *Elder*: I've been stationed at Fort Leonard Wood for one year. I was on duty on January 13, 1977. It was snowing when I got up at five a.m. At eight a.m., I was informed about the Bates' automobile. I checked to make sure my officers were getting descriptions of the kids for broadcast.
>
> At that time, I had no knowledge of a crime having occurred. I later became involved in the investigation.

I notified the FBI when Juanita Deckard was found. I was acquainted with Thornton and had known him for about five months. At the start of the investigation, we knew it was going to be Thornton or someone else acting as an MP. I attempted to call all of the game wardens and asked them if they had any knowledge about Thornton calling into the desk, asking them if they wanted him to come in for duty. I was told, "yes" and that about two p.m., Johnny Lee Thornton reported to the MP command building and drew a weapon as per the normal procedure. Johnny Lee Thornton was the only game warden who didn't report in person to the military police headquarters.

At around six thirty p.m., Thornton called Jensen at the MP building and I listened in on the conversation. I was a little bit late getting to the telephone. I missed the first couple of statements but heard Thornton say he understood we all are looking for him. And Jensen said, "Yes, we need to talk to you." Jensen asked Thornton where he was, and Thornton said he was near H Highway close to the Ballard farm. Thornton asked us to come to the meeting location — unarmed — and told us he had a weapon.

Me, Sergeant Jensen, and FBI Agent Castleberry went to the Ballard farm. After some time, we were able to make contact with Thornton. Thornton came up behind us and caught us by surprise. But we immediately began to speak with Thornton, trying to talk him into a peaceful surrender.

Thornton made numerous comments about his wife, his family, and statements he didn't know what he had done — he didn't know what happened to the people. Thornton told me, "I'm sorry for what I did to your police."

We were finally able to get Thornton to relinquish his weapon, at which time Agent Castleberry made the arrest. The four of us then got into the military police vehicle and drove back to the headquarters building on Fort Leonard Wood.

*

Defense Cross-examination of Colonel Elder:

Defense: Did Thornton ask if his wife was still alive?

> *Elder*: No, he said he knew he had done something bad. But he didn't know what it was. [Thornton] said he wanted to talk to his wife.
>
> *Defense*: Was that granted? Was Thornton allowed to speak with his wife?
>
> *Elder*: I don't know if that wish was granted.
>
> *Defense*: What was Johnny Lee Thornton's reputation?
>
> *Elder*: [Thornton] had a good reputation as a military police officer.

Colonel Elder was released from the witness stand after approximately 30 minutes of testimony. Elder was the last court witness to testify on the 19th of July. Court was adjourned until 9:00 a.m. the next day, July 20, 1977.

* * *

Prosecution witness Michael F. Miller of Fort Leonard Wood:

The first witness on July 20th was Michael F. Miller of Fort Leonard Wood. He testified he'd been at Fort Leonard Wood for three or four years. He was a dispatcher in the motor pool. On January 12, 1977, Miller stated he was on duty and logged out all of the vehicles for that date, including vehicle X37. That particular vehicle was issued out at 2:25 p.m. to PFC David Lee Edwards. It was returned the next morning at 7:30 a.m. on the 13th. Miller stated the vehicle should've been returned at 10:00 p.m, on the 12th.

There was no cross-examination of this witness.

* * *

Prosecution Witness PFC David Lee Edwards:

PFC David Leroy Edwards of the 463rd MP Company, Fort Leonard Wood, was a member of the military game warden detail. Responding to questions, Edwards stated he was on duty on January 12th and 13th. He checked out vehicle X37 at 2:25 p.m. on the 12th.

Edwards stated he rode throughout the area of Fort Wood looking for violators but he didn't go to the game wardens' cabin. Edwards only went there about once a month. Edwards stated the vehicle was dusty when he had it, with no unusual signs of use. There were no bullet holes in the tail gate when he returned the vehicle to the motor pool.

Edwards went off duty on the 12th between 9:30 and 10:00 p.m. Edwards turned the vehicle over to Johnny Lee Thornton at approximately 10:00 p.m. in the MP headquarters parking lot. Edwards told Thornton it had been snowing and the back roads were all snow-covered.

> *Prosecution*: Did Thornton make any comments while he was talking to you? Or did he act in an unusual manner? Was anything else different about Thornton that night?

> *Edwards*: Thornton seemed a little tired and wanted to give me ten dollars to take his duty shift that night. I turned him down. I was there when Thornton was issued a .45 pistol and two pairs of handcuffs.

> *Prosecution*: Did you have any further conversation with Thornton?

> *Edwards*: I asked Thornton why he was checking out two pairs of handcuffs. He said he was "going to play super cop" that night.

Prosecution entered the two pairs of handcuffs into evidence.

*

Defense Cross-examination PFC Edwards:

> *Defense*: Do you know Thornton socially?

> *Edwards*: No, but I've served on tours of duty with him on several occasions.

> *Defense*: Do you have a judgment of Thornton's ability?

> *Edwards*: Thornton is a good cop who's helped me with paperwork. He's quiet.

> *Defense*: Is the term "super cop" used some by others?

> *Edwards*: Yes, it is. If you're trying to be a good cop.

Defense: Was the Scout's exhaust leaking on the twelfth?

Edwards: Yes. It's been leaking for approximately two months.

*

Redirect of PFC Edwards:

Prosecution: Did the exhaust leak into the vehicle make you aggressive or cause you to act in an irrational manner?

Edwards: No, it did not.

* * *

Prosecution Direct Examination of SSG David Paul Cogswell:

SSG David Paul Cogswell was a member of the 463rd MP Company. In response to Prosecution questions, Cogswell stated he'd been in the Army for nine years and was stationed at Fort Leonard Wood. He was the shift supervisor of building 451, the Provost Marshal's office. He was the acting desk Sergeant at the time.

Cogswell testified Thornton came to him and stated he had expended six rounds of ammunition and killed three dogs in Area 20. Cogswell made an entry into the log concerning the dogs. He said Thornton made a written statement on the expenditure of the ammunition. Cogswell had no further conversation with Thornton that morning. He noticed nothing unusual about Thornton's attitude or appearance. Cogswell testified no statement was made to him as to what Thornton had done with the dogs' bodies.

*

Defense cross-examination of SSG Cogswell:

Defense: Staff Sergeant. Did you form an opinion as to the job performance of Thornton?

Cogswell: He was an excellent cop — a good cop.

Defense: Do you think Thornton was a super cop?

Cogswell: No, sir.

Defense: Was there anything unusual about Thornton?

Cogswell: No.

Defense: You weren't looking for that were you, Sergeant?

Cogswell: No, sir.

*

Redirect of Cogswell by Prosecution:

Cogswell was given Johnny Lee Thornton's written statement and was told to read it.

Prosecution: Sergeant, what does the statement say about the dogs?

Cogswell: It says the dogs were killed in the northwest corner of Fort Wood.

* * *

Direct Examination of Sergeant Philip Edward Marketon:

The next witness began testimony at 10:40 a.m. when Sergeant Philip Edward Marketon of the 463rd MP Company assigned to Fort Leonard Wood took the witness stand. Under questioning by Prosecution, Marketon stated he had been stationed at Fort Leonard Wood for approximately two years. He was on duty on the 12th and 13th of January 1977, as the NCOIC in charge of the Armory room. Marketon testified it was his duty to issue weapons, ammunition, and handcuffs to officers going on a duty shift. Marketon testified usually 15 rounds of ammunition were issued at the start of each shift.

Marketon: On the evening of the twelfth, rack number 171 [Exhibit #118–the firearm Johnny Lee Thornton usually carried] was not available. So, I gave Thornton a different firearm.

Prosecution: Sergeant Marketon, is it common for an officer to have extra rounds of ammunition unaccounted for?

Marketon: It's not uncommon at all.

Prosecution: Is it mandatory that an MP carry handcuffs while on duty, Sergeant?

Marketon: They're only required to have one pair. All MPs have to use their own handcuff keys.

Prosecution: Sergeant Marketon, can you tell us about the weapon you issued to Johnny Lee Thornton on January 12, 1977?

Marketon: It was from rack 124 and was a .45 caliber pistol, [Exhibit #117] with the serial number of 2360549. I issued the pistol to Thornton along with fifteen rounds of ammunition at about ten thirty-five p.m. on January 12, 1977.

Prosecution: Can you identify these?

Prosecution then presented handcuffs [handcuff #1, Exhibit # 137 and handcuff #2, Exhibit #138–previously admitted into evidence].

Marketon identified the handcuffs as the ones he had issued to Thornton. Marketon testified Sergeant Thomas W. Connors had relieved him in the afternoon.

Prosecution: Sergeant Marketon, did anything unusual occur during shift change? Was Thornton present during that time?

Marketon: No, [Thornton] wasn't there at shift change. He came in earlier that morning — around seven o'clock.

When asked to identify Thornton in the courtroom, Marketon did so.

Marketon: I remember Thornton's report of using six rounds of ammunition. But Thornton didn't sign the report in my presence.

Prosecution showed Marketon Thornton's written report and asked Marketon if he recognized it. Defense objected to this evidence. The court overruled the objection. Thornton's written statement was admitted as Exhibit #130. Marketon was asked additional questions about the statement.

> *Marketon*: Thornton wrote he killed the dogs at four-twenty that morning.

> *Prosecution*: Did you have any conversation with Thornton or was there anything unusual about his attitude?

> *Marketon*: I asked Thornton how things were going and what kind of dogs they were. He didn't tell me what kind of dogs he'd killed.

> *Prosecution*: Was there anything unusual about Thornton's attitude?

> *Marketon*: I don't know Thornton that well but it's not unusual for a game warden to kill stray dogs.

*

Defense Cross of Sergeant Marketon:

> *Defense*: Sergeant Marketon. Is it common for officers to own their own sets of handcuffs?

> *Marketon*: It is. Sergeant Hildebrand carries two sets of handcuffs — one of his own and one he checks out.

*

Prosecution Redirect of Marketon:

> *Marketon*: Johnny Lee Thornton was given three magazines of ammunition with five rounds in each magazine. The magazines can hold seven rounds of ammunition in each magazine.

*

Defense Recross of Marketon:

Marketon testified there were no regulations against drawing two sets of handcuffs for a duty shift. The witness was then excused.

* * *

Testimony of Sergeant Thomas W. Connors:

Formerly of the 463rd MP Company at Fort Wood, Connors wasn't present in the courtroom. Prosecution read his deposition aloud. His testimony reiterates the facts regarding the issued .45 pistol, the handcuffs, and the ammunition.

Defense read the cross-examination of Connors aloud to the courtroom. In that deposition, Connors made additional remarks about the handcuffs and ammunition issued.

* * *

Testimony of Sergeant Elvin Cole:

Sergeant Cole, was a Military Police Investigator (MPI) assigned to Fort Leonard Wood. Under questioning by Prosecution, Cole testified he'd been assigned to search the stump dump where Thornton said he'd dumped the dogs he killed on January 13, 1977. Cole testified he searched all sections of the dump and found nothing.

Under cross examination by Defense, Cole was asked if it had snowed and if the snow could've hidden the bodies of the dogs.

Cole: Yes.

Defense: Sergeant Cole, do you know Thornton? And, if so, what do you think about him?

Cole: I do know him. He's a good MP who caused no problems and a good worker. He worked lots of hours.

Defense: Were you surprised when you learned about the crime?

Prosecution objected to the question and the court sustained the objection. The witness was excused from the stand.

* * *

Testimony of Thomas Avery:

Thomas Avery was a Civil Service employee working on Fort Wood. He testified he worked at the motor pool. He said he found Linda Needham's billfold and purse in the motor pool's dumpster. These items were entered into evidence as Exhibit #162 (billfold) and #174 (purse).

Under cross-examination by Defense, Avery testified he'd no knowledge of Johnny Lee Thornton's mental state and that he didn't know him. Avery clarified he'd seen Thornton in the motor pool area and knew who he was.

* * *

Testimony of SPC Lora Woods:

SPC Woods was from the Fort Wood motor pool. Woods testified it was her job to keep track of the vehicles' gasoline use. She put gas in vehicle X37. Woods testified that Thornton asked that vehicle X37 be washed on the morning of January 13, 1977, due to the snow on the ground. Woods further testified she saw nothing unusual about Thornton that morning.

Under Defense questioning, Woods stated it was unusual to ask for a wash under the winter weather conditions. Woods testified Thornton was a quiet sort of person. When the Defense attorney asked Woods if she was surprised by the arrest of Thornton, Prosecution objected and the Judge sustained the objection.

* * *

Testimony of Perry A. Knudson:

The next witness was Perry A. Knudson, who testified he was on duty in the armory. It was his responsibility to checkout weapons and issue handcuffs. He testified he was on duty 13 January 1977, and stated Thornton checked out a .45 pistol from the armory at 2:45 p.m. that day because Thornton stated he was coming on duty early.

> Knudson: I asked him why he was coming on early and Thornton said he was going out to look for the four kids who were missing.

> Prosecution: Was Thornton acting different than normal?

> *Knudson*: Thornton seemed quieter than usual. I've known Thornton for a few months and I've never heard him complain of a headache or anything like that.

Under cross-examination, Knudson testified that around 2:00 p.m. o'clock, or so, on the 13th, there were a number of MPs coming in to go on duty early. Knudson said nobody else told him they were going out to look for the missing kids and no one else said Colonel Elder had told them to come in.

Knudson was asked about Thornton's paperwork. Knudson testified the paperwork was accurate and Thornton and never made mistakes prior to that day.

> *Prosecution*: Did you think it was unusual for Thornton to make a mistake like that?
>
> *Knudson*: Yes.
>
> *Prosecution*: PFC Knudson, was it unusual for Thornton to come on duty when he wasn't scheduled. Did Thornton work a lot of extra hours?
>
> *Knudson*: Yes.

*

Author's Note: In addition to Marjorie Bates' notes of the trial testimony, an interview was conducted with PFC Perry Knudson, 463rd MP Company at a later date. This is what he had to say:

Perry Knudson Interview:

I believe I might have even issued the weapon when [Thornton] went out but I'm not sure of that. Because we were in the arms room. And we were doing twelve-hour shifts, so I'm not one-hundred percent sure that I was on duty when we checked it out to him. But I know I was on duty when he checked it back in.

He was calm and cool. He acted like he normally did. He was never one to be joking or anything. He was quiet and reserved, you know? Acting like himself, I should say. Since I emailed you, I've been trying to think back to what his demeanor was and everything. He was always quiet and he never wanted to joke around with the guys or anything.

During the interview, Knudson confirmed that when Thornton came into the arms room on the day after the crime, Thornton told them he'd been called in to help search for the missing kids. Colonel Elder had called him in to duty. None of the other off-duty MPs who were coming in to join the search made statements such as that.

> *Knudson*: Well, Thornton was quite nervous. And he was just kind of a little bit on the paranoid side — which was out of character for him. This was on the afternoon of the thirteenth.

Knudson also confirmed during his interview about Thornton's paperwork:

Thornton rarely ever made mistakes. On this particular day, he'd made a mistake. He always collected his brass when he shot dogs. And he didn't have all of his brass, he just had some of it. Out of the fifteen rounds Thornton had been issued, he probably turned in five or six maybe, yes, that was fired brass.

The standard procedure for game wardens when they shot dogs was, they had to retrieve their brass and turn them in because we need to justify the rounds. Thornton seemed to have a higher count on dog kills than all the other game wardens. The other game wardens did dog kills but not as many as Thornton did. Usually what they did was chase them away.

Once the young lady made it to the highway and then to the farmhouse — and this became known and CID was notified and everything — Thornton was actually a suspect, I was called into the arm's room. I had to pick out his weapon and the brass he'd turned in. I dropped it all in an evidence bag. Because I was actually the last person to have handled the weapon. And I can't remember if it was CID or FBI who did this because we had both of them on post at the time.

I know when I got called up to Springfield to the state mental institute where they were holding him before trial, we had to talk to the psychiatrist. The psychiatrist wanted the full gist of what was going on with Thornton.

The trial itself was just unbelievable. There were people lined up in the hallways and the court room was just full. We went from Fort Leonard Wood to Council Bluffs and we stayed two nights. When we left for Council Bluffs, we were supposed to drive up, get a hotel room, and then get up the next morning to testify and then leave. But I believe there was a glitch in the court, in the trial, and we had to stay an extra day.

Now a friend of mine, Earl Boone — who was also an MP on duty that night — he was the one who was standing guard on the kid's car until the father came by and picked it up. I don't know if that's relevant or not. And another friend, MP Phil Brown stood guard on the bodies in the morgue that night.

*

In order to further amplify the trial testimony of PFC Perry Knudson, we've quotes from the CID interview with him:

About one-thirty p.m., 20 January 1977, PFC [Name redacted], Armorer, 463 MP Company, Fort Leonard Wood, Missouri was interviewed. He related he'd been recently interviewed by investigators concerning Thornton and that he was on duty in the arms room on 13 January 1977, at the time Thornton signed out [Thornton's] assigned US Army .45 pistol.

[Knudson] said he was unable to remember if he'd informed the other investigators that at about two-forty-five p.m. (at the time Thornton signed out the weapon), Thornton was dressed in civilian clothes. At which time, Thornton informed him [Thornton] was going on duty to aid in the search for the four kids reported missing on Fort Leonard Wood. [Knudson] concluded the interview by stating at the time Thornton was at the arms room there was no one else there who may have alerted Thornton about the four missing persons.

* * *

Testimony of PFC George D. Brocious:

PFC George D. Brocious was the base radio operator for the military police command on the 12th and 13th of January, 1977.

Brocious: I've known Thornton for approximately eight months. On the morning of the thirteenth, I received a radio call from Thornton to report an abandoned vehicle near a base entrance. I attempted to check the Missouri license plate number on the vehicle. The plate was a new plate and wasn't yet on file. Thornton gave me the location of the abandoned vehicle. He described it as being on a Range Road and not Cemetery Road.

*

Defense cross-examination:

Brocious: I later learned this was the vehicle the kids were missing from. I didn't dispatch anyone there but I called Thornton back and told him about the new license plate. I'd gone on a tour of duty with [Thornton] at least once.

Defense: PFC Brocious, when you heard about these crimes, did you suspect Thornton? Did you believe he was capable of committing the acts he is charged with? Do you believe he could've killed people?

Prosecution objected. The judge ruled that Thornton admitted to firing the shots. The judge said it was a highly improper question therefore the objection was sustained.

The Defense attorney asked if he could approach the bench and confer with the judge.

Following that conference, the cross-examination continued.

Defense: Do you believe [Thornton] was capable of doing this?

Brocious: No, sir. I'd been with [Thornton] when he made an arrest. I thought he was a law-abiding citizen. [Thornton] was a very good MP.

Defense: Would you rate him one of the best?

Brocious: Yes, sir.

*

Redirect by Prosecution:

> *Prosecution*: PFC Brocious, if you knew the defendant had admitted to the killings, would that change your opinion? If you knew [Thornton] had admitted to the second murder and rape, would this knowledge change your opinion?
>
> *Brocious*: I've never seen [Thornton] handcuff anyone or shoot anyone.
>
> *Prosecution*: Have you ever seen [Thornton] take any of these people and kill them?

The judge immediately instructed the jury to disregard the question. The witness was dismissed.

* * *

Testimony of Charles Gibbs:

Charles Gibbs stated he was in the Army but he was an air traffic controller at the Fort Wood airfield.

> *Gibbs*: On January 13, 1977, I got a call from someone who identified themselves as Wharton or Thornton wanting to know if there were going to be any flights scheduled for that day. I checked and told him, 'no.' The person then asked again if I was sure. So, I called the deputy supervisor and they suggested [the person] call back after seven. The caller said he was with the game warden section, and the request was being made about the southwest corner of Fort Leonard Wood — the area where the kids were found.

*

Defense Cross-examination of Gibbs:

> *Defense*: Was it unusual for game wardens to call concerning this type of flight?
>
> *Gibb*: It was unusual for that time of the year.

The witness was dismissed.

* * *

Testimony of Sergeant Interior Laloula:

Sergeant Interior Laloula. Laloula testified he'd been in the United States Army for approximately three-and-a-half years. He was a game warden stationed at Fort Leonard Wood.

Laloula: I went on duty at six a.m. to patrol Fort Leonard Wood in vehicle X37.

Prosecution: Had you seen the person you were relieving?

Laloula: Yes. It was Thornton.

Laloula then identified Thornton in the courtroom.

Laloula: I'd first seen him about six a.m. in the game warden's office. Thornton still had his firearm on. Thornton was talking about getting back with his wife. Thornton wanted me to wash the vehicle, just in case the Provost Marshal might want to go out and check road conditions.

Prosecution: Did you notice a hole in the jeep?

Laloula: No, I noticed nothing unusual.

Prosecution: Did you see any blood in the floor or the seat in the back of the vehicle?

Laloula: No.

In response to the next question, Laloula stated Thornton made a call inquiring about the flight operations.

Laloula: I couldn't hear the details of Thornton's conversation. This occurred about six-fifteen a.m.

Prosecution: Did you notice anything unusual about Thornton on that date?

Laloula: No, sir. He seemed the same as before. At approximately six-thirty a.m., I left and went out to the vehicle in the front parking lot. I didn't wash the vehicle but I drove away from the MP headquarters in the vehicle.

In response to additional questions, Laloula stated he didn't fire a weapon inside the vehicle and he had the vehicle until 2:00 p.m. in the afternoon.

Laloula: I patrolled the south gate road but I didn't go to the game warden shack that day.

*

Defense Cross-examination of Laloula:

> *Defense*: Are you pretty good friends with Thornton?
>
> *Laloula*: I've been on a duty shift with him many times.
>
> *Defense*: Did you always talk about work? Was Thornton a professional MP?
>
> *Laloula*: Yes, he was one of the best.
>
> *Defense*: Did you ever see him lose his temper?
>
> *Laloula*: No, sir.
>
> *Defense*: Did you ever see him do anything wrong?
>
> *Laloula*: No, sir. Thornton was familiar with the rules and regulations and he was doing his job and he knows what he's doing.
>
> *Defense*: There was nothing unusual about his appearance or mood on that date? He was calm and normal as if nothing unusual it happened?
>
> *Laloula*: No, sir. He didn't talk of personal problems but he'd said he was going to get back with his wife. And I said it was a good idea.
>
> *Defense*: Is it common to check on air flights over the base?
>
> *Laloula*: It is.

The witness was then dismissed.

* * *

Testimony of FBI Agent, Robert Sypult:

Sypult testified to assisting in the murder and assault criminal investigations. He testified about conducting a search during which he found shell casings in the area and an expended bullet which was admitted as Exhibit #117.

> *Sypult*: The slug was found about thirty-three feet from Tony Bates' body.

Defense then asked if they could approach the bench. At the end of the conference, the court was recessed for a period of time.

When court testimony resumed, Robert Sypult was no longer in the witness chair.

He'd been replaced by Alfred J. Jones of the Federal Bureau of Investigation. Jones was sworn in as a witness.

* * *

Testimony of Alfred J. Jones of the FBI:

> *Jones*: I assisted in the investigation. I was at the scene of the crime at the game warden shack, and at the auto scene. I made sketches of the scenes. A bullet and shell casing were found at the site of the car. During the search on February thirteenth, around the rear of the car, a shell casing [Exhibit #116] was found in the area, just to the side of the road across the street from the car. The expended bullet was on a dirt hill ten to twelve-feet high. The bullet was from a .45 caliber weapon.

The bullet was admitted as Exhibit #110.

> *Jones*: During the search on February 14, 1977, two bullets and three shell casings were found behind a log where Tony Bates had been found. In addition, there were pennies found by the log.

The pennies were later determined to have been placed there at the crime scene by a military combat engineer who was attempting to work a mine detector the previous day and tested it by using the pennies as targets. The engineer had been unable to locate all of the pennies in the snow he'd tossed out on previous day.

> *Jones*: Two shell casings and expended bullets were found near the bodies of Wesley Hawkins and Linda Needham."

Exhibits #112, #113, and #115, were admitted into evidence.

The cross-examination of Agent Jones by Defense was brief.

* * *

Testimony of Robert C. Bartley of the FBI:

Agent Bartley testified he was a fingerprint specialist from Washington, DC.

> *Bartley*: I found impressions of palm prints on both the upper and lower portions of the bed springs. I matched the fingerprints of Juanita Deckard.

Following his testimony, these inked impressions were admitted into evidence as Exhibits #5A and #5B.

> *Prosecution*: Agent Bartley, were there any other prints located?

> *Bartley*: I found prints left by a small woman or a child. I didn't have the palm prints of Linda Needham to compare to these impressions.

Prosecution requested the jury be allowed to look at the exhibits and for court to recess while they did so. The Judge approved this request. The judge stated he wanted all attorneys to return to his chambers with him and possibly the government would soon be ready to rest its case.

When court resumed, Judge Collinson stated, "Members of the jury, the government has rested its case. This court will be in recess until tomorrow morning at nine a.m."

12

THE TRIAL

Part Two
Defense Begins

THE CRIMINAL TRIAL OF JOHNNY Lee Thornton continued in the United States Federal District Court at Council
Bluffs, Iowa.

*Defense's Opening Statement on Thursday, July 21,
1977*:

Ladies and gentlemen of the jury, the evidence in this case will
be without question a person in the body of Johnny Lee Thornton
committed some of the most vile, heinous, corruptible criminal
acts ever described in a courtroom. You will hear no evidence
but the facts of the case. And certainly, somebody is to blame.
The evidence will be Johnny Lee Thornton is to blame.

But he is a wretched product from a horrible beginning in his
life — a mind that never fully developed, and all kinds of trauma. You will hear the testimony on both sides that this man
suffers from a mental disability called Borderline Personality
Disorder. This disease is every bit as killing as cancer itself.
You will hear about this Borderline Personality Disorder and
that [Thornton] hasn't learned how to, and has never been able
to become a one-personality person. All people have this, and
they develop it naturally. But the two parts are never entered
into a single person such as Thornton.

The defendant has multiple personalities. One, his work and
dedication — excellent in these. And the other is an angry, violent

personality who isn't rational and is insane. And it inhabits his body. We are not contesting he did all of these things. You will hear testimony from his wife and others where he committed some acts of violence and he didn't remember it afterwards.

The evidence will be a conflict between the government doctors as to whether his condition does exist. Thornton was unable to understand his condition and what he was doing. It was either wrongful or he didn't have the ability to stop his actions. At the end of the testimony, there will be a substantial doubt about this man's sanity. And you will know the government won't have carried its burden of proving his sanity beyond a reasonable doubt.

Authors note: The first witness to testify for Defense was Patti Thornton, wife of Johnny Lee Thornton. However, there was a complication to her testimony. Patti Thornton was in her ninth month of pregnancy and was due to give birth at any moment. As a result of that issue, Defense requested Patti Thornton's testimony be given by deposition. Prosecution agreed with that request. Patti Thornton's deposition isn't in the case file held by the federal court. According to a financial billing statement found in the Thornton trial case file, the government was charged for the production of a deposition from Patti — which is believed to have been 225 pages long.

* * *

Defense Team presentation of Patti Jean Thornton's deposition:

Patti Thornton was living in Los Angeles California at the time of the deposition.

> *Patti Thornton:* I met Johnny when he was living with his mother and father and his brother Jesse Lee Thornton. I am twenty-two years old, and I was sixteen when I met him. I met his mother first — who is married to Bruce Thornton. Both of our families lived in the same area. It was in late 1970, and his brother, Jesse was sixteen at the time when Jesse and Johnny Lee Thornton, and someone by the name of Anna, had broken into a drive-

through milk farm. Thornton was eighteen at the time. It was after September of that year, but their mother wasn't upset about this. They also robbed a wig salon.

Johnny Lee Thornton
High School Yearbook Photo

The police picked them up. And his mother didn't seem to mind it at first for me to see Johnny then. But after a while, his mother didn't want me to see John. Once, we were going to hear some records down the street. His mother asked us where we were going. John didn't hear the question, so I answered for him. Then his mother asked the question again, and again I answered. Mother said, "Let him answer for himself." She got mad at me and went upstairs and got a gun. And said she was going to kill both me and John.

I later became pregnant and I wasn't allowed to live in their home. His mother wouldn't have anything to do with me.

Johnny's mother's name was Ruby Dean Darling. His father was Bruce Thornton. They had moved to Santa Rosa California. When I became pregnant, I called Johnny and told him. He asked me not to write and to have an abortion. I didn't want to. I later got the measles and had an abortion. Johnny was upset about it, and he said he loved me and wanted to take care of me. We lived together in Santa Rosa, California.

Then his parents decided to move back to Arkansas. John wanted to go with them. And so, we did. We continued to live with his grandparents after his parents got a place to live. We both got jobs and went to work. Bruce

Thornton isn't the father of Johnny Lee — his real name is Wharton. I'd seen his birth certificate. His grandfather thought either Johnny or I were hurting one of his dogs. He chased Johnny around the house. He threatened to kill Johnny. Johnny didn't press any charges. He thought grandpa was just getting old. But then, we moved in with Johnny's mother and father.

Great Uncle Herbert was at the restaurant one night and wanted to take me home. He'd never come to the restaurant before. I accepted the ride because Johnny didn't get off work until about an hour later. Herbert said they would go visit his wife. I'd never been to where they were living. On the way, Herbert pulled off the road and attacked me sexually. He kept trying to force himself on me. I pulled a knife out of my purse and he stopped. I told Johnny about this later and he went back to Herbert and Aunt Opal's house. Herbert admitted to the attempt and John told him he'd better not act like that again. And he'd better not catch him hanging around.

I became pregnant and Johnny's reactions were mixed. At first, he wasn't happy about it. But then later, he was happy and continued to be happy. Johnny's mother wasn't at all happy about the pregnancy. We were outside on the porch one day and Johnny said, 'Hi, Grandma' and she glared at him. I told her I was pregnant and she said she would have to beat the baby out of me.

Johnny then began to badgering me to have an abortion. He would discuss it with his mother, and we fought about it. Things would be fine until he would see his mother. And then he would start the argument again. I finally left and went back to California, though we were not married yet. I again asked him to marry me. He said he would but he just thought it wasn't necessary because his uncle Kenny wasn't married.

I left in September 1974, left him a note and I called him later. He was crying and I said I would go back to him if he would marry me. And he promised he would. We got married October 28, 1974. The parents didn't know we were married. We didn't tell the parents we were married for two weeks. And when we did, the parents were not happy about the situation. His mother attempted to break up the relationship between me and Johnny by telling lies.

Johnny was proud of Michael. Johnny had a sister named Julie. Johnny considered Bruce Thornton his father. He didn't see his mother, but he would see Bruce. Bruce would stop by when he was coming home from work. He worked the graveyard shift. Once he had tears in his eyes and asked us to not keep his grandson away from him. But we didn't go to see him. Johnny was proud of Michael. I had never seen him happier and I thought all of our problems were at an end following the birth of Michael because Johnny stood up to his mother.

But later, his mother tried to get him to divorce me. She said she would take care of Michael for him. Then one day father and mother and Julia came to see us and mother was different all-of-a-sudden and offered to take care of the baby and to help me. They didn't stay long, and she kissed me goodbye and told me she loved me.

In May 1975, Johnny enlisted at Fort Leonard Wood, Missouri. He took his basic training there. On May 13, I went to stay with his parents with his consent. It was his idea to do this until we got a permanent station. Then he went to Fort McClellan, Alabama for his advanced military training. While he was there, he stopped writing and didn't call. I contacted the Army personnel and then he began to call me again. He was reprimanded for this. Johnny said he'd a lot of work and later I learned it wasn't true. They went and got Johnny and made him call me. He was off about the base playing poker. He later told me he'd been having an affair. We fought about this at first and I wanted a divorce. He wouldn't have sent for me except I insisted.

Then I found a letter in his wallet — which he wanted me to find. The letter promised to break it off. He never did. After he completed advanced training, he was stationed at Fort Leonard Wood. I was pregnant again. I joined Johnny there at Fort Leonard Wood.

This time, he wanted an abortion again. I was going to do it, but the night before, Johnny didn't sleep any and he told me he didn't want me to have the abortion. I learned he was being unfaithful to me again. When I confronted him with it, we had a fight. Then I filed for a divorce. This occurred when Travis was two-weeks old. Johnny accused me of him not being the father of Travis or Michael. Johnny lived on base and not with me. He didn't complain of headaches but he did have a knot on his forehead where his brother had hit him.

169

Johnny's personality changed when he had these head-aches. On three occasions, he became violent. The first time, we were wrestling — just playing — and Johnny put a pillow on my face and broke my glasses. I kept trying to stop him. Then he would quit and later said he didn't remember doing this. The second time it occurred, he tore up the house. We were wrestling again and I pushed him off of the bed. This made him mad. He started breaking things. This time, he had a headache and he remembered what he'd done. The third occasion, we were in Arkan-sas. He wanted me to go to the grocery store. I didn't want to but finally said I would go anyway, and I did. When I came back to the house, the living room was all messed up. He asked me what I thought about it. I told him I didn't feel it was at all necessary. He acted as if he wanted to hit me.

Then Johnny asked, "What you think about all this?" Then he threw the coffee table in the air. Then he got a pair of pliers and started to bust up the TV. After all of this happened, he said he couldn't remember what he'd done. He talked about seeing a doctor. Then there was a fourth time after Travis was born. Me and the children were living in a trailer at Fort Leonard Wood and he wasn't living with us. Johnny had come over for a visit and was feeding the baby. The baby was crying and Johnny wanted him to stop. Johnny wanted to know what was making him cry. I said he was sitting up too straight and to lower his seat. Johnny did this, but Travis kept on crying. Johnny then yelled at me and said, "What is the matter with him?" Again, I said the seat was still too high. He picked up the little boy and dropped him on the couch. And then threw the baby food jar at me. I fell to the floor. His face looked like he was in pain. After I was on the floor, I saw hatred in his eyes. He had a headache at this time. He got in his car and I called the neighbor and asked her to call an ambulance. I went to the hospital, I was pregnant at this time.

Johnny seem to be having headaches worse. Violence didn't occur when he didn't have a headache. Some-times he wouldn't be violent when he had a headache and sometimes he would be. Johnny never went to see a doctor. He didn't take drugs. He was down on drugs and wouldn't allow them in our house. He wasn't a drinker. Occasionally, I would call him and he wouldn't answer. He'd just be sitting there watching TV and wouldn't even hear me. There was a marked change in his behavior in the latter part of the year before I left Fort Leonard Wood. I last saw him on October 14, 1976, and haven't seen him since."

At this point, Judge Collinson declared a recess for a few moments. When court resumed, one last question from the deposition was read to the courtroom.

Defense: What was the reason for you leaving him?

Patti Thornton: It was because he threw the baby down and threw the food jar at me. I had seen hatred in his eyes at the time, and he couldn't talk about his feelings or his thinking to describe his actions to me.

*

Prosecution cross-examination questions from Patti Thornton's deposition:

Patti Thornton: In 1970, I was sixteen-years old and Johnny was seventeen. I am now twenty-two years old and Johnny is now twenty-three years old. We were both in high school. He'd come to visit his mother but he hadn't been living with them at the time. He went to school in Concorde, California for his senior year. He dropped out of school because of problems about having enough credits to graduate. I also dropped out of school, but we were still in the Concorde, California area living together. Johnny robbed a wig salon and a dairy farm when he was eighteen. We moved to Santa Rosa, California, on May 29, 1972. We had no jobs but we were looking for work. At that time, we stayed with his mother, then lived with his uncle, Kenny. The year before I had had an abortion, and I was pregnant again in February 1972.

Johnny got a job a week after we got there, at Lucky's Grocery Store. He worked for them for over a year 'til we moved to Arkansas. He didn't have any difficulties with his job, no sickness or illness. I worked, too, and we lived with Kenny and Rose for two months. In December 1973, we all moved to Arkansas. The problems with mother were minor. She wanted Johnny to leave me. Johnny got a job in a grocery store and worked for one month, then he went to work for the IGA. He gave no reason for leaving. He worked for IGA until July 1974. We lived with [Kenny and Rose] until we got a place of our own. We loaned money to his parents — twenty dollars now and then. Johnny had started working for Safeway. It was a better paying job. Johnny had no problems with his work and had an increase in salary.

Johnny joined the Army around May 1975. His boss offered him a new position if he would stay with the store but Johnny had already enlisted. After Michael was born, Johnny thought Michael wasn't his but later apologized for this. He was making six-hundred dollars a month and I was making two-hundred-and fifty-dollars a month. I had to stop work before the baby was born. Me and Johnny had a fight about this and he was going to send me back to my father in California. But he didn't get violent. And then, there was a turning point in our relationship. He wasn't able to communicate with me nor me with him about our problems.

I went back to California because of nonsupport in a mental sort of way. Michael was born in September 1975. Johnny had been refusing to marry me for quite some time, but I later agreed to marry him after I had left him and went back to California. Johnny was still working for the Safeway Company, and having no illnesses while living in Russellville, Arkansas. My younger sister was living with us. He was proud to have the baby and stood up to his mother.

In April 1975, he told his mother to stay out of our lives and she did, with no animosity. She stayed away for a while. Later, she came back to visit us for about six days before I left for California. Johnny was going on duty May 13, 1975. He was working at the store and we agreed, but his mother didn't like it. But she didn't say much. It was me and Johnny's idea for me to go to California until he got a permanent location. He knew he was going to be an MP when he went into basic training at Fort Leonard Wood and then to Fort McClellan, Alabama for more training.

The next time I saw him was the Little Rock Airport in Arkansas. He'd been assigned to Fort Leonard Wood starting in September 1975. In October 1975, we moved into a house. I was pregnant again in 1976. And again, Johnny wanted me to have an abortion. He said we had a baby and we didn't need another. Travis was born May 20, 1976. In June 1976, Johnny said the baby wasn't his. I filed for divorce, and a month later he moved out of the house.

Johnny hit me once in Santa Rosa while we were having an argument with my sister. He struck me with the back of his hand. Again, at Fort Leonard Wood, we were arguing and I was pregnant and he struck me. Johnny had said nothing about a headache those times. Later, we reconciled but didn't live together. He wanted everybody to believe we were going to get a divorce. It was his idea and the petition remained on file in 1976. There was lots of talk about each of us having affairs with others.

Johnny stayed at the trailer some nights and had no headaches. I decided to leave when he threw the baby down and threw the baby food jar at me. He asked me not to leave. I said I wouldn't stay. Johnny had frightened me.

Prosecution: Did Johnny complain of headaches?

Patti Thornton: He complained of headaches the first time when he tried to smother me with a pillow in Santa Rosa and didn't remember what he'd done, and he cried when I told him. He was sorry. The second time was when the stereo was knocked over and he broke the clock. Johnny left the house for about twenty minutes and when he returned, he said he just got a headache and he was sorry. He remembered what he'd done but didn't know why he'd done it. Johnny said he couldn't control himself.

The third time was when I was going to the store — he worked at Safeway store — he'd not complained of a headache but he asked me to go to the store at ten-thirty at night. I didn't want to. I didn't get upset and I ended up going to the store at ten thirty at night when I didn't want to. Johnny didn't get upset. He came out to the car and said I didn't have to go. I went anyway and when I got back, the TV was turned over and some other things damaged. I was gone about thirty minutes. When I returned to the house, Johnny was gone. Johnny came back about fifteen minutes later. When he came back, he wanted to know what I thought about what he'd done and the damage in the house. I told him I wasn't proud of what he'd done and he had no reason to do what he'd done. At that point, Johnny did more damage to the living room. He pulled the stereo over and kicked the coffee table across the room while I just stood there looking at him. Johnny made no threatening remarks to me but took it out on the living room.

The next day, he mentioned a headache. I don't know if he had apologized or not. He thought he should go see a doctor. He said he didn't know why he did these things. Johnny went to a hospital for poison ivy. It was when he was in basic training. And once for an ingrown toenail. The last time he got violent was about the baby. He threw the jar at me, he made no comment and no complaint of a headache.

Prosecution: Did your husband drink?

Patti Thornton: Johnny occasionally drank something in his Coke but he didn't drink beer and he didn't drink to excess. He exercised with barbells but he never complained about headaches or bright lights hurting his eyes. Johnny discussed his work. He was happy with his work and he never complained about the Army. Johnny told me why he works so much overtime.

Prosecution: Did you ever have an occasion to become upset about Playboy magazines?

Patti Thornton: Yes.

*

Redirect section of the deposition:

Patti Thornton: We lived at Waynesville. I did, but Johnny did not. Johnny was angry and just took it out on the furniture. We discussed these outbursts. Johnny thought I thought he was crazy, but he wanted my opinion. I became more afraid after the throwing of the baby food jar.

Defense: Was this the first time you were afraid of him?

Patti Thornton: No. The first time was when he tried to smother me with a pillow. I felt there had been a change in his feelings toward me. I talked to him, and after I left, I got letters from him. Johnny said he was planning on coming to get me and the children.

Defense: Did he ever say anything about feeling torn between you and his mother?

Patti Thornton: No.

*

Cross-examination by Prosecution:

Patti Thornton: Johnny didn't stand up for me like he should, but he didn't say he didn't like his mother. I felt it wasn't normal, on occasions. But the last time I had talked to him was on the Thursday before Thursday, the 13th of January 1977. I got a letter written a day or so before the thirteenth. Then, I got one dated 12 January. There were no concerns in the letters and I tried to call him on the 13th, a Thursday, and I couldn't reach him.

At this point in the testimony the court was recessed until 1:15 p.m.

When the court went back into session at 1:19 p.m., a new witness was called to the stand.

* * *

Testimony of Sergeant David B. Webster:

Sergeant David Webster was a member of the 463 MP Company, Fort Leonard Wood.

Webster: I knew Thornton well. He was on duty with me several times. Thornton was the best of the MPs it's been my privilege to know. I've seen him make an arrest. He handled himself well. Nothing violent, good self-control. I've watched him give game warden citations and lots of drug arrests. It was Thornton's duty to do that and Thornton worked overtime on many occasions.

No records were kept on the overtime hours until after this whole thing happened. Records are now being kept. At the end of a duty shift, Thornton would often work over with the incoming shift. I don't know of any arrest Thornton made that he was reprimanded for. Thornton carried two sets of handcuffs and it wasn't unusual for him to do this. The MPs were issued a kit with various tools and plastic handcuffs.

Defense: Was Thornton's proficient with a handgun?

Webster: I'm considered an expert and John could beat me or is better than I am. Thornton has no disrespect for a weapon.

In December 1976, Thornton's general overall appearance was deteriorating and he was losing weight because he wasn't eating properly. He continued to work long hours.

I knew he was having money problems and marital problems and trouble paying his bills. Patti had written a bad check for an airfare back in California but they were making it good at the bank. He sent money to his wife and the children but her and the children were having medical problems.

Thornton called his wife from my residence every Thursday and each call cost between ten to twenty dollars. I talked with him about his mother and his grandparents.

I've heard the term "super cop" used in relation to Thornton. The term was usually applied to a younger cop. It usually meant an energetic officer who a lot of times doesn't show enough common sense and doesn't take enough time in making his decisions. No, Johnny Lee Thornton did not fit the term.

I am aware Thornton was bothered by headaches and both me and my wife had given Thornton aspirins for this problem. Thornton complained about headaches.

I talked to Jensen about giving Johnny a promotion to the rank of sergeant.

I saw Thornton on January 13, 1977, around three p.m. at my residence. I'd called a cab and it didn't come, so I called Thornton at his barracks and got him out of bed to come get me and take me to work. Thornton wanted to know what was going on. I told him about the missing kids. Thornton used my phone to see if they wanted him to come in to help. After he hung up, Thornton wondered if he should go in, too. I suggested me and Thornton go by the Provost Marshal's office and see what was going on. And so, Thornton took me to work.

Thornton was in a good mood. He told me how he was taking care of his bills and made the statement he and his wife were getting back together. When we arrived at the MP headquarters, Thornton told me he had to go up the street and see a supply sergeant about an issue. I got out of the vehicle and when I went into MP headquarters, I was marched into the CID office. Nobody told me what was going on. And then a little later, they said, "No, he isn't the right one."

Under additional questioning by Defense, Webster stated Thornton carried two sets of handcuffs all the time, and that there wasn't anything unusual about checking for helicopter flights over the wooded areas of Fort Leonard Wood.

Webster: We could call and check on the helicopter flights if we wanted to.

*

Prosecution cross of David Webster:

Webster: I worked with Thornton, and it was an accepted practice to handcuff a suspect behind their back. I'd seen other men under stress when they made an apprehension.

One time, Thornton had five or six people up and he called for help. When help arrived, Thornton had three caught and had to chase the other two. He caught them. There wasn't anything unusual about the situation; it was a pot bust. Thornton was a cool, level-headed person and I would still say that in light of what has happened.

Yes, I've seen Thornton with his weapon. Thornton is a better shot than I am. I've never seen Thornton misuse a weapon. A few years ago, I'd have termed myself a super cop but I wouldn't do that now. I think if I'm acting as a "super cop tonight," I may not be acting right and may not use proper judgment. It means you're ready to go out and hopefully to do something proper. Thornton was organized in his personal conduct and everything he did was organized in advance.

Prosecution: Had you noticed anything different about Johnny Lee Thornton's appearance?

Webster: Thornton's appearance had deteriorated. He was always clean-shaven and I'd seen him lately when he wasn't clean-shaven. As far as duty was concerned, he was all right. I'm aware he was living with a member of the Armed Forces by the name of Cochrane up until 31 December, 1976. Following that, his appearance changed. He then lived in the barracks and he discussed sexual problems he'd had with Cochrane. But didn't state what they were or what they stemmed from. He discussed it and said she was super straight about sex. Thornton complained about it on more than one occasion, and he mentioned it five or six times. Thornton complained before and after he moved out. Said she didn't like anything out of the ordinary. Thornton moved out the last of December.

I saw Thornton on the 12th of January. Thornton worked from six a.m. until two p.m. I invited him to come to my house the evening of the 12th. I called my wife and told her I was going to go to the show with Thornton.

Prosecution: Anything unusual about that?

Webster: No, sir. I didn't know of any complaints but if it'd been serious, I would've remembered. I'd seen Thornton on the 13th, going on regular duty. When I couldn't get a ride into work, I called Thornton to come get me. Thornton was advised the kids were missing off Highway 17. I had no knowledge of foul play at that time.

There were three or four kids missing off of Highway 17 and we didn't know if they were dead or alive. Thornton acted concerned. He seemed concerned about their welfare. He couldn't understand what the MPs were doing out there for them. He asked me twice if he could go out there and get in uniform and I told him to call back to the office and get more information and see, and he did. He asked about the kids who were missing, how many and where they were, and where they were from. He reported everyone in the game warden section was out looking for them but no one else was in the back office. He asked if he should go in, but he didn't find out so we decided to wait until later. Thornton wasn't upset but he was concerned about the welfare of the kids. He was still cool-headed during the trip to headquarters.

During the trip to the PMO, the conversation was about money problems and the fact he was getting back together with his wife. Thornton had no expression in any way — it was a normal conversation.

Prosecution: Did you go by the armory?

Webster: No, sir. I didn't see any firearms. I don't remember what Thornton was wearing. He didn't complain of headaches or anything physical, and he was in a good mood. Thornton told me he was going to go up the street to see the supply sergeant, so Thornton stopped to let me out.

I'm sure it was after three p.m., or somewhere in that area. It could've been two thirty p.m. but not any earlier. That was the last time I saw Thornton until after his arrest.

Prosecution: Have you ever carried two sets of handcuffs?

Webster: I have. I've had one set of my own and I checked out one set. I don't do that anymore. I personally have checked three or four times about helicopter flights in the last eleven months. You would be able to see bodies on the ground from these flights.

Thornton scheduled time to discuss relations with his wife. They were having money troubles over bills and his working long hours. Thornton said he believed his wife was unfaithful to him. She'd had a relationship with Mason, Moore, and Wolf at a motel just off the base. Thornton also thought there were others he didn't know about. He was upset and felt betrayed by Mason. I never heard unkind remarks about people or women because Thornton wasn't that kind of a person.

After being let off of the PMO, I spent several hours waiting for Thornton to come back. I was very concerned about the situation and was afraid someone would fire on Thornton with a weapon. I was very concerned and very worried and very surprised Thornton had done this.

* * *

Elizabeth Cochrane for Defense:

Elizabeth Cochrane was a member of the United States Army. In response to questioning, Cochrane told the court she was divorced and she arrived at Fort Leonard Wood in October 1976. She was a neighbor of the Webster family.

Cochrane: I met Johnny Lee Thornton and we began to date. And then later moved in together, that is, he moved in with me, and I knew he was married. Thornton told me his wife had left him and was in California. They had two children. Thornton said he was worried about them.

At various times I discussed work, relations with his mother, and money problems with him. Thornton was kind of rough on my six-year-old boy. We broke up on December 30, 1976. Thornton had talked about his wife with me. He said she'd been unfaithful and she'd hurt him very badly. Thornton said he'd found her in a motel with Moore and Mike Mason and another MP. Thornton said he loved her like someone he'd known a long time, but not as man and wife. He said he wanted his children back. He was concerned about them not having food or shoes.

Thornton discussed things about his work. He wanted to be a good cop, be good at his job. He spent longer hours than necessary working, but so did I. My son, David was with Johnny a lot and they got along well. He said he worked a lot of extra hours and was afraid it would interfere with our relationship. Johnny told me he worked extra hours because he was trying to work extra hard in order to be promoted. He said he wanted to be a better soldier.

Johnny told me he was sending money to his wife every pay day — $115.00 to $125.00. He said he drew $165 a month on them and he was sending more than that. Thornton told me his wife didn't call him, he had to call her. She was always saying, "I need more money." He would say, "Why don't you go to work?" and she would say, "No."

Defense: Were your sexual relations satisfactory?

Cochrane: Yes. Thornton was very happy about our sex life. Thornton would take David out to get haircuts and they would bring flowers back to me. Thornton thought I was making a sissy out of David, and he didn't agree with the way I handled the boy.

We didn't go out on the town. Johnny told me if I wanted him there, I would have to stay home and not go out. We three stayed home and never went anywhere without David.

Me and Johnny had talked about getting married and he was offered a job with the Missouri Department of Conservation. He wanted to quit the army. I said, "No," I wanted him to stay in the army. Thornton said he didn't understand me being so independent. Our relationship ended the day before New Year's. I was working lots of hours and he frequently woke me up at midnight and say I didn't love him. And I would say, "I do love you" and I'd ask him to stay. Later, he said this and I told him to leave. I later learned he received a letter from his wife after he left.

*

Prosecution cross of Elizabeth Cochrane:

> *Prosecution*: Did Johnny ever say to you he wanted to be a super cop?
>
> *Cochrane*: No. I rode with him, and he'd speed. He said he was an MP and no one was going to stop him. He never lost his temper, never struck me. I struck him one time and he grabbed my wrist and said we can talk about it, and [he] was very cool and level-headed in that situation. Thornton was this type of person all the time. He woke me up the night he left at midnight and said, "I can't leave without saying goodbye." And he said, "If you asked me to stay, I will." I told him to leave. Thornton had told me at one time if I broke up with him, I would be hassled by the MPs.
>
> *Prosecution:* Did Thornton ever complain about headaches?
>
> *Cochrane*: He had headaches and was going to go down and see if he needed glasses.
>
> During the relationship with Thornton, I was satisfied and thought he was, too. During relations with Thornton, he didn't ask me to engage in sex acts that I didn't approve of. When I first met Thornton, it was like three or four times a day. One of his favorite places to go on post was the game warden cabin. He also liked covered places down by the trout stream. I've never been at the game warden cabin with Johnny Lee Thornton.

* * *

Testimony of Paul Mara:

MP Paul Mara stated he'd known Thornton for 11 months. He'd worked with him on the same duty shift.

> *Mara:* Thornton was very professional. He made no statements toward violence, none toward women. Thornton was having marital problems, and he discussed his marital problems with me. Thornton had moods. He was extremely moody and depressed at times with regard to his relationships with his wife and children.

Mike Mason was a good friend of Thornton's. After Thornton separated from Cochrane on January 6th or 7th, I'd double-dated with him and nothing unusual occurred.

Thornton told me he'd been living with another woman. He knew his wife was having relations with Mike Mason. Thornton told me he broke up with Miss Cochrane, and she wouldn't let him have his things — like his W-2 form.

Thornton complained a couple times about headaches and said his eyes were getting tired, and maybe he needed glasses. Thornton called his wife from Webster's house. He told me they were getting back together. On several occasions, Thornton borrowed money from me but never told me he was having money problems. I learned Thornton's parents were in Arkansas.

I heard the term "super cop" used in relation to Thornton. It references a bad cop, an individual who would go out and give tickets and do things to look big. Thornton wasn't that kind of person. I don't know anything about the two sets of handcuffs.

I never went up in helicopter flights but Thornton had. Thornton was very professional with his gun. He never flaunted it or tried to show it off. Thornton showed no violence toward anyone that I had observed.

Defense: When you talked with Thornton, did it seem he wanted sympathy?

Mara: Thornton would start something and he wouldn't finish it. He would work over time and it wasn't required — he just wanted to work. On one occasion we had a double date. John told the girl he was with he would show her the back roads while he was working.

Defense: Was there a change in Thornton's behavior in December?

Mara: Yes, he didn't take care of himself and he wasn't sleeping much. He was pale and he worked quite a bit.

*

Prosecution Cross of Paul Mara:

In response to questions Mara testified Thornton never used bad language or got violent.

Mara: He worked on drug cases where people would hide in the woods and use drugs and he would handle these cases himself. Other MPs might've turned these cases over to an investigator, but Thornton preferred to work his own cases. Thornton was good with his weapon. In forty-nine-shots he would get forty-nine — a rather high degree as an expert. As a general rule, it was a good practice not to draw your weapon, fire a shot or do anything else with the weapon unless you intended to use it.

Thornton had moods of depression after October 1976, and he was still in his depressive mood after he began to live with Elizabeth Cochrane. Thornton's moods improved after he said he was getting back together with his wife. I double-dated with Johnny Lee Thornton on the seventh or eighth of January, the weekend before the twelfth and thirteenth of January 1977.

The last time I saw Thornton was that Saturday night, because I left Sunday to go to Jefferson City and I permitted Thornton to use my car while I was gone. Thornton didn't mistreat the car in any way.

Prosecution: Did Thornton ever state he was having headaches?

Mara: I don't remember how many times Thornton said he had a headache but I told the FBI that Thornton asked me for aspirin.

*

Defense Redirect of Paul Mara:

Mara: I told Thornton he should go out. I thought it would be good for him to get out. Thornton's mood seemed to change noticeably when he talked about his wife.

Defense: If a patrolman called in a license check, would you notify the highway patrol?

Mara: Someone wouldn't call in for a license plate check if they didn't want to draw attention to that vehicle. I have no training on fingerprints. I've never pointed a weapon at anyone, or ever threatened to shoot anyone.

*

Prosecution Re-cross of Paul Mara:

In response to one question, Mara testified that around January 1st, Thornton's wife had agreed to come back and live with him.

* * *

Testimony of Kenneth Wall:

Kenneth Wall was an MP stationed in Germany. He testified he knew Thornton before 13 January, 1977, and had worked with him.

> *Wall:* Thornton was one of the most outstanding MPs I've ever come across. Thornton once took in nine [people] at one time. He handled the situation very well and in a very good way. I don't know of any reprimand ever issued to Thornton. He works sixteen to seventeen hours a day.
>
> There were no records kept at that time on overtime hours. Thornton worked this many hours seven days a week. Thornton found he was getting very tired because he worked that many hours from August until December 1976. Thornton worked longer hours than I did. My impression was Thornton loved his work. We discussed personal problems. Both of our wives were pregnant at the same time and we discussed our attitudes about the pregnancy.
>
> I never heard Thornton make any unkind remarks to people but at the end of August, Thornton and his wife separated. Thornton brought it up once about his wife being unfaithful to him. Thornton complained of headaches in my presence and I gave him something for the headaches.
>
> Thornton came over one afternoon. He was pale and laid down and complained about his head. His skin looked cold and clammy. To the best of my knowledge, Thornton never smoked or took drugs of any kind. It wasn't unusual to carry two sets of handcuffs. Thornton carried two sets.
>
> I couldn't say if it was unusual or not to ask about helicopter flights.

*

Prosecution cross-examination Kenneth Wall:

Author's Note: Wall started to testify about deer season being in August, he briefly looked confused, and then changed that to November of the year.

> *Wall*: It wasn't unusual to carry two sets of handcuffs when you go on duty. If you desire to have more than one set, you may request another set. In August, Thornton said he had a headache. And again, in deer season in November, he pulled off the side of the trail and started complaining of a headache. That time there wasn't anything we could do about it. Later on, we got some aspirin.

> *Prosecution*: Did Thornton act abnormal?

> *Wall*: No, sir. Nothing out of the ordinary. He was able to carry on a conversation but he was very quiet. I last saw Johnny Lee Thornton on January 11, 1977. I asked him how he was doing. Thornton gave me Patti's address and said he had several items of clothing that he was going to ship to them out there. Thornton also told us his wife was going to join him.

> He had no complaint of headaches and acted normal on that day. I was with Thornton for about fifteen minutes and observed nothing unusual.

* * *

Testimony of Dr. William Clary:

Author's Note: Defense called Defense Psychiatrist, Dr. William Clary from Springfield, Missouri. He set the stage for presenting the defense team's insanity issue. However, after Dr. Clary testified, Defense put on several other witnesses before they closed. To avoid confusion, I have elected to defer the testimony of Dr. Clary at this time. The two major opposing Psychiatrists duel it out in a following chapter.

* * *

Testimony of Mike Mason:

Mike Mason was an MP who worked with Thornton for 14 months and claimed he was a good friend

> *Mason:* Thornton was one of the most well-liked people, a good MP, and a good game warden.

> *Defense:* Did Thornton have a temper?

> *Mason:* No. He worked long hours sometimes, twenty-four hours without resting many times. He was a good shot, very good with a weapon. He never made a false report to my knowledge and was good with children. I was present in the bar and heard Patti say, "You have never pleased me since we've been married."

> *Mason:* I had an affair with Patti in October, 1976. She went to Arkansas with me. I can't speak to Thornton's mental status. Thornton's marital trouble started in August. Thornton told me that — with tears in his eyes — told me Patti wanted a divorce. Thornton changed after that. He was withdrawn and didn't talk much but continued to work overtime.

The cross-examination by Prosecution of Mike Mason was brief. Mason testified he worked with Thornton on many tours of duty, usually in a vehicle.

* * *

Testimony of Mrs. Deanie (Ruby Dean) Thornton:

Mrs. Deanie (Ruby Dean) Thornton is the mother of Johnny Lee Thornton.

> *Deanie Thornton:* I live in Russellville, Arkansas and I am forty years old. I am married to Bruce Thornton, who is a truck driver. John Wharton Junior is the real father of Johnny Lee Thornton. After my divorce from Wharton, I married Bruce Thornton in December, 1972. I was married in 1952 to Wharton. John Wharton didn't want the child and we hid the baby from his father for four-and-a-half years. Johnny has a brother named Jess who is now twenty-two years old. I had Johnny's [last] name changed to Thornton.

Deanie Thornton described to the jury times when Johnny's real father tried to kill Johnny, gave him a concussion twice, and shot at the boy once.

> *Deanie Thornton*: I thought Johnny was dead once after these assaults. I worked at various jobs. The last time I saw Johnny's real father was when he tried to choke Johnny to death, between shifts. [Wharton] walked by the bed and grabbed Johnny by the throat. That time there was permanent damage done, and Johnny had to have surgery to correct it three years later. Johnny had trouble pronouncing his words right.
>
> I discussed in Johnny's presence the idea of killing his father. I dated other men. Johnny just got into a fight and was going to hit one of the men, and I threw a pan at him.
>
> In Oregon, I left the boys with an eighteen-year-old girl. I found out that girl was bringing boys in and had sex with our little boys too and the other boys in the house. Johnny was seven or eight years old at the time.
>
> Johnny didn't date much in high school — only one girl. Patti was the first girl he really dated very much. Johnny has two little boys and one little girl and he suffered headaches up until he was about fifteen years old. Johnny's brother hit him with a pan and knocked him out and he had a concussion. The past three-and-a-half years, Johnny's had very bad headaches.
>
> Once, coming back from California, he started going all over the road and Patti had to hit the brakes. She grabbed the wheel and he was real pale and complained of a headache at the time.
>
> Johnny had trouble with the law. He broke into a wig shop on Halloween. He took the wigs back. Johnny always wanted to be a policeman even after they were so rough on him about the break-in.

*

Prosecution Cross of Deanie Thornton:

Deanie said she didn't take any of the wigs Johnny brought home.

Deanie Thornton: I didn't know Patti was pregnant. Didn't know she'd had an abortion. Didn't agree with Johnny about living with Patti, it upset him.

Johnny may have left Patti at my request. They moved back to Arkansas where they lived with my mother and father for a time before they could get a place of their own. Me and Patti were always having disagreements. Johnny took sides sometimes. Sometimes he took my side and sometimes he took Patti's side. The arguments would start between me and Patti. I didn't go by their house much but they would stop by mine. Patti had a big mouth and it didn't keep. Me and Johnny got along all right when we weren't arguing about Patti.

It upset Johnny when Patti went to California. After the baby was born, I didn't see them very much because Patti didn't want me around the baby. John would come over to see us and sometimes we argued. John would get upset and say, 'Mom, why did you have to say that? Mom, why do we have to have problems?' Me and Patti just couldn't get along.

Johnny sassed me once and I slapped him. This occurred right after Michael was born and he didn't hit me back. I wished he had. He just stood and looked at me. Johnny was a good worker and I tried to keep him from joining the military. Just because Patti was raised that way, it was no kind of life. Johnny didn't say a lot, didn't want to fight. He and Patti came down and tried to talk to us. Johnny told me he'd always wanted to be a policeman and he could do in the service.

I kept Michael while Patti was in the hospital. Johnny and a friend came to get Michael after Travis was born, I think it was in August. Johnny came back once in December, 1976. He was alone at the time and stayed for three or four days. He seemed awfully upset and told me Patti had left him.

Following the testimony of Deanie Thornton, Defense rested their case.

At this point, Prosecution began their rebuttal testimony.

* * *

Testimony of Dean Neal of St. Robert, Missouri for Prosecution:

Their first witness was Dean Neal of St. Robert, Missouri. Neal testified he was on Fort Leonard Wood on January 12, 1977, and was just passing through on the south gate road.

> *Neal*: I was in the 1974 Chevrolet El Camino which had a camper box on it, and it was around ten-thirty or eleven p.m. that night. I know this because I called a friend and told him I'd been stopped when I got on post. I was headed north, toward post. A vehicle pulled out a red light came on just after we'd passed Bloodland Range Road and Cemetery Road. It was a four-wheel-drive vehicle that stopped me.
>
> The officer approached my vehicle and shined a flashlight in the car. He asked for my driver's license. I handed it to him. The officer asked me if I was Neal. He wanted to know where I'd been. He apologized for stopping me and said they were just checking a few vehicles. The officer was very polite — overly polite. He didn't mention I'd gone over the speed limit, which I had. The officer thanked me and when I left, the officer didn't follow me.

*

Defense cross-examination of Dean Neal:

> *Defense*: Can you identify the officer?
>
> *Neal*: No. I cannot.

Prosecution asked Neal if there was a female in his vehicle. Defense objected. The Judge instructed the lawyers to approach the bench. Following a short conference, there were no further questions for the witness.

* * *

Testimony of George William Palmer:

George William Palmer stated he was in the Army, stationed at Fort Leonard Wood.

> *Palmer*: On January 12, 1977, I was traveling on the south gate road in a Grand Prix automobile by myself. A military vehicle came out of the woods from somewhere along the Bloodline Range Road. I thought the vehicle was going to run me over because it was following so close.

> I wasn't speeding and the vehicle followed me almost to the airport. At that point, the vehicle pulled up real close and put his lights on high. Then, the vehicle made a U-turn in the middle of the road and went back south. I pulled over to the side of the road. The vehicle then made another U-turn, came up behind me, and stopped. I realized it was a military police vehicle. The officer approached and asked me if I had a problem. I told him no. The officer was real polite and didn't ask for a license.

Palmer further stated that the officer was white and he recognized him as an MP or a game warden. Palmer testified he couldn't identify the officer.

At this point, Defense objected to the testimony of Palmer. After an explanation, the Judge sustained Defense's objection and instructed the jury to disregard the testimony of George Palmer. Defense then asked to approach the bench for a conference with the judge.

* * *

Testimony of Colonel Perry Elder, the Provost Marshal of Fort Leonard Wood:

Elder was asked about the vehicle Thornton was driving that night.

> *Elder*: We only had three Scout vehicles on post. The one Thornton was driving was the only one on duty that night. The other two Scouts were in the shop. The one Thornton had was green with a white top — the only one on post like that, the only one on duty and it was issued to Thornton.
>
> When we made the arrest of Thornton, he appeared to be a little afraid and ashamed but was polite and didn't make any threats. However, he did have a weapon.
>
> The conversations with Thornton prior to his surrender lasted approximately thirty minutes. The conversation consisted of us trying to get him to put down his weapon and he wouldn't. We told Thornton we wouldn't harm him.
>
> Thornton discussed the fact he and his wife were separated. He was concerned about her and the family but he said nothing about he wasn't in control of his physical and mental state. Thornton made the following statement

to me, "I know I've done something bad but I don't know what it is." Thornton was crying as he said, "I don't know, I might have done it."

*

Defense Cross of Colonel Elder:

Exhibit #1 was offered by Defense.

Defense: Do you know what this is?

Elder: Plastic handcuffs. I haven't seen a package for MPs with that handcuff included.

Thornton stated he'd known he'd done something wrong but didn't know what.

Elder was then dismissed from the stand.

* * *

Testimony of Bobby Hall:

Bobby Hall testified he lived in Plato, Missouri and he and Stanley Handley were on their way to work.

Hall: We were alone and Stanley was driving when we were stopped by an International Scout. It was green with a white top. It was about fifteen minutes after midnight. We were headed toward the Fort. The MP vehicle was going south and we were going north. The MP vehicle turned around in the middle of the road and stopped us. The officer got out and came up to the driver side of our vehicle and asked for identification.

I asked the officer it if there was anything wrong. The officer said, "No. We are just looking for a certain individual." The officer was polite and he said we could go. The officer followed us a little way and then turned off the road.

*

Cross Examination of Bobby Hall:

Hall stated he couldn't identify the officer. Defense objected, and asked that Hall's testimony be dismissed.
Judge Collinson overruled Defense's objection.

The Judge asked the witness if the vehicle had a red light on it.

Hall: Yes.

The witness was then excused.

* * *

Testimony of Colonel Robert H. Mosebar:

Colonel Robert H. Mosebar was the Commander of the Fort Leonard Wood Hospital.

> *Mosebar*: I was called in to the Provost Marshal's office about eight p.m. I was told they were bringing in a prisoner. They wanted me to examine the prisoner. I got there before Thornton did.

Mosebar identified Johnny Lee Thornton as the prisoner in question.

> *Mosebar*: Thornton wasn't handcuffed but he was being assisted in, and he was in civilian clothing. Our discussion centered on a headache Thornton said he had. Thornton said the headache was very severe. He said light was bothering him. Thornton had his hands over his eyes.
>
> I completed a medical examination of Thornton. During the examination, I asked him to do certain things, such as rotate his neck, to look at me and a few other movements. I asked about the headache and then examined his eyes — checked the eyes to see if they were working correctly. I found no medical problem with Thornton. He was cooperative and polite.
>
> I knew I was going to see Thornton and that the authorities wanted to know if Thornton was physically and mentally able to answer questions.

* * *

Testimony of Dr. Charles Ottensmeyer:

Dr. Charles Ottensmeyer was staff psychiatrist at the Federal Medical Center for Prisoners in Springfield, Missouri.

> *Ottensmeyer*: I examined Thornton during his stay at the Federal Medical Center. On the night of the murders, Thornton knew he was doing wrong and simply set his

conscience aside. I've examined various medical records statements made by victims and reports from other doctors. I saw some things which could be diagnosable as mental illness, a depressive kind of mood, but no signs of psychosis. Psychosis is defined as a mental disorder sufficient to impair a person's capacity to deal with the ordinary tasks of everyday living.

Exhibit #176 was entered into court evidence — the medical records of Thornton from admission through June 4, 1977.

> *Ottensmeyer*: Overall, Thornton knew what he was doing. He was depressed but was able to take responsibility for his actions.

*

Defense Cross of Dr. Ottensmeyer:

Dr. Ottensmeyer testified he wasn't aware Thornton had any headaches and Thornton wasn't given anything for the pain other than regular aspirin and Tylenol.

* * *

Testimony of Dr. Emry Varhley:

Dr. Emry Varhley was Chief of Psychology at the Federal Medical Center in Springfield, Missouri.

> *Varhley*: I talked to Thornton first on January 16, 1977 — on his first day of admission to the center. We spoke for one hour. I found no evidence of mental illness being displayed.
>
> Thornton's first test at the Medical Center didn't show anything except he was mildly depressed and had a more feminine interest in the world than a masculine interest. Each test Thornton took exaggerated his problems and he gained more insight into how to do this [exaggerate].
>
> Thornton was more depressed and had a tendency to be withdrawn, lonesome, and as time went on, he became more and more nervous. Thornton had the capacity to appreciate the wrongfulness of his acts. I believe he could've conformed his activities to the requirements of the law.

193

* * *

Testimony of Juanita Deckard on Recall:

The prosecution asked Deckard a series of questions:

Prosecution: What was [Thornton's] attitude?

Deckard: He was normal. He asked for our driver's license and was polite.

Prosecution: Was he argumentative or did he display any anger?

Deckard: No.

Prosecution: Was there anything unusual about his conversation or demeanor toward the people in the car?

Deckard: His appearance was clean-cut and everything, just like any other officer. Attitude, polite. Did everything in a normal fashion.

Prosecution: At any time when he was talking to you in the car, were you frightened by his actions?

Deckard: No.

Prosecution: Were you frightened by his tone of voice?

Deckard: No.

Prosecution: Compare his voice then with his voice when you got to the cabin. Did he give directions to you in a higher level? A shout?

Deckard: No.

Prosecution: Was any personal violence threatened toward you?

Deckard: He just told us to talk about things in general.

Prosecution: Did he join in the conversation?

Deckard: All three of us were talking.

Prosecution: Were his answers logical and reasonable?

Deckard: Yes. Everything in his actions and voice stayed about the same. He exhibited no hostility or anger toward us. He maintained the same outward composure without change. He asked our names in the cabin. After we told him, he never called us by any other name.

At the end of the testimony by Juanita Deckard, Defense chose not to cross-examine her and she was released from the stand.

The court was then recessed until 9:00 a.m. the next morning because the next witnesses were not available. They had not yet arrived in town.

13

THE SANITY ISSUE

AS PREVIOUSLY RECOUNTED ON THE opening day of the trial, the defense team representing Johnny Lee Thornton stipulated to all of the criminal counts except kidnapping. Their reasoning for leaving one charge open was to keep the trial going.

In the words of Defense Attorney, David Freeman, "We wanted to get down to the real issue in this case: the sanity issue." And so, Defense began their most critical part of the trial.

* * *

Testimony of Dr. William F. Clary for Defense:

Dr. William F. Clary, was a Psychiatrist from Springfield, Missouri. After a long examination of Dr. Clary's professional credentials and qualifications, they addressed questions to Dr. Clary.

> *Clary*: I examined Johnny Lee Thornton on January 26, 1977, to determine if he'd need to be examined in much greater detail—in order to arrive at a diagnosis. I met with Thornton for one hour and then recommended additional studies. I wrote a letter to Thornton's attorney and said [Thornton] needed more time. It was granted. The next time I saw Thornton was on March 10, 1977. I saw him again on March 29, 1977, and again on April 11, 1977. I saw Thornton for about eight or nine hours in total.
>
> I asked Thornton to take some tests. Thornton refused at first but then later agreed to take them. I set up the test.

Dr. Clary described the test to the jury as the use of a truth serum plus hypnosis:

Clary: At first, Thornton didn't want to do this but then last Thursday and Friday he agreed. I'd seen him one or two hours on Thursday and six-and-a-half hours on Friday. The test was done.

I got an extensive history from Patti by telephone. I completed a series of tapes with Thornton for many hours in two interviews. In addition, medical tests were run on Thornton that showed no problem of an organic cause.

We also got medical history from Thornton himself.[1]

Thornton had been accused of having sexual relations with his half-sister. He denied this but he admitted to being unfaithful to Patti while she was in the hospital. Thornton gave the same basic description as Patti had done about the pillow fight where he tried to smother her and didn't remember it when it was over. Thornton told me that when he was little he was being left alone while his mother was a barmaid and his real father threatened to kill him. He'd witnessed sexual relations between his mother and other men. Thornton wasn't completely blank about the crime. [Thornton] came out of the dreamy feeling of hypnosis in the first interview and he said he knew he did [the crimes]. He didn't remember doing some of the things but he did remember stopping the car.

Thornton told me he had difficulty remembering details of the event. The girls represented his wife and his mother. The boys were the men who took his wife and mother away from him or were having relations with them. Thornton's love for his wife Patti was more like the love a toddler has for his mother.

While Thornton was living with Betty, she triggered a relationship memory. He remembered crying in bed with his brother when they were little and their mother was gone.

People with Borderline Personality Disorder dwell on their inner worries of rejection by mother and cruel fathers and not on the facts of present life. Betty triggered what Thornton remembered about his mother. John said, "It made me sick inside." The court case came later, with early childhood memories presented by his mother and the men she found and Patti and the men she found.

Following this bit of testimony, court was recessed until 9:00 a.m. Saturday morning.

---

1 It was basically the same Patti had said in her deposition.

*

On July 23, 1977, the court was back in session. Dr. William Clary was again on the stand talking about his second interview on March 10, 1977, where Thornton had expressed anger at the doctor at the Medical Center in Springfield, Missouri.

> *Clary*: Thornton seemed different. On the first session, Thornton acted as if he was a person. During the second session, he was more interested. Thornton commented he had more feelings. He wanted to know why after he'd done [the crimes], he felt more whole.
>
> Thornton was depressed at first. He stated something snapped when he was with Betty. He was afraid later, afraid of losing his mind. He said, "sometimes I cry, I have never cried before."
>
> Thornton wasn't as vague as before but said he couldn't see the girls. He was afraid of women, afraid he would hit his mother. Thornton said he thought of suicide after Patti left in the fall. This is a common characteristic of his disorder. At the age of fifteen months, a child is able to feel love and warmth. But he isn't capable of feeling remorse. The barriers broke down the isolation wall. This created an identity; a split personality.

Dr. Clary then moved on to the March 29, 1977, session, where Thornton stated he couldn't remember anymore.

> *Clary*: Thornton began looking more withdrawn and confused. Once again, the girls were his mother and, at the same time, he said he was afraid of his guards. He was trying to understand all of it. Thornton said, "I'm tired of everything. Everything is confusion. What would be so bad about dying?"
>
> Thornton felt like a loner. He was closing up. He became more of a paranoid person. Thornton was afraid of women — of them killing him with a knife. He had dreams of this since his last visit. I feel Thornton suffers from Borderline Personality Disorder. In his age, this person was a very poor — just a stick figure. Thornton suffers from acute feelings of loneliness and felt empty.
>
> *Defense*: In your opinion, Dr. Clary, is Thornton competent to stand trial?
>
> *Clary*: I think he can. He understood what he was doing at the time of the murders. I feel Thornton had the

capacity to understand it was wrong but didn't feel he could control his emotions.

Thornton had no premeditation. This was a chance thing which happened. His dual personality took over and if that car hadn't come along at that time, Thornton would've gone back to the barracks and the victims would be alive today.

Thornton was a lonely, rejected child who was unable to develop normal, human relationships. All of Thornton suppressed childhood anxieties surfaced late last year after his wife left him and he moved in with a female soldier on Fort Leonard Wood. When he's in the room, he's not engaged with you. He's talking to himself. There's a lack of commitment to his fellow man. The reason for this is Thornton's belief that if you don't share love, they can't hurt you.

The closest relationship Thornton probably ever achieved was with his wife Patti Jean Thornton. He latched on to Patti like a shark. But Thornton's love for his wife wasn't a normal type of love. It's like the love a toddler has for its mother. Thornton's mother was a bartender who left him alone for long periods of time and was involved with many other men. She was divorced from his real father. Thornton's mother told him his real father would often try to kill him.

The episode which probably triggered Thornton's psychotic behavior was a love affair he'd had with a female soldier who was stationed at Fort Leonard Wood. The female soldier was a divorced mother of a six-year-old boy. She reminded Thornton of his mother. The boy reminded Thornton of himself. The affair dredged up humiliation from Thornton's past which led to his outburst. Thornton had told me, "Something snapped" when Thornton watched the female soldier discipline her son. His personality is tied up in his innards with memories of his mother and his past. You do that to avoid confronting people.

Following a short recess, large-screen TVs were brought into the room. Dr. Clary played video tapes of his sessions with Johnny Lee Thornton. Thornton was alleged to be under hypnosis at the time.

Dr. Clary explained to the jury what the jurors were watching on the videotapes. According to Dr. Clary, Johnny Lee

Thornton had been given a drug commonly known as "the truth serum." While under the influence of that drug and under hypnosis, Johnny Lee Thornton's inner, suppressed personality came forward and could be shown to the jury.

> *Clary*: Thornton has a suppressed personality named "John" who is absolutely ruthless. Sadistic, with no conscience or scruples. Self-centered. Exhibitionist. Grandiose — The kinds of things we associate with small children. Then there is a dominant personality, named "Johnny" who is the Thornton everyone knew — a polite, efficient, rather withdrawn, military policeman. My use of hypnosis allowed me to bring out the suppressed personality of "John" to the forefront for examination. John bragged on the videotape how he conned Johnny into killing the three teenagers on Fort Leonard Wood.

The jury watched the tape, which showed a sobbing Thornton lying on a couch responding to questions from Dr. Clary. During these video sessions, individual incidents and thoughts came to the forefront. Dr. Clary explained these incidents to the jury as a form of schizophrenia.

In a comment, Defense Attorney David Freeman said such schizophrenia was, "Every bit as disabling, every bit as crippling, every bit as killing as cancer itself."

In one videoed incident, a sobbing Thornton lies on the couch and recalled stopping a car containing two guys and two girls on a road on the Army base. In a confused scenario, Thornton repeatedly jumped back and forth from the scene on the road to talking about his wife, Patti Jean Thornton.

> *Thornton*: Patti loves me. She wants to come back. Patti needs to be hurt. She enjoys it. I know she does.

As explanation, Dr. Clary said Thornton was unaware of whom he was killing:

> *Clary*: Thornton felt he was killing the men who took away Patti and his mother. He felt he was in the car with Patti and his mother.

Under hypnosis, Thornton recalled one of the youths in the car had called Thornton an obscene name. He recalls seeing Patti in the car along with his mother, although he appeared confused.

> *Thornton*: Something isn't right. They aren't supposed to hurt me anymore. Patti told me she wouldn't let me get hurt anymore. I can see her looking out the window. I got to do something. Patti and mom are going to get mad they can really hurt me when they get mad.

Dr. Clary told the jury that during Thornton's imprisonment, Thornton told the doctor of a dream he had in which he feared he might be killed by women. In the dream, the women were stabbing [Thornton].

At another point in the tape:

> *Thornton*: I'm not going to hurt them. I'm not going to hurt anybody. Get back in your car and leave me alone.

However, Thornton got upset when Dr. Clary suggests perhaps Patti and his mother will hurt Thornton. Or, the boys will take Patti and his mother away from Thornton.

Thornton's videotaped recollection shifted back to the roadside stop, just after Thornton shot the two boys in his military police vehicle's back seat. As he got back into the vehicle, still holding his firearm in his hand, John said Johnny almost shot himself.

> *Clary*: Part of Thornton's personality was a vicious and hostile personality. This personality known as John took over Thornton's behavior on the morning of January 13th. Under hypnosis, I brought John to the surface and submerged Johnny.
>
> *Thornton as John*: When Johnny sat down, for a fraction of a second Johnny almost shot him and me.

In one section of the tape shown to the jury, John told Dr. Clary how he used images of Thornton's mom and Patti to confuse Johnny.

> *Thornton as John*: He was so confused, a two-year-old kid could've knocked him over. (laughing) I told Johnny the boys in the car had come to take mom and Patti away.

The sadistic-part personality told the confused, real personality to handcuff the boys.

> *Thornton as Johnny*: Please go away. I want to have peace.

John said Johnny drew his .45 caliber pistol and forced the boys into the back seat of the Scout.

> *Thornton as John*: I couldn't get Johnny to draw the weapon. Johnny, as you call him, didn't even know he was holding the pistol.
>
> *Clary*: How are you going to stop them, John?
>
> *Thornton as John*: I'm going to shoot them.

The newspapers reported that during the replay of the tape, Thornton (who had normally sat rigid and impassive throughout the trial at the defense table) buried his head in his hands.

*

> *Clary*: I don't believe Thornton is capable of remorse. He never fully developed his consciousness because his inner personality wasn't aware of what his body was doing. His inner personality is absolutely ruthless and sadistic. He knew the wrongfulness of his acts but was unable to conform to the law.
>
> Thornton once contemplated suicide when his estranged wife left him. Thornton wasn't the kind of depressive person capable of carrying out that act. I don't believe he planned any violence when he went on duty at the Fort on the night of January 12th. But when the carload of teenagers arrived about twelve-thirty a.m., it started a chain of events which triggered a psychotic spell.
>
> If that car hadn't come along at that time, none of us would be here today. It's a chance thing that happened. And if that aspect of Johnny's personality hadn't taken over and become the operator, Johnny Thornton probably would've gone back to the barracks.

Under cross-examination by Prosecution, Dr. Clary told the jury (composed of eight women and four men) it was possible but unlikely Thornton was play-acting while under hypnosis.

* * *

Testimony of Dr. Spiegel for Prosecution:

The trial moved to the testimony of Prosecution's hired psychiatrist to rebut Defense's testimony of Dr. Clary. This prosecution star witness was Dr. Herbert Spiegel — who was associated with Columbia University in New York. Following a lengthy examination of his professional medical qualifications, Dr. Spiegel testified as to his examination of Johnny Lee Thornton.

> *Spiegel*: I gave Thornton two tests. The test revealed that on a scale of from zero to ten, with ten being the most hypnotizable person, Johnny Lee Thornton scored a five. That means he just barely enters into the zone of the capacity for concentrating in the hypnotic at a hypnotic level. It's as if he has one foot in and one foot out of the zone.
>
> I gave Thornton a second test, which is a personality cluster survey test. This test is simply a pretest used to clarify — or to rule out — certain extreme diagnoses. This is the test given to Thornton.

Prosecution Exhibit #181 was admitted as evidence — the results of this particular test.

> *Spiegel*: The second test wasn't an absolute test, but it was a tentative way of giving me some clues as to what else to look for if I got information these conditions were present.
>
> *Prosecution*: Dr. Spiegel, have you viewed the tapes of Thornton being under hypnosis?
>
> *Spiegel*: I have indeed viewed those tapes.

Prosecution took Spiegel through a series of questions to determine exactly how a person under hypnosis should be videotaped. Dr. Spiegel was explicit in his statement as to the proper procedure which should be used in such an examination. Dr. Spiegel was asked about the medications Thornton had been given prior to being videotaped and under hypnosis.

> *Prosecution*: Do you recall what the dosage was?
>
> *Spiegel*: Yes, I was told he was given, prior to that [hypnosis session], ten milligrams of Dexedrine, two-hundred-twenty-five milligrams of Sodium Amytal intravenously, and twenty-five milligrams of ephedrine.
>
> *Prosecution*: What?

Spiegel: Ephedrine, which I assume is ephedrine sulfate, is just a drug to take care of — It's a precaution to take care of too much salivation which may occur by using the drug.

Prosecution: Now, assuming the dosage had been given to Mr. Thornton. What would you believe his state of mind to be when that drug was fully operative on his mind?

Spiegel: I would expect him to get drowsy, and sleepy, and groggy, almost... something like getting drunk without too many alcoholic drinks.

Prosecution: Would it increase or decrease his hypnotizability?

Spiegel: It would decrease, clearly, his hypnotizability.

Prosecution: Now, Doctor, when you saw him, he wasn't under any medication so far as you know?

Spiegel: When I saw him, to my knowledge, he wasn't under any medication nor did he appear to me to be medicated.

Prosecution: So, if he scored a five, I believe you said at that time, his scale would go down as far as hypnotizability would be concerned?

Spiegel: I would expect it to go down to something like two or one under the handicap of such heavy medication.

Prosecution: All right, Doctor. Now, as you viewed the first tape, what were your impressions as to the technique used to attempt to induce a hypnotic state [in Thornton]?

Spiegel: I was surprised and disappointed to see. This was, in fact, not a way to induce a hypnotic state.

Prosecution: Let me advise you, Doctor Clary testified in this courtroom he didn't pretest Mr. Thornton prior to the time he started the interview.

Spiegel: Yes, sir.

Prosecution: I don't know whether you're aware of that or not, but it's been a fact established in this court. But Doctor Clary's testimony, now with that knowledge of what you saw in the videotape, would you describe why you were shocked?

Spiegel: I think I said I was surprised and disappointed.

Prosecution: All right. Surprised and disappointed. Why were you surprised and disappointed?

Spiegel: Because I thought I would be viewing an interview of a man who was in a trance-state, designed to uncover his memory recall of what happened at a specific time in the past. And instead, what I saw was a man who was handicapped by a sleeping medication — a barbiturate, which makes his memory groggy more then it ordinarily is — and there was a ceremonial statement "this was hypnosis" when, in fact, there was no test evidence whatsoever he'd been in a trance state. In other words, it's one thing to go through a ceremony of saying, "this is hypnosis," but it's another thing to test out to see if it's, in fact, the phenomenon you're looking for there.

Following additional question and answers by Dr. Spiegel as to his review of the videotapes completed by Dr. Clary on Johnny Lee Thornton, Prosecution asked the tough question:

Prosecution: Doctor Spiegel, have you been able to form an opinion on whether or not Johnny Lee Thornton was in fact in a hypnotic state?

Spiegel: My opinion is, and was then, he wasn't in a hypnotic state.

Prosecution moved on to an examination of the factors involved in the second tape Dr. Clary had completed on Johnny Lee Thornton.

Prosecution: Doctor Spiegel, have you viewed the tape?

Spiegel: I have.

Prosecution: What's your impression of the procedures involved in the production of that tape?

Spiegel: Well, I didn't get all of the sequences. And I don't know what happened in-between the taping. But the segments I saw at a later time suggested there was a cozy understanding, now that the defendant had picked up that if he now accepts the premise that there are two people, there is a "bad me" and a "good me," and if I can now blame my behavior I don't want to account for on the bad me, I am now free to talk. And I had the impression the defendant had the... he accepted the instructions.

Following a series of objections by Defense, and further clarification that Dr. Spiegel was testifying as an expert on the technique of hypnosis and of how you use hypnosis, he was then allowed continue.

> *Spiegel*:   And the ceremony, the charade of going through the motion of, "Now you're in a trance"—because as I witnessed Doctor Clary encouraging him…and as a doctor, I think it was very appropriate he encouraged him to "do your best." Now, you have this "bad" Johnny doing this — if he accepts that premise, he's now free to state anything at all that he did as long as he can use this as a shield, hopefully to for exoneration. So, rather than seeing this as a testable state of hypnosis — they use the word hypnosis — went through the motions of calling hypnosis, when, in fact, it was making…going through a game, in which, I suspected the subject was, anyway, using his guile to let all this out under the shield of that, "This is that bad me in me."

Later in Dr. Spiegel's testimony, Prosecution had another question-and-answer session:

> *Prosecution*:   All right. What other appearances did you consider to be important in your determination?

> *Spiegel*:   Well, then, this is something about the technique of the inquiry which I felt violate any rules to find out. If there was indeed any memory trying to be tapped which could be brought out, he was instead being told… taught what to state. For example, Doctor Clary at one point said, "You don't want to hurt him, do you John?" Now, that is a total violation of an adequate interrogation technique if you want to find out what is in the reservoir of information available. At another point, he said, "You don't want your mom or dad to see how weak you are and laugh at you?" That's not an admonition or advice you give somebody you're trying to elicit information from. But it is an adequate way of coaching somebody to take on a roll of pretending to have two kinds of mes, a good me and a bad me.

> *Spiegel*:   On another place [on the tape], I heard Doctor Clary say, "Now, that John is a weak, dumb guy. He thinks he can beat you. He's dumb. He's a weak sister. And he will be locked up for that." At another point Doctor Clary said, "He'd like to have me destroy you but I won't." Now, that kind of comfortable liaison between the doctor and patient this way is, in a way, coaching

him to say, "Well, if this is an acceptable way for me to say all this and hide behind the shield that I have two mes, it's a game I'd like to play."

In another telling segment, Prosecution questioned Dr. Spiegel as to how many people he'd hypnotized over the years who could reach the scale of ten. Dr. Spiegel testified there were only ten or eleven people he'd found in his thirty seven-year psychiatric career who reached ten on the ten scale.

A short time later during Dr. Spiegel's testimony, Prosecution asked him the following question:

Prosecution: Now Doctor, in the opening statement made by Mr. Freeman at the beginning of Defense's case, he likened Mr. Thornton — or referred to him as being similar to *Sybil* and the *Three Faces of Eve*. Are you familiar—

Defense objected. The court overruled the objection and allowed the questioning to continue.

Prosecution: Are you familiar with the case known as *Sybil*?"

Spiegel: Yes, I am.

Prosecution: In what way, sir?"

Spiegel: I was a consultant on that case. Doctor Wilber was the therapist who treated the case. And on several occasions, I served as her consultant. During the times when Sybil was very disturbed and Doctor Wilber had to leave town, I took over. I took care of Sybil during those periods but my more important contact with her was when she was one of our research subjects. We did a great deal of work with her in a research lab. We used her as a teaching case at our course at Columbia University.

Prosecution: Was she one of the ten or eleven individuals you have seen who had dual personality?

Spiegel: Yes, sir.

Prosecution: And what did she score on the scale?

Spiegel: Ten.

Prosecution: Did you ever place her under hypnotic state?

Spiegel: Several times.

Later in Dr. Spiegel's testimony, Prosecution asked him a series of questions as to his opinion of the possibility Johnny Lee Thornton was indeed a person with a dual personality.

Prosecution: And do you have an opinion as to whether or not the examination legitimately developed and showed a dual personality of Johnny Thornton?

Spiegel: I have an opinion on that.

Prosecution: And what is your opinion?

Spiegel: I think he didn't demonstrate at all anything like a dual personality. But instead, he demonstrated a compliance to a charade which went on between the doctor and the patient, in which he picked up his cues and accepted this as a con, in a way, to act as if he was two different people — to use that as this portrayal — as a shield to hide behind to win exoneration.

Prosecution: What was it in those tapes you saw which caused you to form that opinion, if you could tell the jury?

Spiegel: Well, number one, he...they gave him a drug which interfered with whatever capacity he had for hypnosis. Number two, I tested beforehand, and because he scored a five on a zero to ten scale, even if he'd not been given the drug, he couldn't possibly have had those characteristics of a highly hypnotizable person. And, number three, the answers about his dual – this, the two people who were, in response to coaching persuasion and the way in which the questions were put to him, rather than a spontaneous discovery he was — had these two different personalities.

Prosecution: Did you see any similarity at all between the responses of Johnny Thornton, the responses of other persons you have found to be people with dual or multiple personalities?

Spiegel: Not only were there no similarities, but, if anything, was what struck me the contrast.

Prosecution: And, would you describe the contrast?

Spiegel: The contrast was he showed no evidence of being in trance. He showed no evidence of living this in the present tense. And he didn't have spontaneity of being with the regressed state and disassociating from the here and now. For example, in one scene the phone rings in the room and he stops talking while Doctor Clary answered the phone. Now, a person who is deeply lost in a trance state and regressed to a scene he is uncovering would be inattentive to a phone call.

Prosecution: All right, sir. Do you have an opinion as to whether or not — from your examination of Johnny Thornton and considering the portions of the tape which you saw — whether or not Johnny Thornton does, in fact, have a dual, or multiple personality?

Spiegel: I have such an opinion.

Prosecution: And what is your opinion?

Spiegel: He does not have a dual personality.

Dr. Spiegel's testimony continued for some time but by this point he'd already rebutted virtually everything Dr. Clary had presented to the jury. Thus, the jury had been shown both sides of the sanity issue.

Dr. Spiegel was dismissed from the witness stand.

* * *

Defense Testimony of Dr. Fleischer from Topeka, Kansas:

Defense witness Fleischer testified he examined Johnny Lee Thornton. He stated he saw Thornton for an hour on 24 January, and the next day gave Thornton a test for some two or three hours. Fleischer's opinion was that Thornton had a personality with borderline personality on competency but not on responsibility.

Prosecution objected to this witness on the grounds Fleischer wasn't qualified to express his opinion on the matter. The court sustained the objection and Dr. Fleischer was dismissed as a witness.

The court recessed until 1:15 p.m.

* * *

Closing Arguments:

Upon returning to the courtroom, the jury prepared to hear closing arguments. Each side was given 45 minutes to address the jury.

Unfortunately, the closing arguments were not recorded. Marjorie Bates had minimal remarks in her transcribed trial notes. The newspapers of the day reported little about what was said by either side. The main comments in the news article were to the effect that during closing arguments, both sides bashed the other side's case.

Prosecution gave a summary of the case: the shots fired; the people killed; the violations committed; the attempts to cover up the crimes. They reiterated the plethora evidence which pointed to the guilt of Johnny Lee Thornton. Prosecution also brought up the number of vehicle stops made by Thornton prior to his stopping of the Bates' vehicle, with the argument Thornton was hunting for his victims.

Defense used their closing argument time to blast the testimony of Dr. Herbert Spiegel. Lead defense attorney, David Freeman did his best to discredit Spiegel's testimony. He told the jury Spiegel was paid $1500 per day, plus expenses, to testify.

Concerning Spiegel, Freeman said, "He got the call and the price was right, so the hired gun showed. Spiegel is a hired gun who is willing to emerge from his ivory tower at Columbia University in New York to testify in any courtroom where he could collect his fifteen hundred-dollars-a-day fee as an expert witness."

Freeman was particularly upset Spiegel gave his damaging testimony after spending only fifteen minutes with Thornton.

*

Prosecution rebutted the arguments of Freeman.

The lead prosecutor was J. Whitfield Moody.

> *Prosecutor*: There had been no attempt to tamper with justice by paying such a sum. Mr. Freeman doesn't tell you how you're supposed to convict one John and set one free. He just wants you to set them both free.

I remind the jury that Thornton had checked out two pairs of handcuffs on the night of the slayings. Thornton said he was going to play "super cop" and he filed a false report of shooting wild dogs to account for the use of the bullets from his gun.

Following the closing arguments, the court recessed.

* * *

When the court was called back into session, Judge Collinson gave instructions to the jury on the conduct of their deliberations. The case rested in the hands of the jury as they retired for deliberations.

* * *

The jury deliberated from 3:45 p.m. until 6:05 p.m.—a total of two hours and 20 minutes. They returned with a guilty verdict on all four counts.

The news media reported that as the verdict was read, Thornton sat motionless with downcast eyes. His parents, Mr. and Mrs. Bruce Thornton refused to comment as they left the courtroom. The news media reported the jurors themselves made no comments but noted four of the female jurors were in tears as they exited the courtroom.

Due to the speed with which the jury returned their verdict, several members of the victims' families were not present in the courtroom when the verdict was read.

Marjorie Bates: I'm relieved but not surprised by the verdict.

I had a lot of thoughts — a lot of different emotions went through my mind as I watched the trial. He took my son's life. He did more than just take my son's life. [The verdict] wasn't unfair.

Defense Attorney, David Freeman said he would file a motion for a retrial within thirty days. "I don't think the verdict would have been different without testimony from Prosecution star witness, Dr. Herbert Spiegel of Columbia University in New York. The jury's verdict didn't stem from the testimony by Spiegel but from the passions invoked by the crimes themselves."

Prosecution Attorney J. Whitfield Moody said the introduction of videotapes during the trial showing the defendant being interviewed by his psychiatrist was, "Unusual in my experience. The way they conducted those interviews left a lot to be desired. Once the jurors got by the issue of the defendant's sanity, I think the case was pretty well settled."

* * *

One final step in the legal process was the pronouncement of sentence upon Johnny Lee Thornton. According to the United States Assistant Attorney, David Jones, this particular court hearing was delayed for at least a month as there were a number of presentence procedures which needed to be completed. He stated the maximum penalty for Thornton's crimes would be life imprisonment.

News reports quoted Judge Collinson as saying, "Under federal law, Thornton will become eligible for parole in ten years or less. To be clear, this case will be reviewed for parole. Not that Thornton will get parole."

On August 31, 1977, Thornton's attorneys filed a motion requesting a directed acquittal by the judge or a retrial based on their arguments that not all of the witnesses in this case had been heard at the trial.

On September 9, 1977, Judge Collinson denied the motions and proceeded with Thornton's sentencing. On count one — the murder of Wesley Hawkins, Thornton was sentenced to life imprisonment. On count two — the assault on Tony Bates, Thornton was sentenced to twenty years in prison. On count three — the rape of Linda Needham, Thornton was sentenced to life in prison. On count four — the kidnapping the four victims for the purpose of rape, Thornton was sentenced to life in prison. Judge Collinson ordered all sentences to be served consecutively.

And with this final hearing, the criminal case against Johnny Lee Thornton came to an end.

At the time this book was completed, Johnny Lee Thornton was register #23293-175 at the United States Penitentiary in Tucson, Arizona, where his release date is listed as "LIFE."

* * *

FBI Agent, Tom Den Ouden:

Because of this case, the Thornton case, I went back to the FBI
Academy for an in-service training. This was right after the
Thornton case, before the trial, so the trial was coming up very
soon. The murder occurred in January and Spiegel didn't come
in until the trial at Council Bluffs. I have no recollection of him
ever coming to Springfield. It was after the competency hearings.

I didn't realize the magnitude of the case, at that point where
it was going in the trial and the preparation for it, and all those
other things. And of course, Bill [Castleberry] did a really wonderful job, as the agent needed to pull it all together, working
with the CID, and so on. He was ready for the trial.

Doctor Spiegel wasn't in Springfield for the hypnosis thing.
We didn't know what was going on with Defense. They don't
have to tell you what's going to happen until the day before the
trial, whereas we had to make known our witnesses. And Spiegel wasn't on the list because we'd not seen video of Thornton
under hypnosis. But when we did see it… and I was there. I said
right there, "Something's wrong here." So, we flew Spiegel
in first-class, and he made a lot of phone calls, and all of his
expenses were paid for. But he did a wonderful job. He really
helped us out.

The reason we got Spiegel was because the trial was in Council
Bluffs and Defense decided they were going to play this tape —
which had been made at the Medical Center in Springfield by
his attorneys and Doctor Clary. Clary was a doctor. He wasn't
a defense attorney. He was a psychiatrist. I don't know what
his background was or the qualifications he had, but Doctor
Clary decided to put [Thornton] under hypnosis, and through
this method find out if he had any recollection of what he really
did to determine whether or not he had the intent, and had any
plan, or had a motive for those kinds of things. And Thornton
agreed to that. We didn't know anything about that going on
until we got to Council Bluffs, Iowa. And then we got to review
the video they took it before the trial, all right.

I had been to the FBI Academy in Quantico (months before the actual trial) and I took this case along — when I was at Quantico — to discuss violent crime on government reservations. And they had a case they discussed from Ann Arbor, Michigan. It was a serial death case. Murder in the hospital and, I forget how many patients had died. But there were some who survived.

So, they put these patients under hypnosis. And Doctor Spiegel was the man, the psychiatrist, who cooperated with the FBI and helped put these patients who survived under hypnosis and talk to them. And they asked them questions and there were several [patients] who said the last thing they remembered before they lost consciousness were the nurses — Filipino nurses —there were two of them in this case. The investigators began to think they must've done something to these patients. I don't know how [the nurses] got the medicine or the chemicals to [the patients] but [the patients] lost consciousness and some of them died.

The same thing happened here in Columbia, Missouri with a nurse named [name redacted]. And so, we were at Quantico Virginia at the FBI Academy and they're discussing this case and how much Spiegel had helped them with regard to hypnosis and really identified the two Filipino nurse suspects who were doing this. They charged the nurses. And it was going to trial. And the defense attorneys brought up an issue that the evidence collected under hypnosis was probably not admissible. Their contention was because of — and I had never heard of this before — post hypnotic suggestion. So, whoever interviewed these people under hypnosis may have suggested that, "Did you remember these Filipino nurses? And can you tell us anymore?" I don't know what these interviews were all about or how much detail but they threw it out because of the post hypnotic suggestion and the two Filipino nurses went free.

When we saw the video of Thornton under hypnosis, I had just come from Quantico — not too long before — and I detected he was really not under hypnosis. Because once, when the door opened and somebody came into the room, which they probably shouldn't have, [Thornton] stopped talking. And another time the phone rang and [Thornton] stopped talking. Now, I didn't think he was really under hypnosis from the limited knowledge I had about what patients are like — what men and women are like under hypnosis — so, I told the prosecutors about Doctor Spiegel and his cooperation with the FBI.

[Spiegel] was probably the foremost psychiatrist in United States with regard to hypnosis. And it all had to do with an examination of eye roll. He would have these patients roll their eyes back as far as they could and he would measure how much white there was after they rolled their pupils up high. This was his test. And he said with regard to Thornton on a scale of one to ten, with ten being the most hypnotizable, Thornton was a two. He wasn't under hypnosis at all! Thornton was just playing along with Doctor Clary.

It looked like a great defense because people had watched *The Three Faces of Eve* and they knew about multiple personalities. But never — and this is what I learned in Quantico — a person who has multiple personalities will never do anything in their unknown self they wouldn't do in their known self. So, that's not a defense.

If they do it in their known self, yeah, then they might do it in their unknown self. But you can't separate those two. And, say this is the bad person. This is the "bad" Johnny. And when he's in that frame of mind and in that personality, yeah, he can do anything. He has no control or anything else and that's where the insanity defense was.

Three or four years later — or longer [after the trial was over], I'm talking to someone who is familiar with the Medical Center. And he said, "Oh, Doctor Clary had a thing about multiple personalities. He thought everybody had them." That was his real deal. He was supposed to be the expert on it, so he pushed it and that's what he did in this case. He was going to use multiple personalities with Johnny Lee Thornton so [Thornton] wasn't responsible for what he did at Fort Leonard Wood that night. Because he'd somehow slipped into this other personality.

Well, the prosecutors were very interested in that. They flew Doctor Spiegel in — and he examined Johnny Lee Thornton before [Spiegel's] testimony.

I believe he gave [Thornton] that test, and talked to [Thornton], and looked at the charts and what the testimony was... and the video. When he took the stand, he blasted Defense. He said [Thornton] was just doing what you wanted him to do when you talked to him. And that [Thornton] wasn't under hypnosis at all. And so, the papers came out the next day and called him the hired gun from the east — Doctor Spiegel, who cooperated with the FBI, and testified on behalf of the US Attorneys, and shot down the defense. So, that's why Bill [Castleberry] said that was monumental with regard to the trial and the defense of insanity.

* * *

FBI Agent, Bill Castleberry:

Their entire defense was that there was a good Johnny and the bad Johnny. And they had their psychiatrist there, Doctor Clary from Springfield who had been hired by the defense [team]. He says he hypnotized Johnny and he found a good Johnny and a bad Johnny... and we had our guy, who was the Godfather of Hypnosis, Spiegel.

Defense didn't realize who we had. And when Prosecution asked the question, "Doctor, are you familiar with multiple personalities like *The Three Faces of Eve*?" Doctor Spiegel's answer was, "Yes, she is my patient." That kind of destroyed the defense because [Spiegel] was saying Johnny Lee Thornton couldn't be hypnotized. And there was kind of funny sidelight when the judge asked from the bench, "Is it true you can be hypnotized to quit smoking?"

I looked at the jury several times during the trial and they were always attentive. They were wrapped up in the case. And they believed the government's witnesses. Of course, it was a short trial because they stipulated to everything. During the trial, Thornton's state of mind was the focus of Prosecution's efforts.

* * *

News Media Comments

At the conclusion of Johnny Lee Thornton's trial, the news media weighed in with their thoughts. From an editorial contained in the Sunday edition of *The News Leader* newspaper from Springfield, Missouri:

Still questions...

Johnny Lee Thornton can't possibly deserve a lighter sentence than he will get, whatever it is he gets.

Thornton got as fair a shake from the rest of us as we could give. We did our best to provide them with a jury of his peers... no small task to find a panel able and willing to give him a cool hearing of the evidence. He had his trial hundreds of miles from the scene of his crime, which was the murder of three Ozark teenagers and the attempted slaying of a fourth.

We can't remember the last time we commented on the court case. It's our policy to refrain from commenting because it says so many things — mostly good — about justice in the US.

We didn't consider Thornton guilty of a crime until the jury said he is guilty. The presumption of innocence, so familiar, is a fundamental part of our obligation to Thornton and to ourselves. But neither have we shed a tear for Thornton — not one, no, not one, perhaps we should be able to do so. We cannot of the available punishments (death isn't among them, government officials say); none strikes us as too harsh for the crime.

What about appeals? No doubt, there will be appeals. But we put little stock in them. United States District Judge, William Collinson appears to have run a trial as neat as a pin. Certainly, his allowance of videotape sessions of Thornton under asserted hypnosis gave Defense a clear, open shot at presenting its evidence. And the cornerstone of the defense — that a dark personality within Thornton did the deeds was a question of fact, classically, a question for the jury. The jury decided the evidence was otherwise, beyond a reasonable doubt. The essence of a fair trial seems to have been had. It is the kind of verdict we hope to see vindicated on appeal.

This case raises two questions we find distressing. First, how in the name of sense is there a hole in the federal statutes which could allow Thornton — the admission of his own lawyers a starkly clear and chillingly present danger to others — to go entirely free on acquittal? Granted, military and state authorities probably could've come up with something to keep Thornton off the streets, had he been found innocent by reason of insanity. But that is a thin reed upon which to lean. Surely, this area of the federal criminal law deserves study.

Finally, how was it that a man like Thornton came to be commissioned by the United States Army as a military policeman? He was provided by the military with his gun, his handcuffs, his [vehicle], and his badge of authority. If there is a psychological screening program for military policeman, surely it, too, merits a searching scrutiny.

* * *

Federal Criminal Charges

Johnny Lee Thornton was convicted on all of the federal criminal charges filed against him. But not all of the federal criminal law violations he committed were filed in federal court. For the Plato community, the question was, "Why?"

The answer? There were many perceived legal problems the United States Attorney would have to face for a successful prosecution of Thornton on those violations.

In any successful criminal case, Prosecution must first determine if, and then later prove, that the court in question has complete jurisdiction over the lands upon which the crimes have been committed.

In the Thornton case, questions quickly arose as to whether or not the United States Government had been fully granted such jurisdiction by the state of Missouri over certain parcels of land acquired from the United States Forest Service and the State of Missouri. These were parcels of land where Thornton committed several of his most horrific crimes.

Johnny Lee Thornton
Courtesy Gatehouse Media,
Daily Guide

However, there was no question as to the land status of locations where Thornton had committed other crimes and, as a result, the United States Attorney presented several, very carefully chosen, specific crimes to a federal grand jury in Kansas City.

The following criminal charges were filed against Thornton:

- Count one: Murder of Wesley Hawkins, Title 18 United States Code (USC) section 1111.
- Count two: Assault with intent to murder for the shooting of Tony Bates under Title 18 USC section 113(a).

- Count three: Rape of Linda Needham under Title 18 USC section 2031.
- Count four: Unlawfully seize, confine, kidnap, and did hold persons for purpose of committing rape under Title 18 USC section 1201.

All of these criminal violations were fully committed on lands the United States Attorney felt he could convict under because the United States Federal Court did have proper jurisdiction over such lands. Three of the charges filed were capital offenses, which means the penalty could be life in prison or a death penalty. The remaining serious charges (such as the actual murder of Tony Bates and Linda Needham) had been committed on lands which may or may not have been under the jurisdiction of the United States Court. Thus, the initial charges filed were limited by the special circumstances of the case.

There were several reasons for this. The case was investigated by the Federal Bureau of Investigation and their proper destination for action on criminal charges was the federal court system. There was also a possible question of double jeopardy as to the charges.

Under the United States Constitution, during a criminal proceeding a person may only be placed in jeopardy one time. Such jeopardy usually attaches when a defendant has been placed in front of a jury and the trial has commenced. The question of double jeopardy as it pertained to Thornton had many twists and turns, and was complex in nature.

One significant concern was, if Thornton had been convicted of an offense on the jurisdictionally questioned lands, and the convictions were later dismissed on appeal (for lack of proper jurisdiction), would double jeopardy attach to Thornton and prevent him from ever being tried for those crimes again?

This was a crucial matter for Prosecution. The United States Attorney's Office was determined to prosecute. They had no intention of losing the case for any reason. But to a large degree, as attorneys like to say, this was a moot point as Thornton was also subject to a court-martial by the United

States Army on any unresolved charges, regardless where the offenses were committed.

Throughout the investigation, the FBI and the United States Army Criminal Investigation Command unit worked the case side-by-side. The Army was in a position to step into the case at any time and place Thornton in front of a military court.

In view of the double prosecution possibility, on Feb. 4, 1977, The United States Attorney for the Western District of Missouri, Bert C. Hurn, sent a letter to the Staff Judge Advocate at Fort Wood. Hurn requested they hold all Army charges until the federal court case concluded, so that any additional charges wouldn't affect the outcome of the ongoing federal trial. The military court would still have jurisdiction on any unresolved charges involving Thornton no matter when they were filed. Thus, no matter what happened to Thornton in federal court, there was a viable back-up plan for justice to prevail.

The legal jurisdiction over some of the parcels of land involved still posed problems for the courts. Thornton's convictions didn't solve those issues. Any future cases of criminal misconduct on those lands would face the same legal, jurisdictional problems. As a result, the Commanding General of Fort Leonard Wood, Richard L. Harris addressed this problem.

In an effort to clarify the confusing set of circumstances, in January of 1978 (well after the trial was over), Harris asked the Missouri General Assembly to enact a new statute which would prevent future conflicts. Harris, in a letter to State Representative, Michael Lybyer of Texas County, said he didn't address the problem until completion of the Thornton trial for fear of interfering with those judicial proceedings.

According to Harris, in the eyes of Missouri law, several parcels of property turned over to the US Army by the US Forest Service sometime after 1957 didn't fall under federal jurisdiction. Harris asked Majority Leader Joe Holt to take the corrective-measure bill under his wing. The sponsors of the proposed bill were Holt, Representative Michael Lybyer, and Representative Richard Hamilton of Pulaski County.

The measure, spelling out US forest land turned over to the Army since 1957 would be included in federal jurisdiction, was presented for action to the Missouri General Assembly in 1978. In an effort to drum up public support for the proposed law, Harris released a public statement concerning the legal problems:

"In January 1977, four teenagers were taken from a stopped civilian automobile on Fort Leonard Wood. Two of the four, both boys, were shot and one of them died immediately. Driven to another location, the two girls were sexually assaulted. At a third location, the wounded boy was shot again — resulting in his death — and the two girls were also shot. Although all four were left for dead, one of the girls survived. All three of the locations were on the Fort Leonard Wood military reservation. Yet, the individual who committed the acts was tried in Federal court only for murder of one of the boys, assault with intent to kill the other boy (whom he had, in fact, killed), abduction and sexual assault. Two murders and one attempted murder went uncharged. The fact he was tried for only a portion of the crimes he committed serves to highlight jurisdictional problems within the Fort Leonard Wood boundaries — which have existed since the post was established in 1940.

"The mere fact the federal government owns land does not in-and-of-itself eliminate the jurisdiction of the state government. No state may interfere with a federal function, such as a military training mission or the activities of a military unit. But unless a state has formally transferred its jurisdiction over federal property, and that jurisdiction has been accepted by the federal government, the state continues to bear the responsibility for all non-federal and nonmilitary activity within the boundaries of the property.

"The State of Missouri has consistently acted to have the federal government exercise exclusive jurisdiction over the land within the state, owned and used for military activities. By act of its legislature in 1943, Missouri ceded jurisdiction to the federal government and reenacted this same legislation twice thereafter. The Attorney General of the state in 1953 formally expressed his opinion state and local law enforcement authorities were without power to exercise their authority within the Fort Leonard Wood boundaries, and this result represented the intent of the legislature.

"The history of land acquisition for Fort Leonard Wood, however, provided legal obstacles which to this day have kept the intent of the legislature from being fully effected. When it was determined to build a military installation at Fort Leonard Wood, an outer perimeter or boundary was drawn. Within that perimeter, numerous parcels of land were already owned by the federal government and held by the US Department of Agriculture's United States Forest Service. The then Department of War, by purchase from private land holders and condemnation proceedings in the federal courts, secured title to the remainder of the land. The United States Forest Service gave the Department of War virtual total right to the use of their land within the Fort Leonard Wood military reservation. In the haste of preparation for the impending World War II, no further thought was given to this land, still held in the name of the United States Forest Service.

"Thereafter, in general terms the Missouri legislature ceded exclusive legislative jurisdiction to the federal government, and this cession was accepted by the Secretary of War. (The state has always retained the right to serve civil and criminal process and the right of taxation on federal military land. Although technically this amounts to a cession of partial legislative jurisdiction, for all practical purposes we may think of it as a cession as exclusive jurisdiction.) The Secretary of War, however wasn't legally capable of accepting jurisdiction from the state over property held in the name of the US Forest Service. That land had been acquired in the 1930's under an act of Congress, which prohibited any federal jurisdiction being acquired over US Forest Service land.

"Subsequent to the last reenactment by the Missouri legislature in 1957 of its cession statute, the US Forest Service and the Department of the Army (as successor to the Department of War) undertook a mutual exchange of land with the result being that now, with only two exceptions, all property within the Fort Leonard Wood boundary is in the name of the Department of the Army. Because the state legislature had referred only to land held at that time for military purposes, the cession legislation didn't apply to the later-acquired property transferred by the US Forest Service. Thus, Fort Leonard Wood is still left with a situation of being spotted with numerous parcels of land over which the federal government and the Federal courts have no jurisdiction. Two of the murders and an attempted murder mentioned at the outset were on such parcels of land, and it was thus not possible for the federal court to try the defendant for those acts.

"The numerous parcels of former US Forest Service land cannot be determined visually. The old property lines follow no topographical features and can be determined only by difficult surveying techniques. It is virtually impossible for an individual on Fort Leonard Wood to know when he has passed from property over which the federal government has exclusive jurisdiction to that over which it has none. For every crime committed on the installation, however, it becomes necessary to pinpoint the location of the crime and do a land survey to determine if a federal court and federal prosecutor or state court and state prosecutor must enter the case. (In most instances this problem does not exist for military personnel who can be tried before a court-martial for any crime committed within the post boundaries, regardless of the jurisdictional status. The question most frequently arises in connection with civilian offenders.)

"It is clear, the State of Missouri intended the federal government exercise exclusive federal jurisdiction over Fort Leonard Wood. The installation is located in a rural part of the state and the population of the installation out-numbers the population of the remainder of Pulaski County – the county in which almost all of the post is situated. It is apparent the state considered the potential drain of providing local law enforcement and other municipal-type services to far exceed the capability of local government to provide. Likewise recognizing this situation, the federal government has previously indicated its willingness to accept jurisdiction and responsibility from the state.

"Fort Leonard Wood has no plans to increase its size. In fact, the installation currently is engaged in restoring approximately 7,500 acres of its land totally to US Forest Service use and making necessary boundary modifications. The new legislation being proposed before the Missouri legislature was drafted to rectify an error made and continued for 37 years. It will provide a clear jurisdiction without the need for future resort to the legislature."

* * *

The Missouri legislature responded to the plea of General Harris, and as a result an existing section of Missouri law was modified to effect the changes requested by Harris. The changed statute became established Missouri law in late 1978. The new section of law was as follows:

"RSMO 12.040: Exclusive jurisdiction in and over any land acquired as set out in section 12.030 or otherwise lawfully acquired and held for any of the purposes set out in section 12.030 by the United States, is ceded to the United States for all purposes, saving and reserving, however, to the state of Missouri the right of taxation to the same extent and in the same manner as if this cession had not been made; and further saving and reserving to the state of Missouri the right to serve thereon any civil or criminal process issued under the authority of the state, in any action on account of rights acquired, obligations incurred, or crimes committed in this state, outside the boundaries of the land but the jurisdiction ceded to the United States continues no longer than the United States owns the land and uses the same for the purposes set out in section 12.030."

* * *

Civil Lawsuits

In the aftermath of the murders, another critical legal issue also went before the federal court system, the issue of the civil liability of the United States Government for the actions of Johnny Lee Thornton. In July of 1978, two lawsuits were filed by the victims' families — the survivor Juanita Deckard, and the parents of each of the murder victims.

At the time these lawsuits were filed, media coverage of the Thornton murder story was extensive and, as a result, quite a few details relating to the filing of the lawsuits were printed in local papers.

The two civil suits filed sought a total of $3,506,269 in damages from the United States government for the actions of Johnny Lee Thornton, a government employee, in regard to the murders of Wesley Hawkins, Anthony Bates, and Linda Needham. In addition, the survivor, Juanita Deckard, also filed for damages from the United States government for the gunshot wounds and sexual assault she suffered.

The parents of Wesley Hawkins sought $750,040 in damages. They stated in their lawsuit petition, their earlier request had been refused and the government had not paid $1,837.15 for Wesley's funeral expenses.

The parents of Linda Needham sought $600,000 in damages — an amount they said the United States government had refused to pay earlier. The petition also asked the government furnish $2,035.35 for Linda's funeral costs.

Tony Bates' father filed a lawsuit asking for damages of $501,815.33, which he stated (in the petition) the government had refused to pay earlier. The government also refused to pay for his son's funeral, costing $1,815.35.

Tony Bates' mother filed a second lawsuit. She sought $150,000 in damages in connection with the loss of her son.

Juanita Deckard requested $105,414.15 and stated the government had refused to pay this amount.

After being turned down by the federal government, the lawsuits were filed and went to trial. The decision of the court follows:

BATES v. UNITED STATES

No. 82-1381.

701 F.2d 737 (1983)

Marjorie BATES, Appellant, v. United States of America, Appellee.

Juanita Ann DECKARD, et al., Appellants, v. United States of America, Appellee.

United States Court of Appeals, Eighth Circuit.

Submitted December 15, 1982.

Decided March 8, 1983.

Attorney(s) appearing for the Case Karl Zobrist, David R. Erickson, Blackwell, Sanders, Matheny, Weary & Lombardi, Kansas City, Mo., for Marjorie Bates.

David E. Wilhite, Lebanon, Mo., for Juanita Deckard.

Dan L. Birdsong, Routh, Thomas, Birdsong & Hutton, Rolla, Mo., J. Max Price, Salem, Mo., for Leroy Arlo Bates and Mr. and Mrs. James Hawkins.

Darrell Deputy, Jr., Lebanon, Mo., for Mr. and Mrs. Hershel Needham.

Robert G. Ulrich, US Atty., Kenneth Josephson, Asst. US Atty., Kansas City, Mo., for appellee.

Before ROSS and FAGG, Circuit Judges, and WATERS, District Judge.

H. FRANKLIN WATERS, District Judge.

These are actions brought by several plaintiffs against the United States of America under the Federal Tort Claims Act, 28 U.S.C. §§ 1346(b) and 2671 et seq., resulting from the murder of three young persons and the serious injury of another by a military policeman at Fort Leonard Wood, Missouri, military base. The parties entered into stipulations of fact and filed cross-motions for summary judgment, and the district court1 denied the motions of the plaintiffs and granted the motions of the United States. Plaintiffs appealed from the judgment of the court. We affirm.

FACTS.

On January 13, 1977, Specialist 4 Johnny Lee Thornton, while a military policeman on the Fort Leonard Wood, Missouri, military base, murdered with his government-issued 45-calibre pistol three teenagers and attempted to murder another. He was later convicted of kidnap, rape, assault with intent to kill, and murder. The plaintiffs are Juanita Ann Deckard, the only survivor of the incident, and the parents of the deceased victims, Anthony Lee Bates, Wesley Hawkins and Linda Needham. In an excellent [701 F.2d 739] and exhaustive opinion, 517 F.Supp. 1350, the trial court set forth the facts stipulated to by the parties as follows:

The stipulations of facts state on January 12-13, 1977, Johnny Lee Thornton was a Specialist 4 in the 463rd Military Police Company, stationed at Fort Leonard Wood, Missouri. At all relevant times on January 12-13, 1977, Thornton was on active duty as a member of the United States Army and as an employee of the Department of the Army, an agency of defendant United States of America. Thornton was a military policeman assigned to the Game Warden Section of the Provost Marshal Office at Fort Leonard Wood, Missouri. All the facts which form the basis of the present action occurred on the Fort Leonard Wood Military Reservation in Pulaski County, Missouri.

Thornton's duties consisted of the random and selected patrolling of Fort Leonard Wood. Thornton checked permits, assisted sportsmen, and patrolled for fish and game violators, poachers, and trespassers. He was also to search for illegal trash dumping; the destruction, dumping or cutting of trees, and the destruction of wildlife food plots.

Thornton's work involved a minimal amount of supervision and a high degree of professional competence. In addition to his game and wildlife duties set out above, Thornton also had authority to arrest military personnel and to detain civilians for any suspected crimes and could make such arrests or detention on any and all parts of the Army base. It was Army policy the detention of civilians for suspected crimes be limited to only such time necessary to release a civilian to federal or state law enforcement officials.

On the evening of January 12, 1977, Thornton reported for duty and was issued several items of United States Army equi pment by agents of defendant United States. He was issued a four-wheel drive military police jeep which was utilized by Thornton while he was on duty on January 12-13, 1977. The vehicle was clearly marked as a military police vehicle and Thornton was in full military uniform at all times during this period.

Thornton was also issued several other items of United States Army equipment by agents of defendant United States. He was given one US Army 45-calibre pistol, several rounds of ammunition, two pairs of military police handcuffs and one military police badge. It was not unusual for someone acting in Thornton's capacity to check out two pairs of handcuffs or several rounds of ammunition before going on duty.

While on duty on the evening of January 12-13, 1977, Thornton stopped a vehicle by using his red emergency lights on his military police jeep. The vehicle was driven by Anthony Lee Bates and occupied by passengers Wesley Hawkins, Juanita Ann Deckard, and Linda Needham. All the occupants of the car were teenagers who lived in the Fort Leonard Wood area. Thornton informed Bates and Hawkins the Southgate Texaco station, a nearby gas station which is not on United States property, had been robbed and Bates' car matched the description of the car involved in the robbery. While the Southgate Texaco station was not, in fact, robbed on January 12-13, 1977, it is agreed if the Southgate Texaco station had been robbed, as Thornton alleged, he would have had the authority to stop and detain suspected vehicles on the military base while he was on duty.

After stopping the vehicle, Thornton ordered the two males, Bates and Hawkins, to get out of the car. He handcuffed Bates and Hawkins' hands behind their backs and placed the two youths in the back seat of the military police jeep. Then, without provocation, Thornton shot Anthony Lee Bates and Wesley Hawkins through the chest with his military issue 45-calibre pistol as they sat handcuffed in the back seat of the jeep.

After shooting Bates and Hawkins, Thornton ordered Juanita Ann Deckard and Linda Needham into the jeep and took them to a cabin on a remote part of the Army base. He then forcibly raped the girls and forced them to commit oral sodomy upon each other and to commit oral sodomy upon him. Afterwards, Thornton shot the two girls. He then buried all four victims in the snow and left them for dead. Anthony Lee Bates, Wesley Hawkins, and Linda Needham died as a result of the gunshot wounds inflicted by Thornton. Juanita Ann Deckard was the only survivor of Thornton's attack. On July 26, 1977, in criminal proceedings before this Court Thornton was convicted of murder in the first degree, assault with intent to kill, rape, and kidnapping for the purpose of committing rape.

II.

DISCUSSION.

None of the parties contend the trial court's summarization of the stipulated facts is in error in any regard, but the plaintiffs earnestly contend the trial court erroneously applied these facts to the applicable law. Specifically, the plaintiffs contend the trial court's granting of the summary judgment in favor of the United States "was clearly erroneous and contrary to the law in that Specialist 4 Johnny Lee Thornton was acting within the course and scope of his employment at the time he committed the assaults and murders on January 12-13, 1977."

These actions were brought under the Federal Tort Claims Act, 28 U.S.C. §§ 1346(b) and 2671 et seq., and the parties agree the issue the trial court had to determine, and this court must review, is whether Thornton, at the time of the shootings, rapes, and assaults was acting in the course of and in the scope of his employment as a military policeman. This issue is to be determined by the application of state law, and plaintiffs do not contend otherwise. See p. 11 of Plaintiffs' Brief, and Stencel Aero Engineering v. United States, 431 US 666, 97 S.Ct. 2054, 52 L.Ed.2d 665 (1977); Bissell v. McElligott, 248 F.Supp. 219

(D.C.Mo.1965), aff'd, 369 F.2d 115 (8ᵗʰ Cir.1966), cert. denied, 387 US 917, 87 S.Ct. 2029, 18 L.Ed.2d 969 (1967).

Thus, the responsibility of the trial court, and the responsibility of this court, is to apply the law of the state of Missouri as announced by applicable decisions of the highest court of that state, and when this is done, this court is convinced the trial court correctly decided these cases.

The seminal case on the law of respondeat superior in Missouri is Haehl v. Wabash R. Company, 119 Mo. 325, 24 S.W. 737 (1893). The law, as announced in Haehl, supra, was the law in Missouri with little change from 1893 until a decision of the Missouri Supreme Court in 1973 in Wellman v. Pacer Oil Company, 504 S.W.2d 55 (Mo.1973).

The landmark case of Haehl, supra, was an action for the wrongful death of a man shot by a bridge watchman employed by the defendant railroad. The decedent was crossing a railroad bridge and, after being halted and turned away by the watchman, he started to leave the bridge and was pursued and shot while still upon the bridge approach. In what has now become an oft-quoted passage, the Missouri court pronounced the Missouri rule on respondeat superior as follows:

The principal is responsible, not because the servant has acted in his name or under color of his employment, but because the servant was actually engaged in or about his business and carrying out his purposes. He is then responsible because the thing complained of, although done through the agency of another, was done by himself; and it matters not in such case whether the injury with which it is sought to charge him is the result of negligence, unskillful or wrongful conduct, for he must choose fit agents for the transaction of his business. But if his business is done, or is taking care of itself, and his servant, not being engaged in it, not concerned about, but impelled by motives wholly personal to himself, and simply to gratify his own feeling of resentment, whether provoked or unprovoked, commits an assault upon another, when that has and can have no tendency to promote any purpose in which the principal is interested, and to promote which the servant was employed, then the wrong is the purely personal wrong of the servant, which he, and he alone is responsible.

After announcing this principle, the court held the defendant company liable and stated "it was not necessary to render the defendant liable, it should have authorized its watchman to kill the deceased or sanction the deed after it was done; and however wanton or malicious it was, the principal is liable if it is done in the course of the servant's employment." Haehl, supra, 119 Mo. at 340-341, 24 S.W. at 741.

After the 1893 decision, the Missouri Court, in a number of cases, applied this principle with almost no change. These opinions are discussed in some detail in the trial court's exhaustive opinion, but the court believes it would serve no purpose to set forth those holdings in any detail in this opinion. Suffice it to say the rule remained relatively unchanged until the decision in Wellman, supra.

In Wellman, plaintiff purchased gasoline at a service station operated by defendant, Pacer Oil Company. An employee of the defendant serviced plaintiff's car, and shortly after he left the station, the hood of his car flew up as he was driving down the road. He returned to the station and accused defendant's employee of "messing up" the hood. In the ensuing argument, the employee pulled a gun and shot plaintiff. Plaintiff stumbled back to his car and got in the driver's seat. The employee followed plaintiff, opened the car door and shot plaintiff again, inflicting serious and permanent injuries. Plaintiff brought suit against Pacer Oil Company, and on appeal, the Supreme Court of Missouri held "the actions of Gamble (the employee) were so outrageous and criminal — so excessively violent as to be totally without reason or responsibility — and hence were, (as a matter of law), not to be within the scope of his employment." Id. at 58.

The Wellman decision modified to a significant extent the court's decision in Haehl. In Haehl, the court stated: "However wanton or malicious it was, the principal is liable if it is done in the course of the servant's employment." 119 Mo. at 340-341, 24 S.W. at 741.

Thus, prior to the Wellman decision, the law in Missouri was that the principal could be liable for the agent's acts, regardless of how outrageous they were, if the agents were actually engaged in the principal's business and not impelled by personal motives. We are convinced the Missouri Supreme Court, en banc, has now modified the law as announced in Haehl, supra, and in order for a principal to be liable for his agent's acts, the acts must not only be taken in furtherance of the principal's business and not impelled by personal motives, but they also must not be "so outrageous and criminal — so excessively violent as to be totally without reason or responsibility."

We are saddened by the outrageous conduct which resulted in these cases, and are not unmindful or unsympathetic to the innocent plight of the plaintiffs and the emotional suffering visited upon them, but the court is convinced to hold the United

States Government legally responsible under the circumstances of this case for the barbarous conduct of its employee would be totally contrary to the law of Missouri which, as was indicated above, this court is bound to apply. We believe and find Thornton's acts in stopping the car, handcuffing and killing the young men and assaulting and raping the young women and shooting them, could not, under any circumstances, be construed to have been in furtherance of his employer's business or incident to any business of his employer. On the contrary, in the words of Haehl, supra, his acts were "impelled by motives wholly personal to himself, and simply to gratify his own feeling..." In any event, just as the trial court found, even if it could be said, for the sake of argument, the acts were within the course of and in the scope of his employment, we cannot escape the plain holding of Wellman, supra. How could it be said Thornton's outrageous and sadistic conduct in this case was not "so outrageous and criminal — so excessively violent as to be totally without reason or responsibility?" Under the circumstances, we have no choice but to affirm the trial court's ruling the conduct of Thornton did not arise out of and in the scope of his employment and, thus, the United States is not liable for his acts.

In support of their contention, the government should be held to be liable in this case, the plaintiffs rely upon Brown v. Associated Dry Goods, Inc., 656 F.2d 306 (8ᵗʰ Cir.1981); Mansfield v. Smithie, 615 S.W.2d 649 (Mo.App.1981); Bova v. St. Louis Public Service Company, 316 S.W.2d 140 (Mo.App.1958); Butler v. Circulus, Inc., 557 S.W.2d 469 (Mo.App.1977); and Panjwani v. Star Service & Petroleum Company, 395 S.W.2d 129 (Mo.1965). We do not believe it would serve a useful purpose to discuss each of these cases in detail. Suffice it to say the court, after having reviewed these opinions, believes that, in each of them, the incidents in question arose out of an attempt by the employee to carry out his employer's business. In each instance, he went considerably further than his employer undoubtedly intended him to, but, in each instance, the act in question occurred as a result of his attempt to carry out his assigned duties. In this case, Thornton did not, by any stretch of the imagination, set out to do his employer's business, and then simply go too far. He set out to gratify his own desires and was impelled by his own motives and did not, at any stage of the incident which resulted in this tragedy, intend to further or actually further to any degree his employer's business. Thus, under the law of Missouri, the employer cannot be held responsible.

III.

CONCLUSION.

For the foregoing reasons, we affirm the district court's denial of the motion for summary judgment of the plaintiffs and its granting of the motion for summary judgment of the defendant.

* * *

Interview with Leroy Bates, father of Tony Bates:

You will know this, it's a little aside to it. I don't think that really I ought to feel that way, but I do. Anyway, the thing which bothered me more about it than, I guess about anything else about it, maybe. It's a selfish thing. But I still think the Army was responsible to reimburse or to pay us something for that. When you look at all that happens around now — things like that how much they get, and so on. Well, you know, here he's using a military vehicle, carrying a military gun, and shoots them with a military gun while he is on duty... And then the judge says, "That's too egregious a crime. I can't hold the Army responsible." At one time they offered me fifteen hundred dollars. They said because it was a traffic-related incident they could give me fifteen hundred dollars. I said, "Forget it!" None of us ever got anything.

14

JOHNNY LEE THORNTON

During the first few days after the murders had occurred, much speculation within the Pulaski County area arose as to what had actually happened, how it could have, and plethora other questions which wouldn't be answered for some time. However, the most frequently asked one was, "Who is Johnny Lee Thornton?"

What did Johnny Lee Thornton do for the United States Army?

Most people say MPs are cops for the military. While that statement is technically correct, it isn't completely. Military police train for a dual role in their military mission. First and foremost, MPs are a combat support arm of the United States Army.

In their role of combat support, the MPs drive semi-armored vehicles with heavy machine guns and roof-mounted grenade launchers. They engage in numerous roles in combat mission support. An MP unit might be stationed at a crossroads to guard it from attack and ensure supply convoys coming up from the rear are directed to the correct road which leads them to the units at the battle front they are to support. Other MP units guard the supply convoy and protect it against attack as the convoy delivers their supplies.

The main purpose of military police on the battlefield is to control enemy prisoners of war. I'm sure most of you can remember the pictures of the tens of thousands of Iraqi prisoners of war herded into camps at the end of Desert Storm. The majority of those camps were guarded by the military police.

Within the military police corps, military occupational specialties (MOS) are broken down into numerical categories. Enlisted men within the military police usually have a designator of 95B, or basic MP. A sub-specialty within the enlisted personnel is a correctional specialist, listed as a 95C. Johnny Lee Thornton was a military police officer whose designator was 95C — a correctional specialist.[2]

The second major MP mission is usually referred to as garrison. This is where most people get the idea that MPs are the cops of the Army. In the garrison role, they investigate traffic accidents, run radar to catch speeders, patrol, look for intoxicated drivers, respond to domestic assaults, take theft reports, arrest shoplifters, and enforce a host of administrative rules and regulations which exist on a military base. Within the garrison mission, there also exists the role of the game warden section. And as we know, Johnny Lee Thornton was assigned to the nine-man game warden detail on Fort Leonard Wood in 1977.

During his Advanced Individual Training (AIT) at the MP school in Fort McClellan, Alabama, Thornton received roughly three months of training, which covered both combat support and garrison roles. Once he reported to his first duty station at Fort Wood, he received more game warden training for that role.

In his official position as a military police game warden, Johnny Lee Thornton had access to all of Fort Leonard Wood — and to some degree, the surrounding civilian community — which was his duty to patrol.

* * *

What exactly is a game warden MP and what are their duties?

---

2   Thornton's MOS designation as a 95C is listed under the system in place in 1977. Currently the designations are: 31A Commissioned officer, 31B enlisted MP, 31C an Internment Resettlement Specialist, 31D a Criminal Investigator, 31K a Military Dog Handler.

A military game warden on Fort Leonard Wood is primarily concerned with the enforcement of the rules and regulations as they relate to hunting and fishing efforts on base. There are other laws they enforce, such as littering, trash dumping, illegal cutting of trees, and some others you might not think of. They are also military police officers. As such, they can make an arrest for bank robbery, or an arrest for the armed robbery of the Southgate Texaco gas station if they found themselves in a position to do so.

To understand the role of a game warden, one must first understand the basics of what they do and how they perform their duties. The job is harder than most people think. In order to enforce the hunting and fishing regulations, one must first find somebody who is actually hunting or fishing. In the case of fishermen congregated along a river bank or around a man-made lake, finding someone who is fishing is simple. But are they violating any fishing laws?

It is relatively easy to walk up to a person standing on the bank of the river holding a fishing pole and ask to see their fishing license. For the most part, they either have it with them or they don't. A simple check may or may not lead to enforcement action. One may also check for any fish the person has in possession or their creel. Which is simply a fancy word for saying whatever method they are using to hold the fish they've caught — be it a 5-gallon bucket filled with water, a specialized fishing basket that hangs at the angler's side in the stream, or a metal stringer one snaps the fish onto in order to retain them. There are regulations in place as to which fish are legal at specific times of the year, the length those fish must be, and so forth. At the time of the check, the fisherman would either be in compliance with the all regulations or not, and enforcement action could be taken.

There are many other rules that deal with fishing and how you may pursue game fish. For example, while fishing on a trout stream, one is restricted as to the number of trout one may keep. Each of those kept fish must be of a specific size or larger. If one does not intend to keep a fish, one is required to release it immediately. Thus, a common tactic for a game warden would be to hide nearby and watch people fishing. The game warden frequently catches a fisherman who has a smaller legal trout in his possession, caught some time ago. When and if the fisherman catches a much bigger fish, he takes the smaller fish out of his creel, throws it back into the river — and puts the larger fish in his creel.

This is a fishing violation in many states, including Missouri. Since the Fort Leonard Wood game laws are modeled after the Missouri game laws, it's also a violation on Fort Leonard Wood. The trauma of being caught and then being handled by the fisherman during the process of removing the hook from the trout's mouth damages the fish. The longer the fish is out of the water, the more progressive the injuries to that fish will be in the long run. Which is another way of saying that when one throws the smaller fish back into the river, its chances of dying an early death are greatly increased. Therefore, the tactic of exchanging one fish for another may actually cost the trout resource stream two casualties for the one fish the fisherman takes home.

When it comes to hunting, the effort needed to find a person in the act of poaching is much harder. Potential hunters don't stand around a riverbank or a lake bed. They are out in the middle of the woods. Many days, finding an active hunter is a major challenge. Once found, the same dilemma arises. By walking up to a person and checking his hunting license and gear, the game warden may have a chance to uncover several violations. Does the hunter have the correct license for the game he is hunting? Is the weapon he's using legal, and does it have a plug in the magazine restricting it to the legal number of rounds of ammunition he can use at one time? Is the caliber of the weapon correct? Is he wearing hunter orange as required? And so on.

If none of the above violations exist, then the game warden's contact with that particular hunter leads to zero enforcement actions.

A game warden must patrol the woods and the thousands of dirt-vehicle tracks on Fort Leonard Wood. It's a rare occasion when one drives over a hill and finds three men dragging a deer out of the woods in plain sight. That would present a duty to check all kinds of restrictions and regulations with regard to the three hunters — and would be what is called a "good enforcement" contact. One may or may not be required to issue citations for any violations in that case.

* * *

Would a game warden make a traffic stop on a vehicle to look for a game violation?

Yes, and no. It would be somewhat unusual for a game warden to make a traffic stop on a main highway such as the south gate road looking for a game violation. But a traffic stop on a nameless, dirt-vehicle track in the middle of nowhere on Fort Wood, with the vehicle driving around in the middle of the night, is plausible. Likewise, the establishment of a roadblock, usually referred to as a checkpoint, on a road out in the woods is another effective way to stop every vehicle driving through to check for hunters with game in their possession. This is also an effective way of discovering violations for enforcement.

In order to succeed as a game warden, Thornton needed several special skills:

- He had to be able to talk to people without confrontation during every contact. Remember, hunters are always armed, and usually with bigger-caliber long guns of some sort versus the MP's lone pistol. Tact is critical.
- Knowledge of the fort and its hunting areas is another skill Thornton needed—shortcuts from one forest track to another and so forth.
- Skilled driving with a four-wheel drive vehicle in extremely rough terrain is also be necessary.
- And patience—for the long, boring shifts on the days and nights when nothing happened.

All of the information available suggests Thornton was a reasonably effective game warden and MP, who worked long hours and had earned the respect of his fellow MPs and game wardens. Much of the information disclosed at his trial suggests that while Thornton's personal life was an ongoing disaster most of the time, his professional standing was solid. As previously recounted, Thornton had been selected as Fort Leonard Wood's MP Officer of the Year due to his professional work ethic.

Testimony from many of his fellow officers at the trial indicates a man who was well-regarded by his colleagues. Many expressed shock and disbelief on hearing about his crimes.

* * *

[Redacted] MP who knew Thornton:

> *Question*: Were you acquainted with SP4 Johnny Lee Thornton?
>
> *Answer*: Yes, I was.
>
> *Question*: How long did you know him and how would you characterize your relationship with him?
>
> *Answer*: I would say we were best friends. I think I knew him better than anyone else there. I knew him for about a year and a half. We went through AIT [Advanced Individual Training] together and arrived at Fort Leonard Wood within a couple weeks of each other. I didn't know him well in AIT. It was at Fort Leonard Wood that our relationship developed.
>
> *Question*: During the period you knew Thornton, did he ever suffer from severe headaches coupled with blackouts?
>
> *Answer*: Never, no.
>
> *Question*: After having been told of the incident for which Thornton has been apprehended, what is your reaction?
>
> *Answer*: Obviously I'm very shocked — surprised. I would never have thought him capable of such acts.
>
> *Question*: How was his relationship with his wife?
>
> *Answer*: I had always thought it to be a good marriage. However, they got divorced. It was very sudden and came as a very great surprise to me. I visited them at their house frequently and saw no outward signs of problems.

Question: Did Thornton's wife ever tell you Thornton beat her?

Answer: No.

Question: Do you know if he did?

Answer: I have heard the rumors he did, but I seriously doubt them.

Question: Would you characterize Thornton as a violent person?

Answer: No, certainly not. I can't remember any single incident in which his temper was out of control.

* * *

Sergeant Marvin Richey:

Sergeant Richey was a member of the 463rd MP Company. As a result of that, Richey had a lot of contact and interaction with Thornton. During an interview, Richey (retired) made the following remarks:

I was his platoon sergeant. Yes, he was a good soldier. In the short time I knew him in my platoon he always had a real sharp uniform. His shoes were always shined, brass was polished, and he would do a good job. He was a game warden on my shift. He was a good soldier. And he worked for me for about one year. And, you talk about shocked. I fell out of my chair when I got the information. It was shocking. Yes, it was shocking. Thornton was from Arkansas. And I am from Arkansas. And once in a while in my office, we would talk about Arkansas.

I had an office in the barracks. I was in charge of forty people — all military policeman. I would hear about their personal problems, and situations, and whatever. And it shocked the heck out of me when this all came down. One of the few things I heard about was the activity which took place in the cabin itself — about the sexual activities. It was a shock to all of the people who knew him. The reason why he went off the barrel was never determined. I thought we had a pretty good relationship on a personal basis."

Richey was living on Fort Leonard Wood at the time of the 1977 murders. His family was with him. Richey had one additional comment:

"Those two kids who went missing were friends with my daughter, and I am so thankful she wasn't with them."

* * *

Marlene Engstrom, Truman Education Center:

In 1977, Marlene Engstrom taught Johnny Lee Thornton.

"I was working for the University of Missouri in Rolla. It was known as UMR at the time. I was teaching a college pre-paratory class and he was one of the students who was in that class. I taught three hours of English each week for twelve weeks.

"He was basically non-descriptive. He came to class and sat there at first. And then he quit showing up regularly. We were required to contact their commanding officers at that time because they were on duty. And if they weren't at class, they should be at work. So basically, that's about it. He never gave me a hard time or anything like that.

"Well, what it was — this was back in the mid-70s and the Army was really pushing college education, and so, the college prep program was designed to give these military students college-level exposure without the worry of failure. There was no pass-fail or anything like that. It was just designed to expose them to college-level courses. They took science. They took math. They took English. They took reading. And they took a social studies-type class. And then at the end of the class, they could try to pass a Quest test, college-level examination program. And if they did pass the exam, they could earn college credits that way.

"And then, when they didn't, when they kind of stopped coming to class — we furnished [the soldiers] textbooks and we tried to get [the books] back because [the soldiers] had not purchased them. We provided the textbooks for free. And so, I do know I tried to contact him several times to get him to return the books but I was never able to get them returned.

"As far as I can recall, there was nothing, no real interaction with the other students and nothing negative about the experience with him. No, he was there. He didn't cause any problems but he also wasn't taking an interest. It was like he was sitting there because that's where he was supposed to be. Sometimes the students were in uniform and sometimes they were not. If they were on duty, they had to come in their military uniform."

When asked about her thoughts concerning Thornton when she heard the news of the murders Engstrom said:

"Well disbelief, for one thing and kind of, 'Wow!' I had him in class and I kept calling him to bring his books back. I kinda wonder what was going on in his head at that time. I guess mostly for me it was mainly because I had him in class. And when I found out the guy's name, it was kind of something you never forget."

* * *

MP Dog Handler, Frank Jung, 208th MP Company:

...one time, Jensen — who was also a game warden — I recall getting invited over to his house one time for dinner....Johnny was there, too. Johnny didn't say a whole lot. During the conversation — they were talking a lot about people going on Fort Leonard Wood looking for Indian artifacts, and things like that.

...the game wardens were always telling us dog handlers, "If you see anything interesting or suspicious, we would like for you to let us know."

So, I do recall being at Jensen's home at least once with Johnny there for dinner. That was the only time I was ever at Jensen's home. My understanding was Jensen and Johnny Lee were really close. After Johnny's wife packed up and took the kids and left him, my understanding was Jensen was always there to support Johnny.

I've heard of the game warden's cabin but I've never been to it. That's where the game wardens would always go because they were always out in the woods. They rarely came into the MP station. And that's why I found it kind of odd that Johnny was there that night at the MP station. Because you rarely saw the game wardens. I would be driving down Airport Road or the south gate road and would occasionally pass one of them. And they waved, you know, and stuff like that. But rarely did you see them, because they kind of had a life of their own. They were on their own. They didn't report to anybody.

* * *

The CID case file yielded another report where a CID Special Agent interviewed the commander of the 463rd MP

Company on Fort Leonard Wood about Johnny Lee Thornton's qualifications with a .45 caliber pistol. As usual the CID report redacted the captain's name. However, the Commanding Officer of the 463rd MP Company at that time was CPT Donald Ryder.

Captain Donald Ryder:

> On January 21, 1977, Special Agent [name redacted] and I interviewed Captain [name redacted], Commander 463rd MP Company on Fort Leonard Wood, Missouri. Captain [redacted name] told us that on October 17, 1976, Thornton, along with other members of the 463rd MP Company, qualified with the .45 caliber pistol. According to Captain [name redacted], Thornton fired a forty nine out of a possible fifty points while firing at silhouette type targets.

* * *

Former MP, James Reist—a fellow game warden serving alongside Thornton:

> In all of my contacts with Johnny, he never displayed any signs of medical issues, headaches, or mood swings. He seemed to be getting his life together and apparently was getting back together with his wife. All in all, he was in a good mood and enthusiastic about his work and life in general.

* * *

15

THE MIND OF A SERIAL KILLER

One of the biggest questions needing clarification in this case is, was Johnny Lee Thornton a serial killer?

There are people who would answer, "Yes, he is." Besides the three murders he committed after the Bates' vehicle stop, they cite the case of Alfred Marshall and TC Gossage. They also have other vague memories of bodies being found on Fort Leonard Wood the same time frame Thornton was stationed on Fort Wood.

Family members of Johnny Lee Thornton say he wasn't a serial killer. He snapped one January night in 1977, due to intense pressures within his mind, they say, and committed those horrible crimes. But those were the *only* crimes Thornton ever committed. These people say no proof has ever been produced that Thornton committed any other murders.

They are correct on the issue of proof.

There has been no proof Johnny Lee Thornton committed any murders other than the murders he was convicted of in federal court connected to the stop of Tony Bates' vehicle.

Author's Note: Thornton was a suspect in the murder of PVT Frederick E. Williams on Fort Wood. However, four other people were convicted of the Williams murder.

But that doesn't stop speculation. The actions and movements of Johnny Lee Thornton raise questions about whether they constitute those of a budding serial killer.

Analysis:

Now that you've read the chapter on Thornton's training, experience, and some of his duty requirements, hopefully you are thinking a bit like a game warden on patrol. So, let's look at a number of actions Thornton performed while working.[3]

1. Vehicle Stop:

The investigating agents interviewed Robert L. Hall Jr., of Plato, Missouri, who told them he was riding to work with his partner, Stanley Handley.

> *Hall:* We worked the midnight to eight thirty a.m. shift at the post commissary. We were heading to work. Approximately twenty minutes after midnight on January 13, 1977, an MP driving a Scout stopped us on the south gate road, in the vicinity of Range 26. We were traveling north when we met the MP vehicle, which turned around to stop us. The MP asked for identification from both of us and shined his flashlight inside Handley's vehicle — a Chevrolet pickup.
>
> Handley always carries a shotgun in the truck. I held it in my lap but the MP made no comment about the shotgun. The MP told us he was looking for a particular person, and let us go.

In this particular interview from the investigation, neither witness could identify Thornton as the man who stopped them — but they were sure it was an MP Scout vehicle on the south gate road just after midnight on January 13, 1977. That could only have been Johnny Lee Thornton as he was driving the only Scout in operation that night.

A vehicle stop like this is unusual for a game warden. After passing an oncoming vehicle on the main road, the MP turned around, pursued the vehicle and made the stop. After approaching the car, he looked at a passenger who was holding a shotgun in his lap. Making no issue of the shotgun in the passenger's lap, he told them he was looking for a particular person — and let them drive away.

Regulations surrounding possession of privately-owned weapons on Fort Leonard Wood are multiple — and they are strictly enforced. For an MP to ignore the shotgun was highly questionable. Thornton should not have been looking for "a particular person." His job was to patrol for poachers — and, here was a car occupied, one could reasonably suspect, by hunters.

---

3   These examples come from the investigation and the trial.

One of the major violations of the Missouri and Fort Wood game laws is the use of artificial light to aid in the detection and shooting of game in the darkness. "Spotlighting" is a citation all game wardens fancy writing. However, Thornton didn't even search the vehicle. If nothing else, the shotgun should have been removed and checked against the stolen firearm list.

After several, non-typical, game warden vehicle stops on the main highway in a row, the most logical assumption is that Thornton was hunting for female victims — not male hunters.

The same basic statement can be made about vehicle stops documented in previous chapters. After Thornton determined there were no females present, they were all released. Until, that is, he came to the vehicle driven by Tony Bates.

2. Total Control:

Examining the stop of Tony Bates' Charger and Thornton's actions in regard to it, one fact becomes crystal clear. Within the first moments of his crime spree, Thornton shot the two boys as they sat in the back of his patrol vehicle.

Why?

Thornton knew full-well that act would bring in the FBI because the boys were civilians. Thornton also knew the blood on the back seat and any possible bullet holes in his vehicle pointed to him. Therefore, from that moment forward, all four kids had to die or Thornton couldn't be sure he could cover up his planned crimes.

There were four people in the Bates' vehicle. Thornton had to prevent them from attacking him to accomplish his desires. And so, we go back to the two sets of handcuffs he requested and his statement, "I'm going to play super cop tonight."

When Thornton stopped the Scout, he was reasonable and matter-of-fact as he explained to the kids that the Southgate Texaco gas station had been robbed, that their vehicle was a match for the suspect vehicle, and he was going to have to take them in for questioning. He handcuffed Wesley Hawkins and Tony Bates without difficulty because they knew they were innocent of any such armed robbery. Once handcuffed, the boys were no longer a physical threat. But then, in order to be doubly sure, Thornton shot both boys where they sat in the backseat of his vehicle.

This action ensured the boys couldn't attack him, no matter what. It also put Juanita Deckard and Linda Needham into a state of emotional shock and fear to where they would obey Thornton's orders without question. At this point, Johnny Lee Thornton was in full control of the situation.

3. Deliberation:

Before Thornton left the site of the vehicle stop (just off of the south gate road), he took his knife and punctured Tony Bates's car tire, leaving an abandoned car with a flat tire for everyone to see. This simple act was presumably designed to delay suspicions about the parked vehicle for quite some time. Everybody could see it had a flat tire and assumed the owner had gone for assistance. A major deception and delay technique — not the action of a crazy man but rather a thinking and plotting one.

4. Eliciting Fear and Confusion:

While sexually assaulting the girls in the game warden cabin, Thornton kept his .45 caliber pistol in his hand to enhance their horror and revulsion. Simultaneously, he made statements in the girls' presence that he wasn't really an MP. That he was leaving the Army — going AWOL. He knew the post like the back of his hand, and so forth. These statements were presumably designed to mislead them.

Thornton's several firewood-gathering trips were also designed to keep the girls off balance. Each time he went outside, they heard him talking to the boys. This made Juanita Deckard believe that the boys were okay — that somehow Thornton had only sedated them. This confusion, of course, gave the girls hope that they all would survive if they cooperated with their rapist.

5. Covering the Tracks:

Following over three hours of repeated sexual assaults, Thornton took the girls to another section of the woods and shot them. He checked on their bodies several times. When he kicked Juanita Deckard looking for a response, she effectively played dead. Then he buried all four of them in the snow. He remained in the area for an additional 30 minutes or so before leaving.

These acts are what a thinking person might do to avoid detection. They imply recognition that his actions were not legal — and awareness of the severity of punishment he would receive if caught.

Once he arrived back at MP headquarters, Thornton went to work establishing an alibi:

a. He called the flight controllers at Forney Field to inquire if there would be any low-flying helicopters in the area that day. (Helicopters with passengers who might see the bloodstained snow or the teens' bodies?)

b. He used his vehicle radio to tell the base radio operator about the abandoned car with the flat tire. (Delaying follow-up questions about Bates' vehicle?)

c. Documenting his shift activities, Thornton filled out a written statement acknowledging he'd fired six rounds of ammunition disposing of "stray dogs in a hunting area on Fort Leonard Wood." (This accounted for the bullets he used to murder the teenagers. To further suppress questions, he told several members in the MP headquarters group about expending several rounds of ammunition.)

d. Thornton asked the officer who relieved him—who was going to take possession of vehicle X37—to wash it thoroughly before departing for patrol. Due to the fact that there were eight inches of snow and ice on the ground and vehicle X37 would be dirty in a matter of seconds after leaving the motor pool area, this was an unusual request. Had the wash job been completed, it would've removed valuable evidence— or at least made it much harder to see. An additional factor, possibly unknown to Thornton at the time, was that due to the low temperatures, the motor pool's vehicle washing equipment was frozen and couldn't be used anyway.

e. Later that afternoon, after the crime was reported, Thornton returned to MP headquarters and checked out another .45 caliber pistol, some ammunition, and disappeared.

f. During the time he was unaccounted for and while the manhunt was active, from roughly 3:13 p.m. until 6:30 p.m., Thornton wrote numerous notes which he put in his pocket. (One such letter, the one which was found in the vehicle he'd borrowed from PFC Paul F. Mara of the 463rd MP Company, was on paper taken from the Fort Wood horse riding stables—after he knew the MPs were looking for him. This letter and all of the notes have appeared in previous chapters. They contain many statements of confusion, headache, and a general lack of understanding as to any crimes he may have committed. In short, they were written to help establish an alibi.)

Similarity to other crimes:

As previously recounted, many of the investigating officers who worked this case believe these notes were written to establish an insanity defense. The sheer volume of these notes required effort to analyze. However, one note in particular deserves attention:

"I don't want to mess up Paul's car, you should be able to follow my footsteps in the snow, I want to write a letter to my wife Patty and pray to God for forgiveness. I really didn't want to hurt anyone. I only remembered after someone I think it was David told me there were four missing persons. I've never done this before at least I don't remember doing it. I've only felt this way, I mean really sick, for only a few months."

The critical statement here is the sentence which reads, "I've never done this before, at least I don't remember doing it."

I have never done this before, as in establishing a defense for the murders of Alfred Marshall and TC Gossage should their bodies ever be found? And he said he'd only been sick for a few months. The disappearance of Al and TC was only a few months prior, so this would attempt to construct a neat alibi for that case.

The people who believe Johnny Lee Thornton is a serial killer look at his statement and believe they know what happened to the two missing kids.

Thornton's behavior at the site where Al Marshall's car was located on October 10, 1976, is suspect. When he came up to the MP Sergeant investigating the parked vehicle, Thornton's statement wasn't, "How can I help you? Do you need help? What you want me to do?" Or any of the other phrases which would most likely be spoken at that time by an officer offering assistance to another officer. Instead Thornton's questions were, "What do you know? What have you found out? Did you find anything? Do you know where the kids are?" In short, was he was fishing for information trying to find out if he'd been careless?

Those who suspect him of murdering Marshall and Gossage also point out that Thornton appeared within three minutes of Moreland's radio announcement that he'd found the vehicle. This means Thornton was somewhere in the immediate area of the car which had once contained the two missing kids. That simple fact by itself is highly suspicious in hindsight.

And finally, we have Johnny Lee Thornton's previously undisclosed report of having fired shots to dispose of dogs. Thornton submitted his report on the morning of October 10, 1976. This report directly related on a time line to the disappearance of Al Marshall and TC Gossage.

Dissimilarity of two cases:

At this point, we have to pause and discuss the difference between the January, 1977, murder case and the October, 1976, disappearance case.

The January, 1977, murders were fully adjudicated in federal court and are now a matter of public record. However, the disappearances of Al and TC in October, 1976, are another matter altogether. It's an open, investigative case — and as such, authors do not have access to those records.

As recounted in previous chapters, federal officers who investigated this case confirm that on the morning of October 10, 1976, Johnny Lee Thornton submitted to MP command a very similar report of shots fired the night before to account for missing ammunition. However, we can't get a copy of the report. We have to accept the officers who say it exists.

And the fact of its existence is devastating to the families of Al and TC.

Many books and articles have been written about the psychology of a serial murder since these two cases occurred. Studies document their progress from youth into adulthood — and the various stages they go through before they become full-blown serial killers. When doing a background on these people, one usually finds that serial killers start out small — torturing dogs and cats, committing arsons, window peeking, Or stealing women's undergarments. A host of sexually-related or violence-themed incidents show up in their backgrounds.

Most of the case studies involving serial killers carefully document the major efforts these men (and they are almost always men) put into looking, acting, and working as a normal person. Words frequently used to describe these men include friendly, charming, personable, and concerned they do their jobs correctly. Or, in simple terms, they try to blend into the surrounding community of people and attempt to not stand out in any way, except maybe as super nice and super normal. And, they stay that way until they lure the next victim into a time, place and situation they cannot escape. Then the monster emerges. At that point, it's too late for the victim(s).

* * *

FBI Agent, Bill Castleberry:

It was interesting. He'd just won the title of Military Policeman of the Year for Fort Leonard Wood. They were surprised. He'd been a model cop, as far as his duties were concerned. He was very enthusiastic about his duties. And so, his motivation didn't become clear until later, obviously.

Most of my thoughts, for me, were, "We have to figure out where those kids are buried so we could find their bodies."

Later, much later, several weeks later, I drove to Springfield and talked to the psychiatrist who interviewed Thornton at the Federal Medical Center. He said most likely the first two victims — and he didn't know about them until I told him — that it was [Thornton's] first time for a human.

Most likely, he's been cruel to animals, has killed dogs and cats and things like that in the past. But most likely, those first two teenagers were his first victims. And being the first, he would've done an extraordinary and strenuous job of hiding their bodies. He might've spent, like a day even, burying them or putting them in a cave somewhere that only he knew about. But most likely, he covered up their bodies in such a way finding their bodies would be extremely difficult.

* * *

Despite an extensive background investigation by the FBI into Johnny Lee Thornton's past, they found nothing along these lines documented by any agency. That doesn't mean these actions didn't occur, it simply means they were never documented and cannot be proven.

However, there may have been other glimpses into the mind of Johnny Lee Thornton.

CID agent interview [Redacted]:

About 3:40 p.m. on January 18, 1977, SP4 [name redacted], game warden, was interviewed. [Name redacted] stated he'd known Thornton since being assigned with him at Fort McClellan, Alabama, during advanced individual training. [Redacted name] considered himself well-acquainted with SP4 Thornton and his wife. [Redacted name] advised on the evening of January 10, 1977, SP4 Thornton was at his quarters and [redacted name] was preparing his income tax.

He stated during the evening, the conversation was brought up about capital punishment and [redacted name] stated the conversation somehow got on the subject of murder. At which time, Thornton stated he could commit murder and get away with it. Thornton stated that he would walk up to someone's house during daylight hours, acting like a normal soldier going about his business, knock on the door, go in and take care of it, and no one would ever find out.

[Redacted name] stated he talked to SP4 Thornton in the game warden office between 2:00 and 3:00 p.m. on January 12, 1977. He stated between 3:00 and 4:00 p.m. on January 12, 1977, he was riding around Fort Leonard Wood with Thornton who said he wanted to talk.

During the conversation, Thornton told him something to the effect he could remember when he was about two years old and sitting on the floor with his arms out reaching for his mother — who wouldn't pay any attention to him. He further stated Thornton told him something about his mother [a fully redacted very long sentence consisting of two lines] couldn't be specific. He stated Thornton appeared depressed at this time and he was surprised [Thornton] even told him this information. He stated after riding around for about one hour, he dropped SP4 Thornton off at the Provost Marshal's Office, about 4:00 p.m. on January 12, 1977.

* * *

The closest we have to any type of criminal background involving Thornton in his mother's testimony at trial. Deanie Thornton said Johnny Lee Thornton robbed a milk farm and a wig salon when he was 18. Money was most likely his motive for the milk farm incident. However, the wig-salon robbery raised questions of whether he took wigs or other such feminine accessories for sexual gratification. At this late date, we have no way of determining.

* * *

Several investigators in this case were familiar with behavioral profiling and serial killer traits. They all expressed a concern that for Thornton to tackle four kids on his supposedly first foray into a murder was highly improbable. These well-trained officers believed it an immense step at a fairly young age. They cannot bring themselves to believe that would be the case. But they also recognize there are exceptions to every theory.

Therefore, if one wishes to conjecture the trail of Thornton as a serial killer-in-training, the trail would go from the burglaries of the milk farm and wig shop to the disappearance of Al and TC, and then to the abduction of the four kids — at which time his career ended. Most officers who study criminal profile behavior say this was still a pretty fast progression — and would be somewhat unusual. They usually see methodical progress over a longer period of time. That doesn't mean it couldn't have happened. It merely indicates it wasn't exactly what the officers would expect to see as a normal progression. However, it could mean Thornton was good at covering up his behavior, never leaving a typical serial killer trail before the 1976/1977 crimes.

While going through Thornton's federal court files, I found a number of psychiatric reports filed by Federal Medical Center psychiatrists in Springfield, Missouri, who examined Johnny Lee Thornton. Since these reports were in the file and I was told I could get copies, I marked for copies. The Clerk of the Federal Court later advised me that Judge Collinson had sealed these copies and I couldn't have them. Therefore, the only psychological views we have into Thornton's mind come from the testimony presented at his competency hearings held in Springfield, Missouri, and the testimony at trial by Defense and Prosecution witnesses.

We also have several comments by the agents who worked this case that the psychiatrists who examined Thornton at the Federal Medical Center for Inmates told them, Thornton would not have confessed to his crimes — no matter what evidence they presented to him nor how effective their questioning. Such a mindset would be hard to understand or to explain, especially since he was caught red-handed and convicted in his role as the killer of the three kids in the Bates' vehicle.

And then, I found a possible answer.

Ann Rule was an author who wrote a lot of books about various true crime cases. One of her first books, *The Stranger Beside Me*, was an up-close and personal account of her job at a crisis prevention hot-line center, working alongside her friend, a man who would soon become infamous as one of the most horrific serial killers in America — Ted Bundy.

As Rule struggled to explain the complex psychological side of Ted Bundy to her readers, she basically concluded that the only thing that mattered to Bundy was Bundy.

And there, in simple words, you have Johnny Lee Thornton. He was all that mattered to him and he wouldn't confess. Nor will he ever set the record straight on Al Marshall and TC Gossage.

I would love to be proven wrong on this point but I hold zero hope he will ever reveal what happened to them, or reveal their final resting location.

The Ted Bundy comparison has also occurred to several other people.

James Reist, a former fellow MP game warden in 1977 said the following in response to a question:

> You know, when you asked what kind of guy JLT was...I almost compared him to Ted Bundy, because they were both personable and quite likable individuals. Johnny never displayed any characteristics of anger or aggression towards anyone. Even when we were arresting or pursuing them on the road or in the woods. He always conducted himself as a professional. And his appearance standards were always of the highest standards. Just goes to show you...you can never tell a person by their appearance or [daily] actions.

16

THE AFTERMATH

THE AFTERMATH OF JOHNNY LEE Thornton's murder spree had a tremendous effect on the Fort Leonard Wood region. In many respects, repercussions from the issues which surfaced during this murder case still plague the Fort Wood region today. From the very start, the case affected both the military and civilian populations of the region. It was a nightmare public relations battle for the Army that was fought on many levels and in several venues.

That isn't to say the United States Army didn't take steps to protect its reputation and to present to the community their side of the story. One of the first steps the military took was to try to eliminate the rumors. In order to do this, they gave the news media at the time unprecedented access to an investigation on the military reservation.

Another effort to address the issues consisted of a letter, written by the Commanding General of Fort Leonard Wood, and addressed to the Honorable Paul Page of the Missouri House of Representatives, to address the thoughts and feelings of the United States military and to call these issues to the attention of the elected representatives of the immediate region.

The letter written by Gen. Harris to Representative Page:

20 January 1977

Honorable Paul Page, Jr.

Missouri House of Representatives

Jefferson City, Missouri 65101

Dear Mr. Page;

I am writing to you as a result of our conversation on Tuesday, 18 January 1977, to provide you with certain information relating to the tragic incident which recently occurred at Fort Leonard Wood. I know you realize I am somewhat constrained in comments I may make so that I will not jeopardize the ongoing FBI investigation or the rights of the individual who has been charged with these most serious offenses.

Almost immediately after the offenses were reported the FBI assumed jurisdiction pursuant to a long-standing agreement between the Departments of Justice and Defense. The direction of all investigative activities remains in their hands with military authorities assisting in every possible way. The suspect, who is currently in federal custody, was apprehended the evening of the incident by military police working in cooperation with the FBI. As you know, he has since been arraigned in Springfield and we expect the jurisdiction will be retained by federal civilian authorities.

I am, of course, acutely concerned such a terrible thing could happen in our community and most particularly with the fact that the person charged with the commission of these offenses is one with whom the law enforcement responsibilities were entrusted. But, after careful personal and professional soul-searching by me and the members of my staff, I am convinced there was nothing we could've done to prevent these senseless deaths or even reasonably to anticipate such a horrible possibility.

Department of the Army constantly strives to improve the quality and effectiveness of the law enforcement personnel and support within the Army. Efforts currently in progress include actions to further improve and reclassification procedures to control, even more stringently, entry into the military police field and to enhance the quality of law enforcement training.

There is nothing apparent in the background of the suspect which is out of the ordinary or indicates any dereliction in his selection for military police duties. He entered the service and conducted his basic training here at Fort Leonard Wood. He then proceeded to the military police school at Fort McClellan, Alabama, and completed eight weeks advanced individual training as a military police correctional specialist. Some of the subjects in which he received instruction were law, investigations, behavioral sciences, and correctional administration. He did very well in his training. He met the regulatory requirements for assignment in his specialty. These requirements are he did not have any disqualifying physical condition, he scored high on his aptitude test, he didn't have a record of court-martial or civil conviction (except for minor traffic violations), and he must have exhibited no pattern of undesirable behavior while as a civilian or during military service.

During the 15 months the suspect worked as a military policeman at Fort Leonard Wood, there was absolutely no indication he would ever commit such acts for which he is now charged. He did his job well and appeared dedicated. He was well thought of and liked by his friends and fellow workers. He had no record of civilian or military convictions, nor were there any indications of physical or emotional illness. He is married and has two children but is currently separated from his family. In reviewing the total picture there is nothing in this man's history, record, or duty performance which could've raised suspicions or questions concerning his capabilities to do the job he was entrusted to perform.

At the time of these offenses, our military police game wardens, of which the suspect was one, operated as one-man patrols as a result of our need for maximum coverage of this extremely large installation. We have since converted to two-man patrols in an effort to visibly reassure the civilian and military communities of our concern and to protect our law enforcement personnel from any emotional overreaction might produce unwarranted accusations against them.

Finally, there are just a few comments I feel compelled to add which I hope will aid all of us in putting this incident in perspective. Fort Leonard Wood is virtually a self-contained city of over 37,000 inhabitants. If incorporated it would be the 10th largest city in the state. Its rural location means it is the center of activity for countless additional people. These circumstances are such one might expect a constant flow of serious crime, yet such isn't the case. Order and safety are the rule. Exceptions are rare. I am proud of my people and my installation for this. In particular, I am proud of the vast majority of hard-working and dedicated law enforcement men and women who are never applauded when all is well but are soundly and collectively castigated when something goes wrong. It would be most unfortunate if people pass judgment on the soldier or Fort Leonard Wood without carefully considering all of the facts and circumstances.

I share in your grief and want you to know all of us have been deeply touched by these senseless killings. I thank you for displaying interest in the welfare and good name of the Army and Fort Leonard Wood and for giving me this opportunity to share my thoughts with you during this most difficult time.

Sincerely,

Richard L Harris

Maj. Gen., USA

Commanding

* * *

The struggle for a better future for the Army, in general, and the MP Corps, in particular, due to the problems arising from the Thornton case went on for years. One of the early proponents to recognize faults and press for a better method for the future was the Provost Marshal of Fort Wood, Colonel Perry B. Elder.

On August 22, 1977, Colonel Elder sent a letter to Colonel Patrick R. Lowery, the Chief of the Law Enforcement Division at Headquarters, Department of the Army, in Washington DC:

*

Dear Colonel Lowery,

I feel a need to share with you some concerns spawned by a recent tragic experience at Fort Leonard Wood.

On 13 January 1977, three teenagers from the nearby community of Plato, Missouri were murdered by SP4 Johnny Lee Thornton, a military policeman assigned at Fort Leonard Wood. Subsequently, in a federal court, Council Bluffs, Iowa, he was found guilty of first-degree murder, assault with intent to kill, rape and kidnapping.

The incident was one of the most heinous crimes I've ever been involved in as a military police officer. The resulting attitudes of the civilian population toward the military police, especially from the area in which the youths lived, was obviously predictable. I, along with other officers of the post headquarters met with the people of Plato, Missouri, within 2 to 3 weeks after the incident. This meeting enables them to vent long-standing complaints and cleared the air for future communications.

From this meeting we established a manned gate at the southern boundary of the post, increased all patrols to two men, and established the point of contact between the post and members of the community. The point of contact was originally the IG, but I'm happy to say since that time the heads of the community have started contacting me personally.

The rapport with the people has steadily improved, and the Provost Marshal's office has even, on two occasions, played the residence of Plato in slow pitch softball. In the near future, I will attend the luncheon of leaders from the area and will present a few remarks. Though feelings and attitudes have improved, it will require continued effort to completely heal the wounds this incident has opened.

To better the law enforcement relations, we have organized a Big Piney Law Enforcement Association. This includes all law enforcement heads and their assistance from the five counties surrounding Fort Leonard Wood. This action has met with outstanding results, and a closer law enforcement effort has already developed.

SP4 Johnny Lee Thornton was considered an outstanding military policeman. In fact, I had, within 30 days prior to the incident, both company commanders check the records of all of our men with the idea of identifying any who should not be military policeman. Specialist Thornton's record was without blemish. Also, later checks on his health record indicated no trouble are areas to cause questions. Using this information as a backdrop, I would now like to focus upon my real concern and the catalyst, for this letter.

At the meeting of Plato questions concerning the selection, qualifications, and the training of military police were repeatedly raised. These were foremost in the minds of our civilian neighbors and they couldn't understand how the Army could give such a man is Thornton a badge, gun, and the authority of the policeman. Specifically, they wanted to know if we required psychological testing. Enclosed is an article which appeared in the Sunday news leader Springfield, Missouri on 31 July 1977, which also focuses on this question.

I have noted on page 66, volume 1, Task Group Report, Provost Marshal and Military Police Activities – An Assessment, that psychological testing was an area discussed. I feel the need for such testing is extremely important to our corps.

Using SP4 Thornton as an example, we can clearly see he apparently had a Borderline Character Disorder, as was brought out during the trial. It took a battery of psychiatrists to make this determination, and, then, they didn't all agree on the term which would best define his deep-seated trouble. However, psychological testing of potential military policeman could identify basic characteristics which would signal the need for further evaluation. If such testing was in effect when Johnny Thornton was trained as a military policeman, this heinous incident may never have occurred.

I understand the Army Research Institute could be levied for a requirement to adopt such an appropriate test. If so, I recommend such action immediately. This part of the PROPLE program, I feel, needs prompt attention, and action should not be delayed any longer if we are to ensure the stability of those soldiers we select as military policeman.

In addition, I feel all persons selected to be military policeman should be given a background investigation. The NAC, and accompanying records check, is inadequate. There are military policemen on duty today who were a source of problems within their communities but not to the point of being arrested with the resultant record. In some cases, they were the ones who local law enforcement agencies encourage to join the service prior to their being arrested or committing an act which would result in an official record. Though a background investigation, the conduct of such people can be properly identified. It is questionable whether they should ever be a soldier, much less a military policeman.

I realize the cost of both psychological testing and background investigations would be high and would cause many to accept less effective selection procedures. However, I do not feel any cost is too great when our core's integrity and, perhaps existence, is at stake. Comparatively speaking, it would be interesting to see what the total cost, from crime to sentencing, has been for criminal acts committed by military policeman.

However, cost isn't the sole criteria. The real reason and over-writing criteria for determining the need for psychological testing and background investigations is the general populace expect, rightly so, the military police corps and the Army will place the best qualified personnel in the positions of trust and authority inherent in the job of all military policeman. I do not feel we are meeting this responsibility with the present selection procedures. To cite cost as a reason for not having such a program, isn't acceptable, as has been found, in the eyes of those we serve.

I feel you must use every resource available to you to ensure a more stringent selection criteria is forthcoming. The need for strengthening our selection criteria was vividly portrayed in the assessment of August, 1976. Incidents of the magnitude described in the Thornton case strongly demonstrated the need for rapid implementation of findings and planned actions outlined in Chapter 5 of the assessment.

I hope my thoughts and comments on this subject adequately express the deep concern I have with the effectiveness of our present selection process. Please feel free to call upon me if I may assist your efforts, in this area, in any way.

Sincerely.

Perry B. Elder, Jr.,

Colonel, Military Police Corps

Provost Marshal

* * *

The Army and CID worked out another way to make sure the lessons learned from the Thornton case were not lost. They set up a lecture presentation at Fort McClellan, Alabama, in front of a new class of MPs in training. In order to present it for training for future classes of both CID and MP Officers, they filmed the lecture. The film was part of the required basic MP course for many years. At the time of the Thornton murders, the military police training school was at Fort Mc-Clellan, Alabama. Since 1999, the military police training school has resided at Fort Leonard Wood, Missouri.

I had the opportunity to review the training film created in 1977, and I had sufficient time to take a few notes during the review.

* * *

Overview of the case by Colonel Perry Elder:

> This morning, it gives me great pleasure to be here at the military police school to present to you the Johnny Lee Thornton murder case. On the other hand, it saddens me to have to come before you and tell you the details of one of the most hideous crimes I have ever been associated with, especially a crime involving a military policeman — a man who was trained by the military police and, in fact, was on active duty with the military police when this crime was committed.

> This morning, the first portion of the story I will tell you isn't fantasy, it isn't a detective story. It's the story of a living victim. A young girl who was shot, but survived, and later told her story in details which are not pretty. But they are details which are accurate and which lent much to the investigation of this hideous crime. Keep in mind, these were young teenagers — happy, having a good time in life just as many of you have done in the past. And many of you probably have children who are doing the same thing today.

Following Elder's opening statements and his detailed description of the crimes, Elder introduced FBI Special Agent, William Castleberry, who gave the audience the details of the investigation from the viewpoint of the FBI. After completing his portion of the lecture, Castleberry was followed by CID Special Agent, George Matthews, who detailed the involvement of the CID agents in this case. Between the two agents, they presented a graphic, extremely detailed, and explicit presentation of the case. Their remarks were backed up by crime scene photographs, autopsy photographs, and much more.

The film is a compelling presentation and one which will not be quickly forgotten. The final result was a film that lasted almost 90 minutes.

* * *

FBI Agent, Bill Castleberry:

> Over the years, I also have had police officers who had served as an Army MP or CID agents, tell me they'd learned about the

Thornton case during training. But I only presented the case one time. I remember the details partially because of what else was going on at that time — the real reason I was assigned at Fort Leonard Wood in the first place.

When I initially arrived at Fort Leonard Wood, I had briefed Perry and Matt of my primary investigative focus. They were always very helpful and supportive, even though they didn't have any jurisdiction off base.

After the Thornton prosecution, there was a lot of interest expressed to present the case to their new training classes at Fort McClellan, Alabama. Just when it was being set up, I got a real break on what I was supposed to be concentrating on and I needed to push hard on that. I explained my situation to Perry and Matt and they were very accommodating. They arranged for an Army plane to fly from Fort Leonard Wood directly to Fort McClellan, Alabama. And after the presentation, back to Fort Leonard Wood the same day.

They taped the presentation. And I was later told the presentation was played for subsequent MP and CID classes.

I remember they told me they had to edit one part out because they had changed their autopsy protocols to not use metal rods to show the trajectory of the rounds because of atypical tissue damage.

With me on the plane was Colonel Perry Elder, George Matthews, and the pilot, of course.

* * *

Retired Military Police Officer, James S. Reist:

We focused on accountability for pretty much every minute of the shift — breaks, report writing, witness interviews, DWI processing, meetings, and nightly training sessions were all accounted for. I had been a one-man unit for most of my career up to that point. Then it became mandatory that all units would consist of no less than two officers. The only exceptions were the patrol supervisor's and the duty officer's units.

Communications checks were conducted every fifteen minutes from the MP base radio, call frequency AAF 725, to each patrol on the shift.

Patrol supervisors did a visual check on every one of their patrol units throughout the shift. Patrol supervisors stashed slips of coded paper at each security check location for their units to retrieve and turn in at the end of the shift.

Leaving your patrol sector without prior approval wasn't tolerated. The units were encouraged to do more static patrol positions that is to be parked in plain sight of the public, as these were considered to be a preventative measure to reduce violations.

Patrols were advised if the vehicle failed to pull over for a traffic stop and was continuing in the direction of the main gate, we were to allow them to continue, radio the main gate, advise them of our approach, and request they stop the vehicle in the safe zone median.

On vehicle stops, other patrols would perform more frequent roll-bys of the stopped unit and its violator vehicle to reassure the public and to promote both public safety and to be in a position to offer assistance to the officer who had the vehicle stopped if needed.

* * *

The aftermath of the Thornton case affected people in many ways around Fort Wood area. People have shared with me their personal accounts of the wide variety of emotions and events which occurred in later years. These personal stories are unique and relevant.

* * *

Former MP, David Kuwamoto:

I was an MP at Fort Leonard Wood with the 208th MP Company from 1979 to 1981, just after these murders happened. It was pure hell trying to enforce traffic laws and, or pull people over at the time — especially around the south gate [back gate] area. People were afraid of us.

Before we could even make the stop, we were required to call our radio dispatch and request authorization from our desk Sergeant for a stop, stating, "requesting Red lights for" and state what the reason was — failure to stop for stop sign, expired license plates, speeding, or whatever the case. Only if permission was granted could we turn on our emergency equipment and make the stop.

During this time frame, we were also required to have two-man patrol vehicles for our safety as well as the safety and comfort of the public. The public just didn't trust the MPs at the time.

While stationed there, I pulled a lot of the south gate duty. I think my platoon sergeant didn't like me very much. The gate did get the occasional gun shot in the middle of the dark nights. The gate had been fortified to help better protect us from the gunfire. These were some long and scary nights. My biggest fear was when a vehicle would approach in the middle of the night. I never knew what to expect. And we were on our own. The nearest back-up was twenty minutes away.

The gate never physically got shot while I was there, but there were shots in the area at night time. And there were physical holes in the gate from the shots. I was never there when it was actually hit. You never saw the duty officer out around the back gate.

I was just a private at the time and I spent three-to-four days a week at the back gate. I saw bullet holes in the gate on several occasions — and I saw where they had repaired other bullet holes. The gate was reinforced to protect us. We sat pretty low in the gate until a car approached. Then, you had to stand up. The gate was about the size of two phone booths at the time, so we stayed inside the gate unless a car approached. They put some steel plates into the guard shack and we also had big, wooden boxes filled with sandbags.

We were pretty much alone out there. We had some patrols come by and the game warden patrols came by. They switched them from the International Scouts to CJ5 Jeeps. The game wardens pretty well kept off the main streets. At that time, they stayed in the wooded areas because of the whole Johnny Lee Thornton issue. The Jeeps kept out on the ranges and in the wooded areas. But most of the time, if something happened to you out there, you had at least a twenty-minute time lag on backup.

I did road patrols. People would run from you all the time. Whenever you wanted to stop somebody, you had to call in and give the reason why — and request to use red lights. Sometimes they sped away and sometimes they just wouldn't stop. Or, they'd go to a gate or some other place where there were lots of people. But I've also had people who wouldn't stop and just went out the back gate. Of course, we stopped at the back gate because we couldn't pursue them off post.

When I first arrived at Fort Leonard Wood, the Thornton story was one of the first things they briefed us on. We were all brand-new MPs straight out of the MP Academy. They had transferred out many of the older men who'd been at Fort Wood during the Thornton incident. They felt those men were tied to the bad incident. They were trying to make the community feel safer, so they brought in a bunch of brand-new privates and everything was brand-new.

They filled us in on the history of the case. And they had us run two-man patrols for our safety and for the safety of the community — because with a two-man patrol there was less chance of one man going rogue.

When I went to MP school, they told us about it but we didn't have the film on it because it had just happened. I think either the trial was going or they hadn't had the trial yet. Thornton had not been convicted, yet. So, when I got here, I talked to some of the CID and MPI officers. They told me about Thornton's multiple personalities and the rest of the story.

The south gate was small — a good target. You're out there in the middle of nowhere. In the nighttime, it was kind of scary but at least you could listen to music. And so, I guess it was all right. Yeah, Johnny Lee Thornton kinda made it bad for everybody.

* * *

In 1992, Kevin Finn, a newly-arrived member of the 4th platoon of the 300rd MP Company, had just been assigned to Fort Leonard Wood. His first two working nights, he did a ride-along with an MP from Fort Wood. However, the third shift he went solo and began patrolling the post. Around 9:30 p.m. that night, as he approached the south gate, Finn noticed a car coming north with only one headlight. Deciding this would be a good warning, Finn did a U-turn and came up behind the vehicle and activated his red lights.

The car didn't stop. Instead, it sped up. Finn followed the vehicle for quite some distance with his red lights on before they got to the Bloodland Range Control building.

At that point, the vehicle made a sudden left turn into the Bloodland Range Control parking lot. A female jumped out of the car and ran into the building. Finn radio advised the MP desk what was happening. They told Finn the people inside Bloodland Range Control would handle the headlight warning and for him to report to the MP desk immediately for a special briefing.

When Finn arrived at the MP desk, the desk sergeant sat him down and told him the story of Johnny Lee Thornton. Finn said at first he thought the desk sergeant was pulling his leg.

"Is this a joke?"

The desk sergeant said, "No. This was for real." The desk sergeant asked Finn where he'd been that he didn't already know about this story. Finn told him he'd been stationed in Germany for the past several years.

The desk sergeant said, "Because of the Thornton case, people have not been stopping for MPs on the south gate road — and many other locations on Fort Wood for a long time now."

Thus, MP Kevin Finn was initiated into the aftermath of the Johnny Lee Thornton case — 15 years after it had happened.

* * *

Mark Ward, a current Missouri State Highway Patrol road trooper and zone supervisor:

Yes, I watched the Thornton film. This would've been early in 1989 while I was at MP school at Fort McClellan. I thought to myself, "How could an MP do this?" You know, because I was still looking with fresh eyes at law enforcement. You know, I thought everybody was going to uphold the law and be law-abiding citizens and it was a shocker to me an MP could do that. This basically shattered my perception of what law enforcement was, or could be.

I grew up in Tempe, Arizona and I had never heard of Fort Leonard Wood. I had never even given Fort Leonard Wood a thought. I didn't even know where it was. Later I got sent to Delta Company, 787th Military Police Battalion at Fort Leonard Wood.

When I arrived at Fort Leonard Wood in June, 1992, I quickly learned that MPs were still not well-liked by the general population. Especially out the back gate, the Evening Shade community and around that area.

The MPs were still looked at suspiciously by a lot of the local people too. I heard stories when we first got here, about how they were shooting at the guards at the back gate. And they had to close down the back-gate guard house because things were not healthy.

* * *

In 2003, Cheryl Keeton, her husband, and daughter moved to Plato, Missouri. Her daughter, Samantha started school in Plato.

In 2005, Cheryl and Samantha were driving onto post. They stopped at the guard shack at the south gate, which was usually manned by civilian police officers. However, on this day there were MPs on duty. Cheryl said her daughter suddenly went frantic in the backseat.

"Mother! Mother! We're at the south gate and the MPs kill people here at the south gate."

Cheryl Keeton got her daughter to calm down and they went onto post. Cheryl asked Samantha where she'd learned this and Samantha said, "They told me in school."

The next time they entered the south gate and there were MPs on duty at the guard shack, Samantha immediately froze stiff in the back seat and didn't move while they went through the gate.

Cheryl asked her daughter, "Why did you do that?"

Samantha replied, "If they think I'm dead, they won't bother us."

Samantha continued to play dead at the back gate for almost a full year, still terrified of MPs.

* * *

CID Agent, George Matthews worked on both the Thornton case and the case of the two missing teens. In retirement, he wrote letters to Thornton in prison hoping to establish a dialogue with him, which might lead to clues about the fate of the missing teens. Matthews never received a response from Thornton.

In the same vein, Renard Ellis, a civilian worker on Fort Wood who lives in Pulaski County heard the story of the Thornton murders and the missing teens. Ellis wrote letters to Thornton in prison hoping to obtain a clue to the whereabouts of the teens. He never received a response from Thornton. Ellis also actively searched the Internet for clues to the case.

While I was researching this book, I kept running into his name in various information locations. Once Ellis learned what I was doing, we exchanged information on the case that has led him to locations on Fort Wood, which he searched at ground level. I suspect we'll continue to exchange information after this book is published.

Eric Lynn Foster grew up in Waynesville, Missouri. At a tender young age, after graduating college, he joined the United States Army and became a military police officer. He'd met a young lady while he was in college named Kathy Elder. In 1981, he married the daughter of Colonel Perry Elder. Eric knew Al Marshall personally but can only vaguely remember TC Gossage. Al was one or two years ahead of Eric in high school.

Eric Lynn Foster:

> I was just a kid in school watching this thing unfold in my community and even then, it was almost like, "It's not possible. This couldn't be possible." This is one of those things you think, "This can't happen in my town or to my family." And then you realize, you are "the other town" and you are "the other family." And then years later, you look back and think, "It was just a bad dream." It could've been real, but it was that bad. The fact the girl survived has always blown me away.

I was dating his daughter when this happened. I never talked to him about this. I went to college, and the Army, and I became an MP. And when I did, he started talking about some of the things. And, of course, we talked about this case — probably three or four times from 1983 to 1986. But he would always mention there were a lot of people around who thought or suspected [Thornton] was involved in the Al Marshall and TC Gossage missing case. He said, "We just never had anything. It's very possible. It could've been. But we just never had any good leads or anything to help us find them or their bodies, you know?

Colonel Elder was also quick to give his MP son-in-law what he considered sound advice on his duties as an MP in a command position.

One of the things in the tape [the MP training video] which stood out to me — [Elder] mentioned to me a couple times — This was the most heinous crimes he had ever seen or been involved with in his entire military career. I think his military career spanned twenty-six years, so he probably saw quite a few bad things in the Army. This stuck pretty heavy on his mind. I would say he told me this when I became an MP. He was always trying to coach me and teach me, whether I wanted to hear it or not.

One of the things he'd done in previous assignments before he got to Fort Leonard Wood and when he got to Fort Leonard Wood as the Provost Marshal — and he told me I should do this as a young Lieutenant, Captain, or Provost Marshal — he said, "I told my Sergeant Major and Company Commanders I wanted to see all of the disciplinary files and counseling folders on every soldier who was an MP, and who was going to work MP duty while he was there." And he wanted to see their medical records. They all thought he was a micro-manager, and that was a little too deep for his level. He'd been accused of being a micro-manager from time to time throughout his career. But nonetheless, they brought all the disciplinary and counseling folders and files on the soldiers. And he was able to gain access to their medical records.

He told me that he personally went over every one of those files to see if there were any disciplinary problems, or health or mental issues. He felt that as a Provost Marshal — a senior law enforcement guy — it was his duty to make sure the people conducting law enforcement on a military installation, who were carrying a weapon and dealing with the public should be mentally and physically in good standing and capable of going and doing that. He didn't want troubled soldiers working on the road. So, he did that the first couple weeks after he landed at Fort Leonard Wood.

I don't know how much time passed between when he arrived at Fort Wood and when this incident occurred. But he told me, one of the things — it sticks out more than anything — one of the first things Army leaders over him asked, "Were there any indications you knew, or anybody knew, that Johnny Lee Thornton had any mental issues, or problems, or challenges, or disciplinary actions?" He said it was easy for him to look them in the eye and say, "No, we didn't know. And by the way, when I got here, I asked to see those files to do that very thing. To take a good look at these young men and women soldiers to make sure they could perform their military police duty. And they were in good standing."

* * *

During the research for this book, I had ladies tell me their dad gave them strict instructions about what to do if an MP tried to stop them. I showcase one small story of a father attempting to protect his daughter, and let this single-story stand for all of the other people who talked to me:

According to Laura Julian Morgan:

Well, after that situation out on post — I wasn't even close to driving at the time, but I started driving in 1981. I can't remember when the court case was. I know it happened like 1977 or 1978, but when I got my driver's license in 1981, Dad said if I went on post and I got stopped, or they got behind me with the lights and everything, I was to drive slowly to the front gate. And I wasn't to break any of the other laws. Dad said he didn't feel comfortable with me driving on Fort Wood after the Thornton situation.

What makes this particular story so remarkable is her father, Thomas M. Julian Sr., wasn't only a proud retired United States

Army member, but following his retirement, Tom Julian had gone to work for the St. Robert City Police Department. The city of St. Robert borders Fort Leonard Wood on one of the main traffic arteries leaving Fort Wood. By 1981, Julian was the Chief of the St. Robert Police Department. So, the advice given to his daughter carries a special note of concern, since it came from a retired Army member and a current police chief.

* * *

Sergeant Mike Watson, of the Missouri State Highway Patrol (Ret.):

I didn't arrive at Fort Leonard Wood until January 16, 1978. I was assigned to the second platoon of the 463 MP Company — which was Thornton's former platoon. About half of the platoon members remaining, at the time I arrived, knew Thornton. And, being so close to the one-year anniversary of the murders, there were lots of rumors going around within the company that the citizens and family members were plotting revenge against the military police.

I don't remember getting any specific training class about the rules of conduct brought about because of the Thornton case, but there were a lot of things we couldn't do. No traffic stop could be made on the south gate road, or the southern part of the Fort. It was very eerie to be assigned to the south gate. You couldn't stop anyone entering the post. You only make contact with them if they stopped and contacted you. And, we had several drivers who refused to stop on the highway. When we would get them stopped, they would claim they were in fear of their life.

Those situations were usually handled by the ranking duty officer, and mostly nothing was done by the duty officer if the duty officer was at the Fort when the murders occurred. Around 1980, that excuse didn't work very well. John Groves was a lieutenant there, but I believe he arrived about 1980 or 1981. He could tell you what he was instructed to do if that situation arose.

* * *

LTC (Ret) John Groves, Military Police Corps:

I got there in 1978. I was originally with the 208th MP Company. It was a Garrison Unit and I was assigned initially when I got there as the physical security officer. All LTs pulled road supervisory duty. I was a Second Lieutenant when I got there — brand-new. Of course, I had a prior enlistment behind me, and I had served as a Joplin City Police Officer for five years, and then two years as a Polk County Deputy Sheriff. So, I did have a clue about law enforcement.

Let me tell you how weird it was back then. My first duty day, my Sergeant tells me, "Hey, sir, it's Sunday. There's nothing ever happens on Sunday, so it'll be quiet." And so, forty-five minutes into my shift, I drive up to the wooded park behind the old bus station and I find a body hanging from a tree, by the neck. And that started it, we had armed robberies and shootings. We were on a twenty-four-hour shift and I ran a straight twenty-four hours. Welcome to Fort Leonard Wood.

I worked quite a bit on the road, plus my other job. When it came to the Thornton case, actually you know, they never gave us anything or told us. So, I found out the hard way. I had one of my patrols. It was attempting to stop a female motorist. And they were not too far from where the Provost Marshal's Office was, and so she drove up close to the Provost Marshal's office —which was lighted and everything. And then, she wouldn't roll her window down. So, they called me to the scene. The patrol told me, "Sir, she won't roll the window down for us or talk to us." So, I said, "Let me go up and talk to her."

I introduced myself to her and she asked me, "How do I know you're an MP?"

I told her, "Well, I have all the equipment on and there are three of us here. I understand what the conditions were when the Thornton incident occurred here. And I understand you're scared. So okay, ma'am, I can tell you we are who we say we are."

And so, I told her, "Right up there, ma'am, is the Provost Marshal's Office. Why don't you just drive up there and park in front of the building where the other MPs and the desk sergeant are located?" And she said, "Okay I'll do that."

This happened quite a bit. It was quite frequent. A lot of them wouldn't stop — especially the female motorists.

Then during the summer of 1979, I was on duty and I was out on the road — not too far from the airport — and it was about one or one thirty in the morning. All of a sudden, this voice came over the radio screaming, "Shots fired! Shots fired! They're shooting at us at the south gate! South gate! Send help now!"

So, I haul butt and I'm the first one there. They are lying on the ground. I jump out with my pistol drawn. I'm looking around. Somebody had fired a high-powered rifle into the guard shack, through the glass — blew the heck out of place. And those guys were, like, down on the ground. I told them to stay down and wait for the other units. Of course, we called Pulaski County Sheriff's Department and the Missouri State Highway Patrol and additional military police units for assistance.

They found some shell casings out in the woods behind a tree, outside of the base, off to the southwest side of the guard shack. Somebody had set up out there and opened fire on the south gate guys with a .30/06 rifle. They pumped several rounds into the building. Those poor guys were just shaking. When it was over, I had to call the Provost Marshal and brief him on the incident.

One of the big things in the aftermath of the Thornton affair were the game wardens. They had to check in by radio constantly. They kept track of [game wardens] like crazy. And we, as duty officers, had to know where the game wardens were at all times. When the call-in came they had better be where they said were.

At the time I was there — after the Thornton affair — besides the three FBI agents on post, we had two full companies of military police officers and the Provost Marshal's office. We had thirteen full-time CID agents and usually three or four probationary agents in training. I had twenty two Military Police Investigators [MPI] in my unit. We were so busy we needed every one of them.

Author's Note: FBI Agent, Jim Holmes was assigned to Fort Wood in the aftermath of the Thornton case in the fall of 1977. He joined agents Castleberry and Den Ouden.

BIOGRAPHY

J.B. KING IS A 1965 graduate of Salem Missouri Senior High School. He attended the School of the Ozarks at Pt. Lookout, Missouri, graduating with a Bachelor's Degree in Sociology in August of 1969. He entered the Missouri State Highway Patrol Academy September 14, 1969.

Upon graduation from the MSHP Academy, his first assignment was to the Waynesville/Ft Wood Zone of Troop I in December of 1969. Pulaski County has been his home since then. He is one of a very small group of troopers the Missouri State Highway Patrol awarded the Medal of Valor. He retired as the local zone sergeant in June of 2001. He then became a reserve officer for the Waynesville City Police.

In 2004, he ran for Sheriff of Pulaski County and won. After being reelected for a second term in 2008, he retired as Sheriff in December 2012. He then became a reserve deputy, currently assigned to the detective division.

He and his wife Cheryl have one son, Taylor. A member of the Missouri Writers Guild, he wrote two books about the American civil war in Missouri — *The Tilley Treasure*, and *Justice*. He has published one short story law-enforcement- humor book, *Tales From the Blue*: *Adventures in Law Enforcement*.

Look for him on Facebook, Author J. B. King, and on his Amazon Author page: https://www.amazon.com/J.B.-King/e/B06XKXV6JK

SANDRA MILLER LINHART WAS BORN in Lander, Wyoming on a warm, summer day in a hospital which has since been turned into a mental institution...which most likely holds no correlation...probably.

Life inspires Sandra in both her writing and her art. Ms. Linhart holds degrees in Sociology, Paralegal, Writing, Graphic Arts, and Private Investigation. She's been featured on radio shows, invited to speak at schools, and participated in conference panel discussions and presentations.

Sandra has five daughters, seven grandkids, and currently resides in the beautiful mountains of Colorado.

Sandra Miller Linhart is an award-winning author and member of the Society of Children's Book Writers and Illustrators (SCBWI), The Missouri Writer's Guild, and the Military Writers Society of America (MWSA). Her award-winning titles include *Diary of an Unkempt Woman*, *Daddy's Boots*, and *Pickysaurus Mac*.

Her titles can be found on Amazon as well as libraries and brick-and-mortar book stores.

Visit her webpage Sandstarbooks.com

APPENDIX

SOURCES

- First, there were my own personal recollections of this case. This includes a three-page deposition taken by the Federal Public Defender's Office in Kansas City, Missouri. They deposed me for the facts of the interview with Juanita Deckard, roadside.

- I conducted numerous personal interviews with Military and Civilian law-enforcement officers involved in the investigations, the families of the victims, and the family and acquaintances of Johnny Lee Thornton. Some are quoted directly in this book.

- Then, we secured written documentation:

1–The 131-page transcript of proceedings held on Thursday, June 2, 1977, otherwise known as the competency hearing for Johnny Lee Thornton.

2–The 85-page transcript of proceedings in federal court held on June 10 and 13, 1977, includes additional testimony from FBI Agents, Paul A. VanSomeren and William Castleberry.

   a. The proceedings also concerned a Defense motion to suppress a military search warrant issued for Johnny Lee Thornton's barracks on Fort Leonard Wood. CID Agent, Thomas W. Byrd completed this phase of the investigation and wrote the affidavit in support of the search warrant.

   b. Military judge, Major Kenneth Miles Mitchell approved the affidavit and granted the search warrant.

   c. Johnny Lee Thornton's living quarters were searched, and a number of evidence items seized.

   d. The search warrant was suppressed by Judge Collinson due to error on the part of the military judge.

3–Judge William R. Collinson's instructions to potential jury members in St. Joseph as to the conduct in proceedings of the trial and the behavior expected of them. The 14-page Document was issued on Monday, June 13, 1977, when the Thornton case came up for trial in St. Joseph Missouri.

4–A 51-page deposition taken on Friday, June 24, 1977, on the testimony of Sergeant Thomas W. Connors. At the time , he was stationed at supreme NATO headquarters in Belgium and reported to St. Joseph, Missouri for the trial.

   a. Connors' duty requirements conflicted with the actual trial date in Iowa and the court allowed his testimony to be done by deposition.

   b. At the time of the Thornton case, Connors was a member of the 208th Military Police Company stationed at Fort Leonard Wood, Missouri, and was pulling duty in the arm's room of the 463rd MP Company.

c. Connors' deposition dealt mainly with the issuance and retrieval of particular firearms to military police officers in general, and specifically to Johnny Lee Thornton.

5–Transcription of testimony of Dr. William F. Clary, the main psychiatrist hired by Defense to examine Johnny Lee Thornton. Dr. Clary's testimony was transcribed in two parts:

a. The first transcription of his testimony was 91 pages in length.

b. The second transcribed part of his testimony was 52 pages.

6–The 59-page transcript of Dr. Herbert Spiegel, who was the psychiatrist testifying on behalf of Prosecution to rebut the testimony of Dr. Clary.

7–The original four-page federal court charging complaint on Johnny Lee Thornton.

8–The two-page grand jury indictment.

9–The five-page military search warrant and the detailed affidavit to supporting the issuance of the search warrant

10–The defendant's advice of rights form, better known as the Miranda waiver—one page; an exhibit at trial #D1.

11–The Defendant's Exhibits list entered into evidence at the trial. This is one legal-sized page long.

12–The Prosecution's Exhibits list entered into evidence. This list is four legal-sized pages long.

13–The Defendant's Motion for Judgment of Acquittal, made immediately after Prosecution rested its case. This document is three pages long.

14–The federal court docket for the Johnny Lee Thornton trial—includes 18, legal-sized pages listing every order, motion, and date of proceeding of the entire case.

> NOTE: The last entry in this docket is dated October 1, 1981 and it is shown as an order for the partial transcript of the proceedings to be printed. There may be more to the court docket but this is all we found.

15–A five-page legal-sized document from the federal court files listing 102 potential witnesses for the Thornton case.

> NOTE: These witnesses are listed by name and address.

16–Army Regulation 27-10, issuance of search warrants by military judges is seven pages.

NOTE: Exhibit #P1 at trial.

17–Twenty-eight pages of unofficial trial notes compiled by Marjorie Bates, mother of victim Tony Bates.

18–Two articles written by CID Special Agent, George Matthews, right after the cases concluded, for the in-house CID agents' magazine.

    a. The first one was 20-legal-sized pages long on the Freddy Williams murder case. Matthews was one of the primary agents who worked this case.

    b. Matthews wrote a 37-page article on the Thornton case. The CID magazine published an abbreviated copy of the Freddy Williams case but it did not use the Johnny Lee Thornton case.(Agent Matthews was gracious enough to donate a copy of both articles to me for the research file.)

19–Roughly 363 newspaper articles from papers all across the United States. Some are just two-to-three paragraphs and some are three-to-four pages.

20–The Freedom of Information Act (FOIA) request to the United States Army Criminal Investigation Command.

    a. The result was 203 pages of detailed CID reports and notes on this case. The reports are heavily redacted—all DOBs, SSNs, and all names, except for the deceased victims, are blacked out. This includes the names of the agents who completed the reports. (When you have all of the recorded interview memories and all of the documents at your command (listed above) you can pretty much accurately fill in the redacted names on the CID reports.)

    b. Those reports, which deal with a major issue in the case, are easy to identify when compared to the trial testimony. Many others who talk about a key detail or a single issue are easy to ID when compared with the trial documents, and backed up by the newspaper accounts and Marjorie Bates' trial notes.

21–Minor reports, like the one which details an event where Thornton and Captain [unknown name] went to the residence of Thornton's former girlfriend, Elizabeth Cochrane, after their breakup to allow Thornton to repay her for several long-distance phone calls he'd made from her house, can produce a "best guess" situation. Since the Commander of the 463rd MP Company at the time was CPT Donald Ryder, a best, and very probable, guess would be CPT Ryder was the unknown name in this report. But we cannot be 100% positive we have it correct.

a. There are other reports, such as the interview with Thornton's eye doctor to review his eye care history. The unknown eye doctor advised Thornton's vision was quite good and Thornton had not complained of any headaches or blackout spells during the doctor's examination of Thornton. This medical record on the headaches could've been critical at trial to rebut Defense, but the doctor wasn't called to testify. A guess could be made after looking at the 102 names on the witness list. There were several doctors listed and no field of practice was given with some of the names. So, the eye doctor's name remains unknown.

NOTE: The CID reports also helped the formulation of this book in another way. Several of the officer interviewees had referred to a timeline of events during our talks. In the middle of the CID documents, I found a three-page report which started at 10:00 a.m. on January 11, 1977, and ran to 10:30 p.m. on January 13, 1977. This report presented an hour-by-hour account of Thornton's whereabouts at all hours during that period of time. While, again, the names of the people who saw him and reported him at each time and location are redacted, the information itself wasn't. This was a very useful tool in keeping our storyline straight.

22–*True Detective Magazine*, December 1977 issue, Volume 108, number 3) by "Steve Hamilton."

NOTE: Several of the retired CID agents told me about the Thornton story inside a "detective" magazine. They suspected it was written by one of their own agents (completely unauthorized.) The editors inserted a disclaimer into the story indicating the use of the false name for the surviving victim.

a. The contents of the story and the actual crime scene photos used with the story match up almost perfectly with the CID case file referenced above. Except in the CID file, the graphic photos are redacted, and all I got was a blank page telling me what the photo displayed. In the detective magazine, the actual graphic photo was used. Every CID agent who told me to find this article also gave me his best guess as to which agent wrote the article. Everyone named the same guy—who won't be named here.

b. In many ways, this article was most helpful. One example, when Thornton shot the boys in the back seat, common sense told me he had to have fired three shots since two bullets were found in the back seat of the Scout and one more in a snowbank across the road. But I couldn't find a report that stated that as a fact. The detective magazine story flatly said that three shots were fired. A small, but crucial detail which could only be known to someone who was neck-deep in the case.

c. More agent names and actions were also exposed, giving me even better ability to read the redacted CID file. All in all, this "True Detective Magazine" story was extremely helpful. Having researched this case for 32-plus months, I can now tell you the author of the "True Detective Magazine" story knew his facts and told the story well and in detail. Complete with dozens of actual exact quotes straight from the mouths of people who were there. As the saying goes, it had to be an inside job.

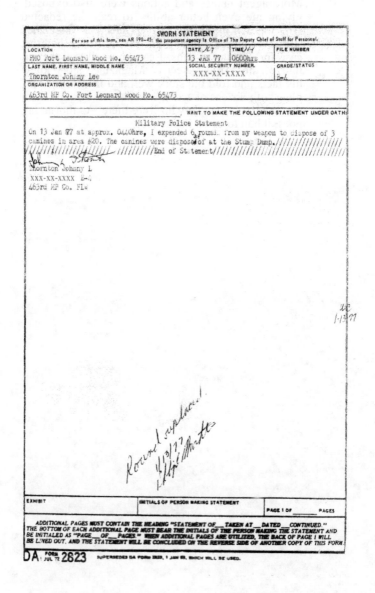

SWORN STATEMENT

For use of this form, see AR 190-45; the proponent agency is Office of The Deputy Chief of Staff for Personnel.

LOCATION	DATE	TIME	FILE NUMBER
PMO Fort Leonard Wood Mo. 65473	13 JAN 77	0600hrs	

LAST NAME, FIRST NAME, MIDDLE NAME	SOCIAL SECURITY NUMBER.	GRADE/STATUS
Thornton Johnny Lee	XXX-XX-XXXX	E-4

ORGANIZATION OR ADDRESS

463rd MP Co. Fort Leonard Wood Mo. 65473

_____, WANT TO MAKE THE FOLLOWING STATEMENT UNDER OATH:

Military Police Statement

On 13 Jan 77 at approx. 0440hrs, I expended 6 rounds from my weapon to dispose of 3 canines in area #20. The canines were disposed of at the Stump Dump.///////////////////
///////////////////////— //////////End of Statement////////////////////////////////////

Thornton Johny L
XXX-XX-XXXX E-4
463rd MP Co. FLW

Round explaned!
1/13/77

EXHIBIT	INITIALS OF PERSON MAKING STATEMENT	PAGE 1 OF PAGES

ADDITIONAL PAGES MUST CONTAIN THE HEADING "STATEMENT OF ___ TAKEN AT ___ DATED ___ CONTINUED."
THE BOTTOM OF EACH ADDITIONAL PAGE MUST BEAR THE INITIALS OF THE PERSON MAKING THE STATEMENT AND
BE INITIALED AS "PAGE___OF___PAGES." WHEN ADDITIONAL PAGES ARE UTILIZED, THE BACK OF PAGE I WILL
BE LINED OUT, AND THE STATEMENT WILL BE CONCLUDED ON THE REVERSE SIDE OF ANOTHER COPY OF THIS FORM.

DA FORM 2823
1 JUL 72
SUPERSEDES DA FORM 2823, 1 JAN 68, WHICH WILL BE USED.

Samples from Marjorie Bates'
Trial Notes

Note: Mrs. Bates was taking down this information while it was happening using shorthand. She then typed out her notes. These pages are reproduced as Marjorie Bates created them including font, capitalization, spelling, and punctuation.

Page 4:

2:25: RECESS WHILE JURY LOOKS AT PICTURES.

3:10: COURT IN SESSION, EXHIBITS OF FINGERPRINTS OF JUANITA AND THORNTON.

3:12: CALL CAPT ROBERT DEWITT, COMMANDER OF CID AT FORT LEONARD WOOD, ON DUTY 13TH HE DID VISIT THE PLACE OF WHERE THE CAR HAD BEEN ABANDONED. HE TOOK PICTURES OF THE VEHICLE. LEARNED IT WAS THERE AT 9:00. WENT OUT AT 10:00. EXHIBIT OF AUTO IN PICTURES. 72 LIGHT COLORED-CHARGER. DID HE EXAMINE IT, HE DID. HE NOTICED RIGHT FRONT TIRE WAS FLAT, HE DID NOT FIND A SLICE OR NAIL IN IT. EXHIBIT 40 FRIENDSHIP CEMETERY ROAD, CAR ON NORTH SIDE OF ROAD HEADED WEST FOUR AND A HALF FEET TO FOUR FEET FROM A SIGN ABOUT ONE FOOT FROM SNOW BANK. HE INSTRUCTED CAR NOT TO BE MOVED OR LET ANYBODY BOTHER IT AS A POSSIBLE SCENE OF A CRIME.

3:20: CROSS EXAMINATION: HE WAS ACQUAINTED WITH THORNTON, KNEW HIM ABOUT SIX MONTHS. HE WAS CHIEF OF MP INVESTIGATION. HE WAS ASKED IF HE COMPLIMENTED HIM ON HIS WORK, SAID HE COULD NOT REMEMBER DOING THAT. HE SAID HE DID PERFORM HIS DUTIES FARELY WELL.

REDIRECT: HE WAS REPRIMANDED ONCE. HE MADE AN IL-LEGAL SEARCH. HE WAS ENTHUSIASTIC. HE WANTED TO BE A POLICEMAN.

CROSS EXAMINATION: WITNESS STATED HE LEARNED FROM HIS REPRIMAND AND THAT HE WAS A GOOD M.P. BUT WOULDN'T STATE AS TO HIS DEDICATION.

3:30: RICHARD R. JENSEN, THORNTON'S IMMEDIATE SUPERVI-SOR, NINE MEN WERE UNDER HIS SUPERVISION, THORNTON WAS ASSIGNED A 1972 SCOUT FOUR-WHEEL DRIVE NUM-BER X-RAY 37, STANDARD SHIFT, EXHIBIT 48-49-51. 1972 SCOUT WAS FOR MILITARY USE ONLY, HAD A RED LIGHT AND A SPOT LIGHT. HE IDENTIFIED PICTURES OF VEHICLE. HE DID OBSERVE THE VEHICLE LATER AND THAT IT HAD A HOLE THROUGH THE TAILGATE, SHOT FROM THE INSIDE ON THE 13TH.

DID COL ELDERS ASSIST ON THE INVESTIGATION? HE DIDN'T KNOW. JENSEN WAS AT THE SCENE OF THE CRIME. EXHIBIT OF MAP WAS ENTERED, HE RECOGNIZED THE MAP OF FORT LEONARD WOOD. HE WAS ADVISED OF LOCATION OF TONY'S CAR, HE SAID IT WAS 13 MILES FROM THE CEMETERY ROAD (?) TO THE CABIN.

(THORNTON JUST SITS THERE LOOKING DOWN AT THE TABLE HE HARDLY EVER LOOKS UP) HE IS FAMILIAR WITH THE GAME WARDENS SHACK. EXHIBIT 33-34-30- ASKED IF HE RECOGNIZED THE SCENE. HE DOES. NO. 34. HE SAID THE CABIN WAS THE GAME WARDENS CABIN BY ROUBIDOUX RIVER, NO ELECTRICITY IN CABIN, HAS TWO BEDS WELDED TOGETHER AND A POT BELLIED STOVE, ONE OR ONE AND A HALF MILES FROM THE CABIN WHERE THE KIDS WERE FOUND. (THORNTON WOULDN'T OR COULDN'T LOOK AT THE PICTURES WHILE HIS DEFENSE ATTORNEYS WERE LOOKING AT THEM.) HE HAD KNOWN THORNTON A YEAR AND HE CALLED HIM ABOUT 6:00 IN THE EVENING, HE SAID HE WANTED TO TALK TO JENSEN AND COL. ELDERS, ASKED HIM WHERE HE WAS AND HE TOLD THEM THE BALLARD FARM AND THEY AGREED TO GO OUT THERE TO TALK TO HIM, HE JUST SAID HE KNEW THERE WERE LOOKING FOR HIM AND WANTED TO TALK TO THEM, DID YOU HAVE KNOWLEDGE OF THE SUSPECT? IT WAS THORNTON. HE WANTED THEM TO COME UNARMED AND ALONE, DID HE RELATE THAT REQUEST? HE DID. COL. ELDER, JENSEN AND CASTLEBERRY WENT OUT, — ANOTHER AGENT WENT OUT THERE. (THORNTON SCRATCHED HIS HEAD) IT WAS ABOUT FIVE MILES FROM PROVOST MARSHALS OFFICE, BUT LOCATION WHERE HE WAS TO MEET HIM ON WAS BASE, DROVE A — COL. ELDER IN FRONT SEAT, JENSEN WAS DRIVING, CASTLEBERRY WAS IN BACK. IT WAS DARK, COLD, AND CLEAR THEY WERE ALL ARMED THEY KNEW HE WAS ARMED, HE SAID TO CO ELDER YOU KNOW WHAT I'VE GOT AND COL. ELDER SAID DO YOU STILL HAVE YOUR WEAPON AND HE SAID AND HE SAID YES, AROUND 7:00 THEY DID MEET HIM WHAT HAPPENED THERE — WHEN THEY GOT THERE NOBODY WAS THERE, AND THEY DROVE ON AND CALLED FOR HIM IN THE PATROL CAR AND THEN COL. ELDER AND HE GOT OUT AND CALLED SEVERAL TIMES AND THEN HE ANSWERED THEM BEHIND THEM. NO FIREARM VISIBLE. I ASKED HIM IF HE HAD A WEAPON AND HE SAID IT IS IN MY RIGHT HAND, THEY TALKED TO HIM 15 OR 20 MINUTES, TRIED TO GET THORNTON TO GIVE HIM THE WEAPON AND HE WANTED TO KNOW WHAT THEY WANTED HIM FOR, AND TALKED ABOUT HIS WIFE AND KIDS, HE WANTED THERE TO BE NO HAND IRONS AND NO M.P.S. AND WANTED TO CALL HIS WIFE HE WAS TOLD HE COULD CALL HIS WIFE WHEN THEY GOT IN. 4:00 GUN ENTERED AS EXHIBIT 1 US ARMY 45 CALIBER RACK 171, SERIAL NO. 1092358, GUN WAS NOT LOADED KNIFE ENTERED AS EXHIBIT 7 WEAPONS CARD

ENTERED AS EXHIBIT. JEEP WAS PLACED WHERE HE COULD
GET GAS, OIL OR TO BE WASHED.

Page 16:

3:15: Lt. Cochran; Army, Miss Elizabeth, divorced, may I call you
Betty? She came to ft. wood in October of 1976. She is a neighbor to
Webster. They began to date and then moved in together, he moved
in with her, she knew he was married. He told me his wife left him
and was in California and they had two children and he was worried
about them. She discussed work, relation with mother, money with
him. She thought he was kind of ruff on her 6 year old boy. They
broke up December 30, 1976. He did discuss wife with her. He said
she had been unfaithful she had hurt him very bad. He had found
her there in a Motel with Moore and Mike Mason and M.P. he said
he loved her like someone he had known for a long time, but not as
man and wife. He wanted his children. He was concerned about them
not having food or shoes. He did discuss things about his work. He
wanted to be a good cop at his job. He did spend longer hours than
necessary but she did too. David was with John they got along well.
He said he worked extra hours and was afraid it would interfere with
their relation he worked extra hard to be promoted he wanted to be
a better soldier. He was sending money to his wife every payday
$125 or $115, he draws $165 on them and he was sending more than
that, his wife didn't call him, he called her, she was always saying
I need more money, he would say why don't you go to work and she
would say no.

Was their sex relations satisfactory? (Betty and Johnny Lee) Yes,
he was very happy about their sex life. He would take David to
get haircuts and they would bring her flowers. He thought she was
making a sissy out of David. They didn't agree about the way she
handled the boy. They didn't go out. He said if she wanted him she
would have to stay home and not go out. The three stayed home never went anywhere without David. They were talking about getting
married and he was offered a job with the Missouri Conservation
and he wanted to quit the Army and she said no, she wanted to stay
in. He said he didn't understand her being independent. They split
up the day before New Years. She was working lots of hours and
he woke her up at midnight and said she didn't love him and she
would say I do love you and ask him to stay. Later he said this and
she told him to leave. Later she learned he had a letter from his
wife after he left.

CROSS EXAMINATION: He did want to be an outstanding Military
Police, did he say to you that he wanted to be a super cop? No. She
did ride with him and he would speed and said he was an MP and
no one was going to stop him. He never lost his temper, never did
strike her. She did strike him and he grabbed her wrist and said
we can talk it over, very cool and level headed, he was this kind of
person all the time. He woke her up the night he left at midnight
and said I can't leave without saying goodby and said if you ask
me to stay I will, she told him to leave. He told her one time that
if she broke up with him she would be hasseled by the M.P.s. He

said that someone wanted to go out with him. He said he wanted to go live with her. He did have headaches and was going to go down and see if he needed glasses. No, never complained of anything. During relations with Thornton she was satisfied and thought that he was. No he did not ask her to engage in things she did not approve of. How often? When she first met him it was 3 or 4 times a day. One of his favorite places to go was the game wardens cabin. He liked covered places down by the trout place he also liked the game wardens cabin. The M.P.s took their families there and it was by a stream. No she had not been there with him.

RECESS FOR 20 MINUTES:

Thornton talking to Att. seemed a little more alert, very down, now looking down at the table. He does this all the time.

COURT IN SESSION: Paul Mara an M.M. He knew Thornton for 11 months, he worked with him, He worked same shift duty with him. He is very professional. No statements towards violence, none towards women. He was having martial problems, he did discus this...

Example of CID Report

SYNOPSIS: Continued   0018-77-CID043-09009

and ▮▮▮▮▮ to a nearby wooded area where he shot and wounded ▮▮▮▮▮ with his service weapon; shot and killed HAWKINS and NEEDHAM with his service weapon; and left the four persons partially buried in the snow.

EXHIBITS:

A. ATTACHED

1. Agent's Investigation Report (AIR) by SA ▮▮▮▮▮ 13 Jan 77, reflecting that he had gone to the scene where the bodies were located; that ▮▮▮▮▮ pronounced the three victims dead at the scene; and that he ▮▮▮▮▮ accompanied the bodies to the General Leonard Wood Army Hospital (GLWAH), FLW, MO.

2. AIR by SA ▮▮▮▮▮ 13 Jan 77, reflecting that he had discovered what appeared to be blood and a bullet hole in the MP vehicle which had been used by THORNTON, and that he had assisted photographing the crime scene and the location of the bodies at the crime scene.

3. AIR by SA ▮▮▮▮▮ 13 Jan 77, reflecting that he proceeded to the crime scene and photographed the crime scene with Polaroid film.

4. AIR by SA ▮▮▮▮▮ 13 Jan 77, reflecting his examination of the crime scene.

5. AIR by SA ▮▮▮▮▮ 14 Jan 77, reflecting that what appeared to be blood and a bullet hole was found in the vehicle which had been used by THORNTON, that the vehicle was to be secured at Transportation Motor Pool, and that the bodies of the deceased persons had been photographed at the GLWAH.

6. Letter of SA (b)(6)(b)(7)(C) 13 Jan 77, reflecting that the FBI had assumed investigation jurisdiction.

7. AIR by SA ▮▮▮▮▮ 13 Jan 77, reflecting his initial interview with (b)(6)(b)(7)(C) and that THORNTON had been examined at the GLWAH.

8. AIR by SA ▮▮▮▮▮ 13 Jan 77, reflecting that he had interviewed (b)(6)(b)(7)(C) who related aspects of being contacted by (b)(6)(b)(7)(C) and what (b)(6)(b)(7)(C) had told him about the incidents.

9. AIR by SA ▮▮▮▮▮ 13 Jan 77, reflecting that he observed (b)(6)(b)(7)(C) at the Pulaski County Memorial Hospital, Waynesville, MO. and requested that Dr ▮▮▮▮▮ conduct a rape test on (b)(6)(b)(7)(C) efforts to obtain (b)(6)(b)(7)(C) clothing; and his initial interview with (b)(6)(b)(7)(C)

10. AIR by SA ▮▮▮▮▮ 13 Jan 77, reflecting that A. BATES had never been employed on FLW, MO; that ▮▮▮▮▮ was interviewed and said that THORNTON had been operating the military vehicle N-37 at the time of the shooting, and that there had been blood and a bullet hole found in the vehicle.

000006
9

291

United States Department of Justice

UNITED STATES ATTORNEY
WESTERN DISTRICT OF MISSOURI
549 UNITED STATES COURT HOUSE
KANSAS CITY, MO. 64106

September 19, 1977

Clarence M. Kelley, Director
Federal Bureau of Investigation
JEH Building
Washington, D.C. 20530

      Re: United States v. Johnny Lee Thornton
            United States District Court
            Western District of Missouri

Dear Director Kelley:

From information I have received from members of my staff
who conducted the prosecution of the murder, assault with
intent to murder, kidnapping and rape charges involving
Johnny Lee Thornton, a member of the United States Army
stationed at Fort Leonard Wood, Missouri, I feel that I
should call to your attention the most commendable and
professional manner in which Special Agent in Charge Bill
D. Williams and the many Special Agents assigned to the
Kansas City Division investigated the heinous crimes per-
petrated by the defendant on the Fort Leonard Wood Military
Reservation in January 1977. The very careful and thorough
investigation, particularly the gathering of a great number
of items of physical evidence, enabled the Government to
build an unimpeachable case against the defendant. In that
regard I am advised that the reports of several laboratory
agents who participated in the examination of many of the
items of physical evidence were so clear and convincing that
defense counsel agreed to stipulate at trial to many of the
findings of the laboratory experts.

I would like to especially commend Special Agent William
Castleberry, the case agent, not only for the excellent
manner in which he coordinated the investigation of the
many agents involved therein and for the reporting of that
investigation to our office, but also for the invaluable
assistance he rendered to the trial attorneys in the preparation for and trial of the case. Without that assistance
the results obtained would have been much more difficult, if
not impossible. Also assisting in the preparation and trial
of the case was Special Agent Thomas Den Ouden who was very

Clarence M. Kelley, Director
September 19, 1977
Page 2

helpful in obtaining the services, on very short notice, of
one of the most qualified medical doctors specializing in
hypnotic psychiatric diagnosis, Dr. Herbert Spiegel. As a
prosecution witness, Dr. Speigel was devasating in rebuttal
to the defense of insanity of the defendant at the time of
the crimes.

Because of this outstanding work of the agents of the Federal
Bureau of Investigation in the field and in the laboratory,
the defendant was found guilty of all counts and was recently
sentenced to imprisonment for three consecutive life terms
plus a consecutive term of twenty years, the maximum sentences
provided by law.

As a recently appointed United States Attorney I look forward
to many more pleasant experiences with agents of the Federal
Bureau of Investigation in our combined and continuing efforts
against crime.

Respectfully yours,

RONALD S. REED, JR.
United States Attorney

cc: Mr. Bill D. Williams
     Special Agent in Charge
     Kansas City, Missouri

Form A. O. 91 (Rev. 12-1-53)

Complaint

United States District Court
FOR THE

WESTERN DISTRICT OF MISSOURI

F I L
JAN 1 4 1977

Magistrate United States No.

UNITED STATES OF AMERICA

v

JOHNNY LEE THORNTON

Case No. B77-7M

COMPLAINT for VIOLATION of 77-2002-01-E

U.S.C. Title 18

Section   1111(a)(b)

BEFORE **Honorable James C. England**,   **Springfield, Missouri** ,
      Name of Magistrate   *Address of Magistrate*

The undersigned complainant being duly sworn states:

That on or about **January 12** , 19 77 , at **Ft. Leonard Wood, Missouri,**

in the

     Western District of **Missouri, on land within the maritime and terri-
torial jurisdiction of the United States,**
(1)
     JOHNNY LEE THORNTON

did (2) **, with premeditation and malice aforethought, and by means of
shooting, unlawfully killed ANTHONY LEE BATES, all in violation
of Title 18, United States Code, Section 1111(a)(b).**

And the complainant states that this complaint is based on **information furnished to
Special Agent George C. Scruggs, Jr. See attached affidavit.**

And the complainant further states that he believes that
     1) **James B. King, Missouri Highway Patrol, Troop I, Waynesville, MO**
     2) **Alex Kerekes, CID Agent, Ft. Leonard Wood, MO**
     3) **Paul VanSomeren, Special Agent, FBI**
     4) **William Castleberry, Special Agent, FBI**
     5) **Col. Perry B. Elder, Provost Marshal, Ft. Leonard Wood, MO**
       (see attached sheet)
are material witnesses in relation to this charge.

GEORGE C. SCRUGGS,   *Signature of Complainant.*
Special Agent, FBI

Official Title.

Sworn to before me, and subscribed in my presence,   1-14   , 19 77

United States Magistrate.

(1) Insert name of accused.
(2) Insert statement of the essential facts constituting the offense charged.

FPI-LC-100M-8-72 9611

294

Material witnesses (continued)

6) Robert E. Lee, Military Policeman, Ft. Leonard Wood, MO
7) David Cogswill, Military Policeman, Ft. Leonard Wood, MO
8) Dr. Gerald Rappe, M.D., Ft. Leonard Wood, MO
9) Juanita Deckard, Plato, MO
10) George Matthews, CID Agent, Ft. Leonard Wood, MO
11) Brooks Black, Special Agent, FBI
12) Phillip E. Marketon, Military Policeman, Ft. Leonard Wood, MO
13) David Leroy Edwards, Military Policeman, Ft. Leonard Wood, MO
14) Interior Laloulo, Military Policeman, Ft. Leonard Wood, MO

AFFIDAVIT OF SPECIAL AGENT GEORGE C.
SCRUGGS, JR., FEDERAL BUREAU OF INVESTI-
GATION IN COMPLAINT ENTITLED UNITED STATES
OF AMERICA v. JOHNNY LEE THORNTON

On January 13, 1977, JUANITA DECKARD advised Missouri State
Highway Patrol Trooper James B. King, and CID investigator
Alex Kerekes, and on January 14, 1977, advised Special Agent
Paul VanSomeren of the Federal Bureau of Investigation, that she
and her three companions, Linda Needham, Anthony Lee Bates and
Wesley Hawkins, were stopped on Southgate Road on the Ft. Leonard
Wood reservation by a military policeman in military uniform and
driving a four-wheel drive military vehicle bearing red emergency
lights and containing a military police radio which was on. She
further advised the military vehicle was believed to bear the
numbers 327.

Ms. DECKARD further related the vehicle operated by her and
her companions was stopped by a person in a military uniform
identifying himself as a military policeman for the reasons
stated by the military policeman, that the car occupied was
similar to one used in an armed robbery. Ms. DECKARD further
reported the military policeman removed ANTHONY LEE BATES from
the automobile and placed him in the military police vehicle
and at that time she observed the military policeman shoot, with
a large handgun, the above-named ANTHONY LEE BATES. JOHNNY LEE
THORNTON was the only military policeman on duty during the night
hours of January 12, 1977, and the morning hours of January 13,
1977, who was driving a four-wheel drive military vehicle, the
number of which was X37.

David Leroy Edwards, a military policeman at Ft. Leonard
Wood, Missouri, reported that THORNTON received from him at
approximately 2200 hours on January 12, 1977, a four-wheel
drive military vehicle, to wit, an International Scout military
police vehicle designated X37. Interior Laloulo, a military
policeman at Ft. Leonard Wood, Missouri, reported that THORNTON
turned over to him at 0600 hours on January 13, 1977, a four-
wheel drive military vehicle, to wit, an International Scout
military police vehicle designated X37. Subject vehicle is the
only military police vehicle bearing the designation X37. At
the time THORNTON picked up the subject vehicle and turned it
back in he was in full military uniform.

THORNTON, upon completion of his term of duty at 0600 hours
on January 13, 1977, surrendered his weapon back to Sgt. Phillip
E. Marketon, military police control, and executed a sworn statement that he had expended six (6) cartridges from his weapon
while killing dogs which he reported he had dumped at the
Ft. Leonard Wood dump. The executed statement was delivered to
David Cogswill, a military policeman at Ft. Leonard Wood. Thereafter, Robert E. Lee, military policeman, 463rd Military Police
Company, conducted an investigation at the Ft. Leonard Wood
dump and was unable to locate any dead dogs. Ms. DECKARD further
provided a description of the subject which generally fits that
of JOHNNY LEE THORNTON.

During the afternoon of January 13, 1977, THORNTON contacted
the Provost Marshal Colonel Perry B. Elder at Ft. Leonard Wood,
indicating he had heard a serious crime was under investigation
and that his, THORNTON's, services were required. Col. Elder
instructed THORNTON to appear for duty but THORNTON failed to
ever make an appearance. On January 13, 1977, in a 1971
Chevrolet bearing Minnesota license JY4-278, being utilized by
THORNTON at Ft. Leonard Wood, Special Agent Paul VanSomeren of
the FBI, located a letter signed by JOHNNY LEE THORNTON addressed

to his wife which read as follows:

> "I don't remember doing what I did.
> Sometimes I get these headaches, I
> want to die from the pain. I don't
> want to hurt people, but when these
> headaches comes something snaps in
> me.....I have never done this before,
> at least I don't remember it. I've
> only felt this way, I mean really
> sick, for a few months."

On January 14, 1977, a search by Special Agent George
Matthews, CID, Ft. Leonard Wood, Missouri, and Special Agent
Brooks Black of the FBI, of military vehicle X37 revealed
a bullet hole and a substance which, on preliminary examination,
appeared to be blood. The military vehicle carrying the designation X37 was operated by JOHNNY LEE THORNTON during the night
hours of January 12, 1977, and the morning hours of January 13,
1977. Ms. DECKARD further reported she was taken by the subject
to a cabin in an isolated area of Ft. Leonard Wood. The cabin
is known on Ft. Leonard Wood as a game warden refuge. THORNTON's
assignment as a military policeman was presently that of a game
warden. Gerald Rappe, M.D., pathologist, Major, AMC, General
Leonard Wood Army Hospital, Ft. Leonard Wood, Missouri, pronounced ANTHONY LEE BATES dead on January 13, 1977. On January
14, 1977, Gerald Rappe, M.D., determined the cause of death as
gunshot wounds.

George C. Scruggs, Jr.
Special Agent, FBI

Sworn to before me, and subscribed in my presence,
January 14, 1977.

United States Magistrate

Military Police Disciplines

The Military Police tasks can separated into three disciplines and one integrated function:

Security and mobility support operations (Area Security/Battlefield Circulation Control)

Police operations (Law Enforcement)

Detention operations (Enemy Prisoners of War)

Police intelligence operations (integrated function across all disciplines)

* * *

Career

The Military Police Corps has six career paths within the Army, one for commissioned officers, one for warrant officers, and four for enlisted soldiers: Currently 31 series, formerly the 95 series, and before that, 1677.

31A Military Police Officer

311A Criminal Investigations Warrant Officer;

31B (95B) Military Police

31D (95D) Criminal Investigations Special Agent

31E (95C) Internment/Resettlement Specialist

31K Military Police Working Dog Handler

Note: In 1977 Thornton's MOS of 95C would have been correct. The MOS change did not come about until around the year 2001.

INDEX

141, 163, 212, 219, 225,
227, 228, 229, 246

J

JLT Murder Victims

Linda Needham 4, 7, 22, 25, 33,
58, 66, 69, 80, 90, 121,
124, 133, 134, 135, 136,
137, 154, 163, 164, 212,
220, 225, 226, 227, 228,
229, 247

Tony Bates 4, 7, 22, 25, 33, 58,
66, 69, 80, 90, 121, 124,
133, 134, 135, 136, 137,
154, 163, 164, 212, 220,
225, 226, 227, 228, 229,
247

Wesley Hawkins 4, 7, 22, 25, 33,
58, 66, 69, 80, 90, 121,
124, 133, 134, 135, 136,
137, 154, 163, 164, 212,
220, 225, 226, 227, 228,
229, 247

L

Law Enforcement

CID Special Agents

Adams, George 49

Blasingame, Lee E. 99

Byrd, Thomas W. 20, 22, 64, 82,
87, 88, 281

Cagle, Donald E 77, 78

Caldwell, Michael A. 57, 61, 63,
84, 85, 99

DeWitt, Robert, CAPT 142, 286

Kerekes, Alexander 61, 63, 84,
120, 121

Matthews, George T. x, 21, 29,
30, 79, 80, 98, 99, 100,
121, 123, 141, 263, 264,
270, 283

Moriarity, Matt 27

Oster, Robert 20, 27, 99, 100

Rodery, Larry R. 76, 88

FBI Special Agents

Adams, George 49

Bartley, Robert C. 142, 164

Black, Brooks 121, 123

Browning, Roger D. 84

Castleberry, William "Bill" x, 15,
27, 29, 44, 45, 46, 47, 48,
50, 52, 56, 73, 99, 106,
110, 113, 119, 120, 127,
130, 139, 144, 147, 213,
216, 251, 263, 275, 281

Cummere, Thomas 142

Den Ouden, Tom E. x, 22, 23,
24, 29, 50, 56, 74, 82, 86,
104, 139, 213, 275

Hazelwood, Roy 113

Holmes, Jim 275

Jones, Alfred J. 131, 163, 212

McDonald, Don 28, 74, 84

Palladino, David A. 84

Reid, Gary W. 28, 87

Scruggs, George C. 49, 74, 120,
121, 123

Sypult, Robert 162

Teten, Bud 113

Trammell, Emmet 28, 74

Van Someren, Paul A. 65, 86,
121

Williams, Bill 96, 97, 98, 99,
103, 106, 107, 108, 110,
244, 283

Missouri State Highway Patrol

King, J.B. 5, 277

Ward, Mark Road Trooper 268

Watson, Mike Retired 273

St. Robert Police Department

Julian, Thomas M. 272

Legal Proceedings

U

US Army

V

Vehicles

W

Witness

Printed in the USA
CPSIA information can be obtained
at www.ICGtesting.com
LVHW021143210624
783650LV00011B/992